Palgrave Macmillan's Postcolonial Studies in Education

Studies utilizing the perspectives of postcolonial theory have become established and increasingly widespread in the last few decades. This series embraces and broadly employs the postcolonial approach. As a site of struggle, education has constituted a key vehicle for the "colonization of the mind." The "post" in postcolonialism is both temporal, in the sense of emphasizing the processes of decolonization, and analytical in the sense of probing and contesting the aftermath of colonialism and the imperialism which succeeded it, utilizing materialist and discourse analysis. Postcolonial theory is particularly apt for exploring the implications of educational colonialism, decolonization, experimentation, revisioning, contradiction and ambiguity not only for the former colonies, but also for the former colonial powers. This series views education as an important vehicle for both the inculcation and unlearning of colonial ideologies. It complements the diversity that exists in postcolonial studies of political economy, literature, sociology, and the interdisciplinary domain of cultural studies. Education is here being viewed in its broadest contexts, and is not confined to institutionalized learning. The aim of this series is to identify and help establish new areas of educational inquiry in postcolonial studies.

Series Editors:

Antonia Darder holds the Leavey Presidential Endowed Chair in Ethics and Moral Leadership at Loyola Marymount University, Los Angeles, and is professor emerita at the University of Illinois, Urbana-Champaign.

Anne Hickling-Hudson is associate professor of Education at Australia's Queensland University of Technology (QUT) where she specializes in cross-cultural and international education.

Peter Mayo is professor and head of the Department of Education Studies at the University of Malta where he teaches in the areas of Sociology of Education and Adult Continuing Education, as well as in Comparative and International Education and Sociology more generally.

Editorial Advisory Board

Carmel Borg (University of Malta)
John Baldacchino (Teachers College, Columbia University)
Jennifer Chan (University of British Columbia)
Christine Fox (University of Wollongong, Australia)
Zelia Gregoriou (University of Cyprus)
Leon Tikly (University of Bristol, UK)
Birgit Brock-Utne (Emeritus, University of Oslo, Norway)

Titles:

A New Social Contract in a Latin American Education Context
Danilo R. Streck; Foreword by Vítor Westhelle

Education and Gendered Citizenship in Pakistan
M. Ayaz Naseem

Critical Race, Feminism, and Education: A Social Justice Model
Menah A. E. Pratt-Clarke

Actionable Postcolonial Theory in Education
Vanessa Andreotti

The Capacity to Share: A Study of Cuba's International Cooperation in Educational Development
Anne Hickling-Hudson, Jorge Corona Gonzalez, and Rosemary Preston

A Critical Pedagogy of Embodied Education
Tracey Ollis

Culture, Education, and Community: Expressions of the Postcolonial Imagination
Edited by Jennifer Lavia and Sechaba Mahlomaholo

Culture, Education, and Community

Expressions of the Postcolonial Imagination

Edited by

Jennifer Lavia and Sechaba Mahlomaholo

CULTURE, EDUCATION, AND COMMUNITY
Copyright © Jennifer Lavia and Sechaba Mahlomaholo, 2012.
Softcover reprint of the hardcover 1st edition 2012 978-0-230-33825-8
All rights reserved.

First published in 2012 by
PALGRAVE MACMILLAN®
in the United States—a division of St. Martin's Press LLC,
175 Fifth Avenue, New York, NY 10010.

Where this book is distributed in the UK, Europe and the rest of the world, this is by Palgrave Macmillan, a division of Macmillan Publishers Limited, registered in England, company number 785998, of Houndmills, Basingstoke, Hampshire RG21 6XS.

Palgrave Macmillan is the global academic imprint of the above companies and has companies and representatives throughout the world.

Palgrave® and Macmillan® are registered trademarks in the United States, the United Kingdom, Europe and other countries.

ISBN 978-1-349-34128-3   ISBN 978-1-137-01312-5 (eBook)
DOI 10.1057/9781137013125

Library of Congress Cataloging-in-Publication Data

   Culture, Education, and Community: Expressions of the Postcolonial Imagination / edited by Jennifer Lavia and Sechaba Mahlomaholo.
      p. cm.—(Postcolonial studies in education)
   1. Education—Social aspects—Cross-cultural studies. 2. Education and state—Cross-cultural studies. 3. Educational change—Cross-cultural studies. 4. Community development—Cross-cultural studies. 5. Postcolonialism. I. Lavia, Jennifer. II. Mahlomaholo, Sechaba.

LC191.C777 2012
306.43—dc23   2011040687

A catalogue record of the book is available from the British Library.

Design by Newgen Imaging Systems (P) Ltd., Chennai, India.

First edition: May 2012

Contents

List of Figures and Tables	vii
Series Editors' Preface	ix
Anne Hickling-Hudson, Antonia Darder, and Peter Mayo	
Preface	xiii
Acknowledgments	xv
Introduction: Imagining the Postcolonial *Jennifer Lavia and Sechaba Mahlomaholo*	1
1 Postcolonial Thought: A Theoretical and Methodological Means for Thinking through Culturally Ethical Research *Laurette Bristol*	15
2 Validating Community Cultural Wealth: Toward Sustainable Empowering Learning Environments *Sechaba Mahlomaholo*	33
3 Rethinking Education in South Africa: Amplifying Liberation Pedagogy *Milton Molebatsi Nkoane and Jennifer Lavia*	49
4 The Politics of Restrictive Language Policies: A Postcolonial Analysis of Language and Schooling *Antonia Darder and Miren Uriarte*	69
5 Súil Eile: A Different Perspective on Migration, Language Acquisition, Belonging, and Multicultural Society *Simon Warren*	103

6	Reimagining Lines of Flight in Schooling for Indigenous Students in Australia *Bob Lingard, Greg Vass, and Elizabeth Mackinlay*	125
7	Border Crossing: Conversations About Race, Identity, and Agency in South Africa *Dennis Francis*	147
8	Constructing a Nation: The Role of Arts Education in South Africa *Lorraine Singh*	163
9	Calypso, Education, and Community in Trinidad and Tobago: From the 1940s to 2011 *Gordon Rohlehr*	183
10	More in de Mortar dan de Pestle: Recruitment into Secondary Teaching in Trinidad and Tobago *Joyanne De Four-Babb*	211
11	Comparative Collaboration: A Transgressive Academic Practice of Being and Becoming *Laurette Bristol, Joyanne De Four-Babb, Talia Esnard, Jennifer Lavia, and Lisa Perez*	235

Conclusion: Postcolonial Strivings   255
Jennifer Lavia and Sechaba Mahlomaholo

List of Contributors   261

Index   265

Figures and Tables

Figure

4.1 Annual high-school dropout rate, comparing EP and LEP in Massachusetts from the 2002/2003 to the 2007/2008 academic years   95

Table

7.1 Summary of participants' identity   154

Series Editors' Preface

Culture, Education, and Community: Expressions of Postcolonial Imagination takes us on a variety of postcolonial journeys that explore issues of identity, domination, and change in education. The contributors to the volume wrestle thoughtfully with the problems of how to bring about equitable change in education in a world that continues to be marked by the injustices of the colonial aftermath. They confront these problems in several global contexts—Africa, Australia, the Caribbean, Ireland, and the United States. The complexity of the problems is made particularly vivid by the South African man who challenges academics by asking what meaning there is in the highsounding ideas of reconciliation, equity, and educational change for a person like him, who was deprived of an education under apartheid, who is now 52, unemployed, uneducated, living poverty-stricken in his mother's home, and unable to provide a promising future for his children (Mahlomaholo, chapter 2).

The conditions decried by this man vividly come to mind when one watches the film *Invictus,* which highlights the Mandela-led policy of national reconciliation and "unity" in support of the South African rugby union team, the Springboks—a team that had excluded blacks during the apartheid period. Although many praised Nelson Mandela for his effort, others saw the policy as a politics to sanitize the country's racist colonial past. In light of similar postcolonial concerns, the book offers a multilayered look at educational problems, in places where people under colonialism were, in the words of another South African man, "hated, despised, detested on the basis of...physical makeup...made to feel inferior and incapable of challenging the colonial order"—and whose indigenous culture/ knowledge, including ancestral knowledge, was denigrated and pathologized, in contrast to the exaltation of the imported and imposed dominant one. Moving beyond critique, the authors take us into the terrain of attempted solutions and the implications for those who now have a chance to "rediscover [their] own genius and reassume [their] life history" (Nkoane and Lavia, chapter 3).

How do societies confront the imperative of paying the enormous debt owed to those deprived of an education by the former colonial system, and or denied an equitable education by the current system? What are the prospects for those determined to resume their rightful place in their societies? What forms should equity measures, affirmative action, and cultural restitution take in these contexts? The mesh of neoliberal governance that currently entraps governments globally means that these governments are less able and less willing than previously to provide the support services and affirmative action that would allow disenfranchised and oppressed people a fighting chance, let alone their inalienable right to redress the social imbalances created by colonialism and concomitant policies of cultural invasion, linguistic racialization, and economic exploitation.

The debt stemming from the educational neglect of people in formerly colonized and enslaved societies remains massive. The market economics and small government of neoliberal policies betray the idealistic objectives of independence movements and liberation struggles to create more equitable societies, where the rights to high-quality educational and other essential services were to be accessible to all, irrespective of social class, race, creed, or gender. This volume describes how educational conditions remain inequitable, whether in newly democratic South Africa or older independent nations, such as those of the Caribbean and Ireland, or in settler societies with indigenous and other multicultural minorities, such as Australia or the United States. The postcolonial critique of the authors shows that, although educational opportunities have grown, the system still reflects in many ways the gross inequities, disparities, and distortions of the educational system under colonialism or apartheid. Although the processes involved are perhaps more covert than in previous times, they generate persistent inequalities nevertheless.

What would it be like if a curriculum were to draw on the strengths of impoverished communities, rather than remaining mired in the neocolonial perspectives of Europeanized dominant cultures? Would this be akin to the notion of "inverse hegemony"? Toward this end, the book argues for a curriculum to be shaped by forms of community cultural wealth that are "aspirational, navigational, linguistic, familial, and resistant" as well as sociocultural (Mahlomaholo, chapter 2), and to draw inspiration from projects in which universities, parents, students, and teachers use the everyday life stories and practices of schools and their communities to learn, to teach, and to research (Nkoane and Lavia chapter 3). The colonial shaping of the curriculum continues to be contested in these and other ways. Unfortunately, it is remarkably successful in persisting with the troubling legacies of the past and resisting change, as Rohlehr points out (chapter 9). Political independence for new nations does not necessarily mean decolonizing minds and the structural legacies of the discriminatory and differentiating colonial state.

Deep racial, cultural, and identity problems are manifested in the complex struggles for equitable education in the various contexts examined in the book. The linguistic issue is particularly difficult, partly because of its complexity in the societies of former colonies. The neoliberal state discourages effective bilingual language learning in U.S. schools, where working-class immigrant communities desperately need it; yet encourages it in wealthy schools preparing students for careers in a globalizing world (Darder and Uriarte, chapter 4). This linguistic inequity is part of a broader system of racialized economic and political oppression that positions immigrant learners of English and their families as unworthy of the kind of high-quality education that includes multilingualism, making a culture of and programming for academic failure more likely. In the context of Irish-speaking Ireland (Warren, chapter 5), many parents insist that their children's schools operate as English-dominant (given that the colonizing English language is the language of power and international currency, as with other former colonial states) rather than bilingual, seeing the maintenance of the indigenous Irish language as a private responsibility. Yet, the native Irish language is the one of indigenous belonging.

How then to utilize educational resources to help preserve and expand the mother tongue? As with other educational issues examined in the text, authors offer a variety of suggestions. Warren, for example, considers both educational and community contexts to explore how the society could construct a popular cultural politics, and argues for an approach that is of relevance for multicultural societies—that is, building the political and public defense for living in and with diversity as a public good. In Australia, reforming indigenous schooling takes us on the dangerous terrain of who can speak about whom. The terrain is negotiated by Lingard, McKinlay, and Vass (chapter 6), discussing the strengths and weaknesses of three important approaches to educational change, contested by Indigenous educators themselves—the demand for personal effort and a pedagogy of direct instruction; the advocacy of high motivation, self-pride, teacher effort, and indigenous context; and the Federal government's aim of funding the direct teaching perceived as needed to close the gap in achievement between indigenous and other learners.

At a time when educational contexts around the world have become ever more contested due to neoliberal policies that propose the increasing instrumentalization and privatization of schooling for those populations most dependent on public means, *Culture, Education, and Community: Expressions of Postcolonial Imagination* provides readers with key insights into both theoretical and practical aspects of the postcolonial experience in education. With themes centered on autobiography, citizenship, curriculum, pedagogy, community development, language politics, indigeneity, changing identities, postcolonial aesthetics, and resistance, the book provides a much needed multifaceted analysis of education and community, through a postcolonial lens. The volume's exploration of curriculum decolonization and research collaboration in terms of social equity, racism, cultural and gender identity, language policies, and knowledge paradigms is important for constructing a broad interdisciplinary and postcolonial view of education and culture in the world today.

ANNE HICKLING-HUDSON, ANTONIA DARDER, AND
PETER MAYO

Preface

We live in an era defined by rapid shifts and flows in peoples, ideas, capital, and cultures, in which identities and experiences are constantly being transformed and rewritten. Arguably, education occurs within community, and as an academic discipline, it continues to be a contested site in which the imperialist intent of modern capitalism continues to thrive through crisis and becomes manifest in a parade of neoliberal policies and practices. How these policies and practices are experienced as epistemic outcomes of hegemonic knowledge can be seen as having a globalizing effect. Yet it can be argued that education occurs at the local site, and, as dangerous as these times are, they do provide challenges and opportunities for developing a politics of recognition in which voices of subaltern professionals can struggle to be articulated within multicultural settings.

It is within this context that this book has emerged. Out of conversations and reflections on professional practices among and between the contributors of this volume, have come a series of interpretations of the postcolonial condition. As editors of this book, we became preoccupied through email exchanges and face-to-face conversations with the urgent and unfinished business of postcolonial discourse, and more so, in striving to push the boundaries of postcolonial theories to glean deeper and more critical understandings of how such theories can contribute to how we think about education and schooling. The aim of this book therefore is to reexamine how postcolonial theories might contribute to understandings about education, and we pose two questions to provoke the debate: Can education contribute to cultural confidence of peoples and communities who have endured centuries of oppression and marginalization? If so, what is education, and what is education for given such historical circumstances? Our hope is that the book has provided a critical space in which to interrogate the ways in which postcolonial voices are imagined and struggle to be valued, heard, and responded to. The book takes the imagination of the postcolonial and the experience of postcoloniality as its focus, acknowledging that postcolonialism is a troubling, unsettling, and ambiguous concept requiring revisiting and reinterpretation. Through these chapters, the book seeks to promote the opportunities for, and begin to remove the limitations of, articulating postcolonial theories to understanding education and all the other aspects of the human condition and draws upon the lived experiences of postcolonial scholars to provide interpretations that foreground missing perspectives that are often marginalized, silenced, ignored, or denied.

By bringing together postcolonial understandings as well as critical theories that are allied to postcolonial thinking, we have sought to work through studies of culture and learning in human and social sciences. Autobiography, citizenship, curriculum, pedagogy, community development, indigenous perspectives, changing identities, postcolonial aesthetics, and resistance are examples of unifying themes throughout. By addressing the contested, yet related, themes of culture, education, and community, we are aspirational in our outlook that the impact of a postcolonial agenda for understanding education and for changing cultures and communities will be significant to those working in and for education and community development. Such an agenda, therefore, is central to this book and is considered in the book, from a number of different postcolonial and critical perspectives informed by the personal, professional, and research experiences encountered by its authors.

Acknowledgments

We wish to recognize that no endeavor is ever really an original starting point. In this way, we acknowledge the work of those who have gone before us and paved a way so that we could have the knowledge, skill, and most of all, the moral agency to navigate these complex times.

We also extend sincere gratitude to all contributors for their commitment to advancing a postcolonial agenda.

During the preparation of the manuscript, we were privileged to have the support of critical friends and colleagues, especially Caribbean Educators Research Initiative (CURVE), Dr. Vussy Hongwane, Ms. Themesa Neckles, Dr. Willy Nel, Professor Nareadi Phasha, the National Research Foundation for sponsoring the Sustainable Learning Environments (SuLE) research team, and Professor Pat Sikes.

Finally, we are grateful to our families for sustaining us during this process: Leon and Leon-Omari, and Nkhatho, Lillian, Mabasia, Maleke, Lerato, Nkhatho (junior), Realeboha, and Palesa (senior and junior).

Introduction:
Imagining the Postcolonial

Jennifer Lavia and Sechaba Mahlomaholo

"...*For the power to create and innovate remains the greatest guarantee of respect and recognition.*"

—Nettleford, 1970, 227

We begin by imagining! Perhaps more accurately stated, we begin by "reimagining"¹ as we take the opportunity presented in this book to realize two aims. First, we want to contribute to reinvigorating postcolonial discourse with these chapters serving as a dialogue among contributors and with the reader. The book also serves as an epistemological and methodological encounter with the wider social discourse, underlining urgent and unfinished business. Our second aim is to push the boundaries of postcolonial perspectives, seeking to expose and provoke, deconstruct and reconstruct, centering education as cultural practice and acknowledging it as occurring within community. During our preparation of this book, we have come to recognize that imagination is essential when considering postcolonialism, because it is necessary to accommodate a wide range of critical perspectives, which are potentially allied theories concerning the conditions of postcoloniality.

Our contributors offer, in a single volume, disparate critical assessments that challenge traditional Western accounts of knowledge and engage in a cultural politics of education. Indeed, we set out to highlight the importance of culture as a human right for communities that have been traditionally treated as if they mattered less than others, showing how these communities conceive of their lived experiences as cultural expressions of marginalization, oppression, and resistance.

When we invited contributors to this volume, we asked them to consider these central, interrelated questions: Can education contribute to the cultural confidence of peoples and communities who have endured centuries of oppression and marginalization? If so, what is education, and what is education for, given such historical circumstances? In responding to these questions, we hoped to find, like Kanu, "multiple modes of theoretical representations [emerging] from alternative perspectives on postcoloniality grounded in a dynamic variety of life experiences" (2006, 4). Not only do the chapters provide expressions of postcolonial imagination, they do so by making central to the postcolonial discourse the voices of the colonized through autobiography, citizenship, curriculum critique, critical pedagogy, community development, indigenous perspectives, changing identities, postcolonial aesthetic, and resistance. Interwoven in these critical spaces of engaged difference are analyses of theory and practice of the postcolonial—community cultural wealth, liberation pedagogy, indigenous schooling and knowledge systems, language acquisition, race, class, identity, and agency. We acknowledge the link between culture and learning in the attainment of knowledge and accept that this link is central to the process of decolonization.

Before highlighting the contributions in this book, we wish to unpack how we have chosen the title. The title, *Culture, Education, and Community: Expressions of the Postcolonial Imagination*, brings with it five interrelated themes—culture, education, community, postcolonialism, and imagination. In elaborating on our meanings, we will address culture, education, and community as a collective theme to mediate the epistemic power of everyday lived experiences. The latter two themes will be discussed subsequently to explore how we have come to understand the power of imagination within postcolonial contexts.

Culture, Education, and Community

According to Bourdieu (2006), "[t]he social world is accumulated history and if it is not to be reduced to a discontinuous series of instantaneous mechanical equilibria between agents who are treated as interchangeable particles, one must reintroduce into it the notion of capital and with it, accumulation and all its effects" (105). Central to the statement by Pierre Bourdieu is the idea that individuals do not come to a social encounter as *tabula rasa*, but rather, they embody an accumulation of knowledge, skills, and experiences—social energy, which has a potential capacity for reproduction and transformation. Education as a cultural practice, read in light of Bourdieu's claims, positions our discussion in the realm of cultural inquiry and contributes to an understanding of our practice as critical arrangements of community, commitments, obligations, and connections.

By positioning the book as a representation of a cultural politics of education, we adopt a mode of cultural inquiry, like Kanu to engage in a practice to destabilize "taken-for-granted categories, representation and truths in educational discourses and practices" (Kanu 2006, 5; see also Hoffman 1999, 464). For example, Darder and Uriate in chapter 4, provide contrapuntal reading of the dominant discourse about new and emerging language acquisition programs in the United States to expose how racialized projects serve the exclusion of working-class communities and are functioning to redress the gains of the past. Here they argue, "There has been a failure to consider the education of English-learners and their language rights with greater analytical depth, despite the manner in which workers are positioned within the U.S. political economy". Bristol, DeFour-Babb, et al. (chapter 11), focus on the notion of practice, claiming that theirs is not content with technicist, instrumental accounts and strategies, but rather, they move toward a "collective praxis," prevailed upon by knowledge generation and action. We acknowledge, therefore, that within these contexts, and those articulated by other authors in this volume, cultural critique facilitates: radical inquiry into how culture and society shape us and how we shape culture and society; the necessary exposure of power and control "exercised through a corpus of knowledge"; deconstruction of traditional categories to understanding the nature of unequal distribution of resources; reconstruction of new ways of thinking and acting; and the centrality of situated practice to fulfilling the project of postcolonial imagining (see Kanu 2006; Hoffman 1999; Apple 1996; Giroux 1983; and Young 1971). It is here that we make the link between culture and learning.

As readers will come to realize, one of the epistemic pillars of this book resides within practice theory and more so in advocating for situated practice. Nkoane and Lavia (chapter 3), Bristol et al. (chapter 11), and Singh (chapter 8), and Lingard et al. (chapter 6), for example, all refer directly to the importance of studying indigenous forms of knowledge, thereby emphasizing that learning takes place within multicultural and cross-cultural knowledge exchanges that make public the specificities of the lived experiences of individuals and communities (see Masemann 1990). However, McCarthy (1998) in writing about the uses of culture sends out a caution not to treat "topics of culture, identity and community simplistically" (148), because we run the risk of becoming complicit with minoritized and under-theorized reading and writing of these phenomena. Rather, in support of the idea of situated practice, McCarthy claims, "the dynamism and heterogeneity of everyday life of the myriad human encounters that produce and reproduce cultures and identities are thwarted in education" (148). Lee shares in signaling the danger of reifying culture when she claims that approaches to understanding practice as cultural difference, cultural deficits, cultural mismatch, and cultural repository all, although locating culture as central to learning, can lead us to miss the opportunity to interrogate that "people participate in different ways in multiple communities" (2007, 10). The cautions of both McCarthy and Lee warrant that we perhaps take a closer look at the culture –learning dialectic of situated practice to establish its circulatory logic.

Theodore Shatzki in forthcoming work, *A Primer on Practice* (2012), provides a comprehensive account of the field of practice theory, identifying its three central tenets. The first is that practice always occurs within rules and regulations, and we would argue that these act as vehicles through which power and control are exercised. In this way, practice is organized and systemic. The second tenet is that practice as organized activities is rooted in human activity, meaning that its study is essential to understanding "matters such as reason, identity, learning, and communication" (2012). Third, Shatzki refers to "teleoaffective structures," which can be construed as habits, attitudes, dispositions, feelings, and ways of being, doing and communicating. He offers a societist view of practice, to convey the idea that practices are located in sites that occur in bundles of sayings and doings. In summarizing the field, Shatzki (2012) writes, "The domain of 'practice theory' is delimited by a conception of practices as organized activities, the conviction that both social phenomena and key 'psychological' features of human life are tied to practices, and the idea that the basis of human activity is nonpropositional bodily abilities" (n.p.). In a related manner, making direct reference to education as a practice, Kemmis (1995) asserts that it is a form of power mediated by self-understandings of those who practice and who are affected by that practice. He further argues that practice is constructed in the sense that first, no practice is neutral but rather brings intention with it; second, practice is interpreted; third, it is historically constructed; and fourth, it is politically constructed. These criteria are useful in understanding the relationship between culture and learning, demonstrating that critical cultural inquiry will of necessity turn our attention to the "cultural situatedness" (Kanu 2006, 6) of all learning. And, as a corollary, all learning holds the potential for the production and construction of knowledge.

Let us reflect here on the Funds of Knowledge Project (see Moll and Greenberg1990; Gonzales, Moll, and Amanti 2005) and its contribution to our understanding of the relationship between culture, education, and community. Setting out to expose the messiness, yet potential for knowledge production of everyday life and by extension research, Gonzales, Moll, and Amanti (2005) elaborate how the Funds of Knowledge Project evolved organically. These researchers, mindful of the proliferation of research that is so often disconnected from the communities about which they write and do research, claimed and named a commitment to facilitating teachers in learning about the communities of their students. Teachers in this sense became the learners, willing to strip back their preconceived notions of their students' lives to become alert and sensitive to a corpse of knowledge that resided within the students' everyday experiences. The student experience was central to their ethnographic study that initially involved ten teachers in California. As the study unfolded through the process of paying home visits to students, it was found that the home/household-based artifacts, environments, and encounters generated different types of knowledge. Acknowledging that "the interaction between text and social life, between word and worlds is a constant process," the project generated its own creative praxis and lexicon, causing participants to develop a new and different attitude (2005, 22) to cultural resources that were to be found within the households. Seemingly inspired by the notion that teaching requires curiosity (Freire 1998), the Funds of Knowledge Project has contributed a material and discursive space to interrogate educational practice, stating in clear terms that the requirement for transformation and change are constitutive of cultural action for social transformation based on the everyday lives of individuals and communities. Learning in this sense can be read as a process of conscientization through deliberate and conscious action. This act, as direct interference into cultures of silence that are perpetrated by dependency social exclusion, is identified and contextualized by several contributors to this volume.

By extending the critique on the ideas of funds of knowledge, Carol Lee credits the Funds of Knowledge Project with providing the groundwork for what she conceptualizes as her notion of cultural modeling. She argues, however, for a different focus for her cultural project by foregrounding "learning as an ecologically situated practice" (2007, xxiii). In addition to paying attention to the knowledge reservoir gleaned from the social context of everyday experiences, she also articulates a framework for examining and deconstructing how culture occurs within classrooms.

Postcolonial Imagination

We turn our attention now to the subtitle "Expressions of the Postcolonial Imagination." The word *expressions* is offered as a space of creativity where specific cases of colonial encounter are represented by various authors. Not all chapters use postcolonial theories in their analysis; however, we believe that in pushing the boundaries of postcolonial thought what we have done is to allow for eclectic expressions that find common ground in their quest to trouble, confront, contest, dismantle, and reconstruct old and new enclaves of colonialism. It is in this sense that we articulate that the postcolonial resides in a field of complexity and contestation. As Stuart Hall (1996) has advised, when he asked the question, "When was the postcolonial?," in occupying a deconstructed mode, we speak truth to power through our spaces of liminality, allowing for theoretical and methodological rendering of this misnomer. These spaces are interpreted in this book through narratives that relate to the struggle for language rights, critical pedagogy and praxis, cultural identity and the role of teachers and academics, indigenous rights and education, and curriculum reform and change.

As Bristol has highlighted in this volume, "postcolonialism offers the possibility of a new story, a different story, and a contested story," and it is in this sense that we accept responsibility for positioning the discourse to allow a postcolonial theoretical orientation that can lead to and accommodate other critical perspectives, since most deal with power and uneven relationships (Kanu 2006; Althusser 1971). We share the claim that the scope of postcolonial thought can been seen in its different interpretations and emphases of colonial encounter. These locations include accounts of the struggle for independence and the transformation of colonies into autonomous states riding on the waves of intense anticolonial movements. They also include consideration of the contemporary context, learning from the historical and projecting alternative ways of knowing, doing, and being. By expanding the discourse, we agree with Kanu that "the 'postcolonial' becomes the site where a variety of assumptions accepted on individual, academic and political levels are called into question in the struggle for more democratic social relations" (68).

We wish to emphasize two central ideas in this book. First, historical accounts serve to contextualize and present a framework for postcolonial imagining, and second, by developing a cultural politics of education is to directly link a central concern of postcolonialism, that being unpacking the relationship between knowledge and power. Further Rizvi et al. (2006) disclose: "It is only through education that it is possible to reveal and resist colonialism's continuing hold on our imagination...Education is also a site where legacies of colonialism and the contemporary process of globalization intersect" (257). In this book, therefore, we have explored this intersection, imagined through common concern for exploring historical and contemporary sites of resistance that lead to the re-installation of cultural confidence for colonized communities.

Structure of the Book

Fenway and Fahey (2009, 2) ask two important questions that could guide us to understanding the importance of imagination. They ask: How do we commonly imagine the imagination? How do we understand it in the everyday? The chapters in this book present ways of imagining through collective interpretations of specific circumstances. We would hope that we have forged a community of ideas and practices that have privileged the "generating [of] conceptions of personhood and identity" (Kanu 2006, 68; also see Popkerwitz 2000; Rizvi 2000).

In chapter 1, "Postcolonial Thought," Laurette Bristol seeks to explore how the theory and methodology of the postcolonial is decolonizing and arguing for its application to education research. Bristol makes connections between culture, education, and research to show how cultural confidence can be forged through what she describes as culturally ethical practice. Positioning education as cultural practice, Bristol comments on the capacity of teachers to become conscious of what their practice reproduces. By providing this cultural account of education and educational practice in the context of Trinidad and Tobago, Bristol's analysis is important.

The agency of educational researchers is taken up by Sechaba Mahlomaholo in chapter 2, "Validating Community Cultural Wealth Toward Sustainable Empowering Learning Environments," where he reflects on how far the rhetoric of the Truth and Reconciliation Commission has addressed the promise of a better and more humane and democratic life for South Africans. Using Yosso's notion of community cultural wealth, Mahomaholo proposes a role for intellectuals and academics—that of forging links with the community to imagining new futures.

Like Mahomaholo, Nkoane and Lavia discuss in chapter 3, "Rethinking Education in South Africa, the country's context, where they emphasize the role of education as liberatory practice. They begin by providing an historical overview of education in South Africa, showing how in 1953 the Bantu Education Act legalized a separate and racist education system. They draw upon a Freirean notion of liberation pedagogy, arguing that education occurs in community and is hopeful practice. They provide an autobiographical account to show the lived experience of apartheid that rendered the Black masses as less than human and have advocated critical practice—liberation pedagogy as an effort of recovery in a democratic South Africa. In this way, their analysis is important in that, these authors have made explicit that cultural confidence is to be gained through respectful relationships between students and teachers engaged in a critical pedagogy and seeking change on the basis of an anticolonial agenda. Such an agenda is to be found in the developing intellectual curiosity around African indigenous knowledge systems (AKIS).

In chapter 4, "The Politics of Restrictive Language Policies," by Antonia Darder and Miren Uriarte, who turn our attention to a specific struggle of language restriction in the United States. By historicizing the case of Boston, they illustrate how restrictive language policies have contributed to marginalization of communities of English language learners. The choice of Boston was twofold. First, as they have stated, Boston and Massachusetts schools were among the first to enact legislation making provisions for transitional language programs for the new and increasing Spanish population. Second, the majority of English learners are from histories "that have been deeply marked by colonialism." Their concern is that the gains made by the previous legislation, where a civil-rights agenda was given privilege, are being displaced by conservative neoliberal measures of restrictive language policies. By elaborating this postcolonial analysis through an empirical study, Darder and Uriate present an important account of social exclusion by examining the relationship between class and race, implementation of restrictive language policies and the location of English language learners within the economy, politics, education, and wider social fabric of American society.

The ideas of indigenous curricular, minority language and language acquisition come together in chapter 5, "Súil-Eile," by Simon Warren, who focuses on the Irish context. He positions the specific case of Ireland within a more general context of "the fate of threatened or endangered languages." While in the case of Darder and Uriate in chapter 4, they focus on how exclusion occurs systemically through restrictive policies around English language acquisition, Warren draws our attention to issues of colonial power with regard to languages that have been minoritized. He articulates a stance that moves beyond the binary of how do Irish people construct a popular cultural politics in the context of opposition between the language of the people and the language of the colonial power. In addition, he argues for confronting the reality of English as the common vernacular of Irish people. Further, Warren challenges the notion of cultural confidence, suggesting instead that interrogating "the sustainability of pursuing a cultural politics of language based on the assertion of minority rights" can be more reliably formulated around a notion of solidarity.

In chapter 6, "Reimagining Lines of Flight in Schooling for Indigenous Students in Australia," Lingard, Vas, and Mckinlay focus their analysis on schooling for indigenous communities in Australia and provide a critical analysis of contemporary policy concerning these students. They unpack the offering of Noel Pearson's radical vision, Chris Sarra's "strong and smart" strategy, and the national and regional policy of "closing the gap." They also interrogate what it means in their work to take a postcolonial stance and how this stance becomes appropriate as an aspirational project in respect of indigenous education. In reflecting on the central question of the book, these authors conclude that schools alone cannot compensate for centuries of violence and oppression on indigenous peoples. Rather, they argue that reclamation, reconciliation, and resuscitation of indigenous rights and schooling must be pivotal within: a recognition of "the colonial violence of the past and ongoing colonial present," the conviction that schools can and must make a difference in the lives of indigenous people, "the need to work with Aboriginal funds of knowledge within schools and their communities," and that a movement toward policy and practice that is decolonizing is essential if "local epistemologies and ontologies are taken up robustly in the culture and practices of schooling relevant to that particular setting."

In chapter 7, "Border Crossing," Dennis Francis continues with the theme on race to highlight the experience of nine Indian-white biracial youths in South Africa. Admittedly, a much under-researched topic, Francis presents his findings from empirical study of how these young people articulate their experience of social life. By using life-history research, Francis shows how preoccupied society is about race as identity pointing to the elements that contribute to the cultural confidence of the biracial young people in the study. In this case, Francis uses postcolonial analysis to historicize the experience of apartheid South Africa, showing the persistent preoccupation with race and the resultant expression of these biracial youth to internalize complex representations of their identity.

Basing her thesis on the work of Frantz Fanon, in chapter 8, "Constructing a Nation," Lorraine Singh continues the discussion of culture, identity, and the South African experience. Singh begins by signaling the need to interrogate cultural difference in light of the colonial experience. Making the point that South Africa "suffered doubly under centuries of colonialism and apartheid," she argues for "reconstruction and cultural reimaginings," and begins by scrutinizing the history of education-policy documents with particular reference to arts education. Critical of both the notion of the "rainbow nation" and the "rhetoric of the African renaissance," Singh engages in a comparative analysis of three versions of the arts education curriculum, illustrating the transient understandings of the notion of "culture" with the most current curriculum policy agenda, dropping the word *culture* entirely in preference for *creative arts*. Singh argues that is not merely a matter of semantics but represents a fundamental shift in ideology. Agreeing that school arts curriculum in South Africa has been influential in resistance and countenancing oppressive regimes, Singh makes claims for a South Africans' funds of knowledge—a curriculum that "offers a space and a way of knowing about our world and how we act in it." One of the conclusions that Singh comes to in her chapter is that the double oppression of South Africa and the corresponding strategies for reclamation and resurgence indeed provide spaces for hybrid forms of culture—new ways of thinking, writing, reading, being, doing, and relating.

It is an example of this hybrid space, a liminal space, which is highlighted in chapter 9, "Calypso, Education, and Community in Trinidad and Tobago," where Gordon Rohlehr has produced a creative chapter, using an array of calypsos to provide an historical analysis of education in the Republic of Trinidad and Tobago. Rohlehr's chapter arises out of a public lecture that he gave in which he used over 100 calypsos to illustrate the power of the genre to exemplify an indigenous form of knowing and being. In this published form, Rohlehr's chapter is written as three movements. The first provides an historical background to understanding a text written by Eric Williams, entitled *Education in the British West Indies*. The significance of this text is to be found in its explanatory power and guidance in shaping post-independence education within the Anglo-Caribbean region and more so because of its anticolonial stance for national and regional development. The text, as Rohlehr explains, cannot be read in isolation to understanding the historical colonial encounter, and it is in this regard that Rohlehr interweaves calypso commentary in the second movement about the aspirations, frustrations, successes, and failures of the national and regional educational experience. Calypso is used as indigenous and practical philosophy that theorizes the postcolonial through other eyes. The third moment gives an account of the final years of Eric Williams of the post-independence problematic and how these "troubles" and challenges have been configured through the lyrics of the calypso.

In chapter 10, "More in de Mortar dan de Pestle," Joyanne DeFour-Babb, continues to explain the educational context of Trinidad and Tobago, albeit turning her attention to secondary-school teachers. Central to her argument is the notion of teacher identity more so, she offers empirical insights into how secondary teachers as postcolonial subjects have come to understand their own professional identity. Drawing upon similar historical precedence as Rohlehr in the previous chapter, DeFour-Babb addresses the issue of cultural confidence in three ways. First, she presents an analysis of how the state perceived that the graduate secondary teacher and how the state-imposed configuration shaped the teacher. Second, DeFour-Babb asks: "What [were] the dominant cultural-discursive, material-economic and social-political arrangements (Kemmis and Grootenboer 2008) [that] enabled or constrained the recruitment process for graduate secondary teachers in Trinidad and Tobago?" Third, she represents how secondary-school teachers perceived their recruitment as teachers and their practice in an era of independence. De Four-Babb combines a postcolonial perspective with a Foucauldian analysis to amplify the colonizing process of teacher recruitment.

In the final chapter, chapter 11, "Comparative Collaboration," the writers have returned to some common themes running through the book. In this chapter, Bristol, De Four-Babb, Esnard, Lavia, and

Perez present an unfolding narrative of how the five authors have been collaborating in a fledgling research network (CURVE) to advance an aspirational agenda around educational and social research that is *from* and *for* the Caribbean, rather it being *on* the Caribbean. Claiming the right of their subjectivities, they locate their work eclectically, asserting that cultural confidence occurs within transgressive practice. Like Mahomaholo in chapter 2 and Nkoane and Lavia in chapter 3, they position the teacher, academic, and researcher as architects and agents of transformation. None of these authors are under the illusion that the right conditions will simply present themselves without some form of agency. Making reference to Edward Glissant (1999), Bristol et al. establish that, "For us being and becoming is not only an aspect of *orchestration and prefiguring* but a characteristic of social, political and economic alliances /affiliation." In naming "comparative collaboration" as decolonizing practice, they join Lingard et al. in chapter 6 in urging that postcolonial discourse is not enough to irradicate centuries of violence, oppression, and marginalization. Comparative collaboration as decolonizing practice is implicated as cultural and historical obligation decided on the basis of privileging a stance from the colonized. For these authors, being and becoming are given shape through epistemic, axiological, and methodological projects.

We present a collection of critical essays in this book that offer disparate accounts of colonial encounter through which we have attempted to show the tensions, possibilities, and capabilities of cultural inquiry. Positioned within the critique of the postcolonial, we have subjected education as cultural practice to interrogation to expose the necessity for making public, private concerns.

References

Althusser, L. 1971. *Lenin and Philosophy*. New York: Monthly Review Press.
Apple, M. 1996. *Cultural Politics and Education*. New York: Teachers College Press.
Bourdieu, P. 2006. "The Forms of Capital." In *Education, Globalization & Social Change*, edited by H. Lauder; P. Brown; J. Dillabough and A. Halsey, 105–118. Oxford: Oxford University Press.
Freire, P. 1998. *Pedagogy of Freedom: Ethics, Democracy and Civic Courage*. Lanham, MD: Rowman and Littlefield.
Giroux, H. 1983. "Theories of Reproduction and Resistance in the New Sociology of Education: A Critical Analysis." *Harvard Educational Review* 53: 257–293.

Gonzales, N., L. Moll, and C. Amanti, ed. 2005. *Funds of Knowledge: Theorizing Practices in Households, Communities, and Classrooms.* New Jersey: Lawrence Erlbaum.

Hall, S. 1996. "When Was the Post-Colonial?: Thinking at the Limit." In, *The Post-Colonial Question: Common Skies, Divided Horizons,* edited by I. Chambers & L. Curti, 242–259. London: Routledge.

Hoffman, D. 1999. "Culture and Comparative Education: Toward Decentering and Recentering the Discourse." *Comparative Education Review* 43 (4): 464.

Kanu, Y. 2003. "Curriculum as Cultural Practice: Postcolonial Imaginations." *Journal of the Canadian Association for Curriculum Studies* 1 (1): 67–81.

Kanu, Y., ed. 2006. *Curriculum as Cultural Practice: Postcolonial Imaginations.* Toronto: University of Toronto Press.

Kemmis, S. 1995. "Prologue: Theorizing Educational Practice." In *For Education: Towards Critical Educational Inquiry,* edited by W. Carr. Buckingham, UK: Open University Press.

Kemmis, S. and P. Grootenboer. 2008. "Situating Praxis in Practice: Practice Architectures and the Cultural, Social, and Material Conditions for Practice." In *Enabling Praxis: Challenges for Education,* edited by S. Kemmis and T. J. Smith. Rotterdam: Sense 37–62.

Kenway, J., and J. Fahey, ed. 2009. *Globalising the Research Imagination.* London, Routledge.

Lee, C. 2007. *Culture, Literacy, and Learning: Taking Bloom in the Midst of the Whirlwind.* New York: Teachers College Press.

Masemann, V. 1990. "Ways of Knowing." *Comparative Education Review* 34 (4): 465.

McCarthy, C. 1998. *The Uses of Culture: Education and the Limits of Ethnic Affiliation.* New York: Routledge.

Moll, L. and S. Greenberg. 1990. "Creating Zones of Possibilities: Combining social contexts for instruction." In *Vygotsky and Education,* edited by L. C. Moll. Cambridge: Cambridge University Press, 319–348. Funds of Knowledge Project.

Nettleford, R. 1970. *Mirror Mirror: Identity, Race and Protest in Jamaica.* Kingston: LMH Publishing.

Popkewitz, T. S. 2000. "Reform as the Social Administration of the Child: Globalization of Knowledge and Power." In *Globalization and Education: Critical Perspectives,* edited by N. C. Burbules and C. A. Torres. New York: Routledge, 157–186.

Rizvi, F. 2000. "International Education and the Production of Global Imagination." In *Globalization and Education: Critical Perspectives,* edited by N. C. Burbules and C. A. Torres. (New York: Routledge), 205–225.

Rizvi, F., B. Lingard, and J. Lavia. 2006. Postcolonialism and Education: Negotiating a Contested Terrain. *Journal of Pedagogy, Culture & Society,* 14 (October 2006): 249–262.

Shatski, T. 2012 (forthcoming). "A Primer on Practices." In *Practice-Based Education: Perspectives and Strategies,* edited by J. Higgs et al. Rotterdam: Sense Publishers.

Young, M. 1971. *Knowledge and Control.* London: Collier Macmillan.

1
Postcolonial Thought: A Theoretical and Methodological Means for Thinking through Culturally Ethical Research

Laurette Bristol

Introduction

Colonialism as a story of European legitimacy, control, enlightenment, and civility has used research to claim and maintain its hold over the psyche of the colonized. This research strategically functioned to erase and reassign great moments in history, knowledge capacity, and technological advancement; as such, it became the means through which the colonizer told colonized peoples about themselves (see Smith 1999; Williams 1962 for the ways that research has attempted to construct the identity and capacities of the colonized).

Against the meta-narrative of European colonialism, postcolonialism stands as a set of perspectives in which the contemporary world is reinterrogated, reinterpreted, and repositioned discursively through practices and policies *of* and *for* social justice. If research is constructed as a dominant story, told about a particular moment, in which a particular group responded to social, economic, political, and historical forces, then postcolonial research offers the possibility of a new story, a different story, and a contested story. This new research can address not only the illusion of colonialism as a universal perspective but interrogates itself as something framed within the systems it functions to disrupt. Beyond the sphere of cultural studies, a postcolonial perspective has often been forced to confront itself through the varied experiences and interpretations of globalization, neocolonialism, and imperialism. These discourses are typically used to interrogate the identity formation of societies, and the economic, social, and political means through which colonial identities are perpetuated and challenged within the institutional practices of societies, governments, and transnational corporations. Postcolonial theory has demonstrated its application and usefulness to the field of comparative education. In this space, postcolonial theory has been used to construct a critique of the relationship between development and education and the ways in which such a relationship has served to foster a new form of imperialism through a repositioning identities and affiliations, reinscribing a progressive dualism between the developed and developing world.

This chapter contributes to the postcolonial debate by examining the ways in which postcolonial theory can provide both a theoretical and methodological framework for the design of educational research that actively works to interrogate ideas of what counts *as* and *for* research in contexts with a history of colonialism. In this chapter, I suggest that postcolonial research that fails to make use of the indigenous knowledge and modes of sense-making from the community under consideration can contribute to a form of "new imperialism," as proposed by Tikly (2004, 74). Failure to recognize the value of indigenous ways of knowing to the design of research has the potential to implicate postcolonial researchers in postcolonial contexts, such as the Caribbean region, in the maintenance, reproduction, and dominance of Westernized ways of coming to know the world through conducting research. The aim of this chapter, then, is to discuss how postcolonialism, as a cultural account for society, facilitates and provides a theoretical framework for educational analysis and a methodological orientation for culturally ethical and aspirational postcolonial-educational research. In order to achieve this aim, I move through three spaces of discourse.

In the first instance, I will address the intentions of a theory of postcolonialism and its demand for a critical cultural consciousness. Second, I will engage with culture as the way in which individuals represent themselves through the construction of a social imagination. I argue that the social imagination of teachers is shaped through the traditions of education and teaching that are specific to the context in which they practice. Understanding the relationship between culture and education and how they reciprocally embrace each other has implications for educational transformation and the practice of postcolonial research. In the last movement of this chapter, I propose a postcolonial approach to educational research that provides a cultural perspective for ethical research.

The central argument of this chapter is that postcolonialism helps to excavate the interrelationships and tensions between education, culture, and research. In suggesting this, I invite Appadurai (2000) into the discourse as he challenges those of us within the academy to:

> Contest, interrogate, and reverse...and create forms of knowledge transfer and social mobilization that proceed independently of the actions of corporate capital and the nation-state system (and its international affiliates and guarantors). These social forms rely on strategies, visions and horizons for globalisation on the behalf of the poor that can be characterised as "grassroots globalisation", or, put in a slightly different ways, as "globalisation from below" (3).

Postcolonial-educational research, because it inherently challenges and tackles the problems inherited from colonialism, is then ethically charged to participate in a practice of *globalization from below* through a consideration of the historical and cultural politics of education and the particularities of the society within which education is the field of interest. Postcolonial-educational research that is culturally ethical (re)presents education and its associated research practices as a dialectical and dialogical space for political and ideological struggle. In so doing, it creates the opportunity for a community of teachers to reconstruct their roles as teachers and cultural workers (Freire 2005).

Postcolonial Thought: A Theoretical Positioning

Postcolonial theory for cultural studies and postcolonial theory for education has different applications. The former interrogates the construction and contradictory nature of the colonized identity; probing into the ways in which that identity is rehearsed historically through constructions of hegemonic and subaltern cultures. It provides an emancipatory discourse and privileges cultural consciousness as the means by which the colonized, through an interrogation of the dominant discourses around race, ethnicity, colour, gender, and class transforms and creates a counter narrative against oppressive structures (Jefferess, McGonegal, and Milz 2006). It provides an account of the customs, traditions, and values of societies that experienced the influence of colonial development. In doing so, it explores the ways in which particular relationships within these societies have arisen and the ways in which individuals and mechanisms within these societies maintain or resist their presence (Fanon 1952; Fanon 1963; Fanon 1964; Bhabha 1994; Lamming 1995; Won Lee 1997; Farred 2001a; Fuchs and Baker 2004; Chandra and Larsen 2006).

For Rizvi, Lingard, and Lavia (2006) postcolonial discourse is a 'highly contested political and theoretical terrain' (249). Recognizing the field as problematic, some scholars suggest that the term *postcolonialism* is misleading and contradictory in its suggestion of the end of colonialism (Shohat 1992; Majid 1996; San Juan 1999; Chowdhury 2000; McLeod 2000; Farred 2001b; Hassan and Saunders 2003; Mishra and Hodge 2005; Mezzadra and Rahola 2006; and Wehrs 2004). Others argue that the theory has a "guilty conscience about depending upon Western-derived analytical matrices [which] exhibit a lack of interest in non-Western cultures' articulations of meaning and value" (Wehrs 2004, 761).

Proponents of using postcolonial theory for education realize the practicality of postcolonial thought as a vehicle for pedagogical transformation (Appadurai 2000; Crossley and Tikly 2004; Hickling-Hudson 2004; Hickling-Hudson 2010; Rizvi 2006; Rizvi, et al. 2006). Lavia (2007) argues that postcolonial theory promotes an aspirational agenda and generates:

> A set of lenses through which the persistent and insidious legacies of European colonialism can be made visible. [It] posits a decolonizing discourse about schooling and educational practice putting on the table a productive, critical and engaged role of educating students and radicalizing of teachers' practice' (286).

For Hickling-Hudson (2010), postcolonial theory provides educators with interrogative tools that lay pathways into and a response to "questions of why so many curriculum practices and educational programs appear still far away from consensus on the goals, contours and implementation of equity" (299). Hickling-Hudson (2010) also suggests that:

> Since postcolonial theory identifies the colonial roots of many of the problems of our globalizing era and deconstructs the aftermath, it throws light on how the curriculum can be problematized and challenged within its historicized context (299).

Lavia (2007) and Hickling-Hudson (2010) point to the importance of making visible contemporary structures, policies, texts, technologies, and institutions that continue to execute dominant discourses and practices that prefigure the practice of the educator and the critical capacity of students as oppressed, acritical, or apolitical (see also Tikly 2004). In this way, they recognize the value of postcolonial theory to an interrogation of the cultural-discursive (sayings), material-economic (doings), and sociopolitical (relatings) conditions (Kemmis and Grootenboer 2008) constructed within experiences of postcolonial subjectivities in an era of globalization that work to constrain as well as enable the practices of educators and researchers in the face of neoliberal demands. For postcolonial educators to engage in a practice of emancipation, they must begin to challenge, by making visible, their dialectical location within the historical, political, economic, and social conditions that frame their view of the world. The practice of making visible the discursive structures that frame the agentic capacity of teachers can be realized through a research practice that looks at the world not only from *below* as suggested by Young (2003) in Preece et al. (2008), but more problematically from *within*.

Looking at the postcolonial problematic from within has implications for the development of a postcolonial research methodology. Returning to Appadurai (2000), a postcolonial methodological design can be one that actively works to counter the emergence of a Westernized discourse around what counts as research and how it could be enacted; it encourages and demands that researcher pose "questions about the nature of knowledge itself" in a postcolonial-educational context which intersects with the experiences of globalization (Tikly 2004, 178). Building upon the arguments of Preece et al. (2008) and Tikly (2004), postcolonial methodology as a discursive practice can:

> Provide [the] necessary starting point for those interested in social critique and transformative action because it is within this terrain that shared understandings about the nature and implications of economic, political and cultural change are constructed and contested (Tikly 2004, 177–178).

In addressing the educational and research implications of our social, political, and economic existence within the intersection of the global and the local, cultural understandings become the resource with which the postcolonial-educational researcher recreates a methodological orientation that recognizes the historical rootedness of globalization in postcolonialism and colonialism. Privileging culture not only as a pedagogical force (Giroux 2003), but as a methodological resource, allows the researcher to interrogate enacted assumptions about educational practice from within the traditions and practices of education and the society. In so doing, it has the potential to limit the ways in which educational research in collaboration with educational provision is able to realize a new form of imperialism (Tikly 2004).

Culture in Education: The Value of Postcolonial Thought

In this section, I argue that the intersection between culture, education, and postcolonial thought provides the postcolonial-educational researcher with pedagogical and methodological tools. In addition, I suggest that the intersection between the three areas of thought constructs the intellectual framework needed to interrogate forms of production perpetuated through a collection of ideas and practices that undergo constant struggle and compromise within classroom practice. To do this, I examine notions of culture as a form of knowledge production and the lens with which to interrogate postcolonial subjectivity.

Teachers, as members of a community of educators, are brought into the habits of educating through personal experiences, schooling incidents, and encounters with other teachers who are already embedded or being initiated into their roles as members of a teaching community. The practice of organizing members, defining identity, determining roles, and maintaining group integrity is considered to be the cultural habits of a group. To speak of the transformation of teaching requires an awareness of the teacher's cultural role as well as the development of a critical cultural consciousness that allows the teacher to interrogate the meanings of images and concepts represented within the shared linguistic turns of the culture of teaching. This signifies that educational transformation requires first the recognition that "the educator's practices are also the product of other practices" (Kemmis and Grootenboer 2008, 37) that make up the culture of the society of which the teacher is a part. These understandings help us as teachers to understand the cultural function of education and the ways in which educational culture can be made intelligible, be contested, and made more relevant to the educational needs of postcolonial societies in the twenty-first century. My intention here is to relate this idea to the context of the Caribbean region and the educational research challenges it must meet in responding to global imperatives. The action and processes involved in making educational culture intelligible, explicitly contested and more relevant to our postcolonial context as a group of developing nations is a part of the "pedagogical force of culture" (Giroux 2003, 54) for which teachers are responsible.

Teachers and researchers are members of a particular culture to which they are called to account, interrogate, challenge, and reproduce through pedagogical and research practices. An awareness of the political force of culture and the ways in which it frames our view of the world and our position in that world becomes important when culture is in itself a "form of production" (Giroux 2005, 123). Culture frames "the ways in which human beings make sense of their lives, feelings, beliefs, thoughts, and the wider society. [It is a] set of practices and ideologies from which different groups draw to make sense of the world" (Giroux 2005, 123). Cultural understandings make individual and community existence intelligible. This process is repeated over generations, and so culture is the "intellectual inheritance" of a society (Gilroy 1993, 8). Edward Said (1995, 95) presents a more "territorial" view of culture. His position takes into consideration the stance of both Gilroy (1993) and Giroux (2005). Said (1978), however, extends the analysis by bounding culture within a geographical field, observing that each culture is different and distinguishable by geography, language, and ethnicity. Constructing culture and the study of culture in this way provides culture with a sense of "utility" (Said 1978, 54) that serves two purposes. In the first instance, it satisfies the mind's demand for order, and in the second instance, it distinguishes our culture from theirs. In giving claim to culture, the mind:

> Requires order, and order is achieved by discriminating and taking note of everything, placing everything of which the mind is aware in a secure, refindable place, therefore giving things some role to play in the economy of objects and identities that make up an environment. [In so doing the mind makes use of] imaginative geography and history [to] help the mind to intensify its own sense of itself by dramatizing the distance and difference between what is close to it and what is far away (Said 1978, 53).

From Said's (1978) position, differences among and between cultures are constructions of the mind. The extent to which this view can be fully accepted is limited as it suggests that cultures are able to isolate and insulate themselves from the influence of other cultures through constructions of mental mapping. I believe, however, that the ways in which cultures are formed is what makes culture as a set of intergenerational social practices unstable, especially, in the face of encounters with other peoples in possession of a different conception of what stands for culture. This contestable characteristic of culture, like postcolonial thought, does not suggest that it is not constant or very easily changed. What it does suggest is that these are political fields where struggles for cultural compromises and supremacy are waged.

Taking up the issue of vulnerability and dynamism in culture, from a postcolonial perspective, involves a consideration of theories of "creolization," "hybridity," and "syncretism." These theories speak of the linguistic and social spaces where two or more cultures meet and exchange cultural understandings. Like Said (1978), Gilroy (1995) characterizes this exchange as cultural borrowings, while Wilson Harris (1998) describes cultural interactions as the "gifts [one culture] offers to another culture" (29). The cultural vulnerability that allows for exchange is also a form of resistance for cultures that were overtaken by force and suppressed. Bhabha (1994) constructs cultural vulnerability as a "camouflage, as a contesting, antagonistic agency functioning in the time-lag of sign/symbol, which is a space in-between the rules of engagement. [It is a form of] political agency" (277). It is in the negotiations or struggles between cultures that cultural supremacy is called into question. To resolve this, cultural compromises are made in which some elements of one culture get assumed into the culture of another. In these negotiations, compromises, and struggles, what occurs is a redefinition of the collective images that represent a culture. For postcolonial-educational research, the possibility of such a redefinition of images could be extended to include a reconceptualization of postcolonial-educational research design and methodologies.

Another feature of culture that I consider to be valuable to a discussion on the work of the postcolonial teacher and educational researcher revolves around the value of culture as a pedagogical and methodological tool. To engage with this, we must return to Giroux's (2003) argument that culture has a pedagogical force that can be accessed through classroom teaching and research. On the point of pedagogy, Giroux (2005) states that culture can provide the teacher:

> With the critical categories necessary for examining school and classroom relations as social and political practices inextricably related to the construction and maintenance of specific relations of power (Giroux 2005, 194).

These critical categories of examining school culture provide the teacher with what Giroux (2000) calls a "cultural pedagogy" (Giroux 2000, 162). Cultural pedagogy is a method of evaluative teaching about school culture and the way that the practices of the school perpetuate or contest standardized relations of power that support structures of social order. Cultural pedagogy can serve social reproduction as well as facilitate the transformation of cultural practices through education. The teacher engaged in cultural pedagogy is engaged in promoting cultural consciousness. A critical cultural consciousness lends itself to what Ramchand (2000) calls "cultural confidence" (515).

> [It is] knowing who you are and why you are in the midst of all the convulsions that are changing your life. It is difficult to achieve... and it can never be final. The outcomes of post-independence education, politics and economics suggest that a more serious look has to be taken at the possibilities inherent in the works of the creative imagination (Ramchand 2000, 515–516).

Here Ramchand (2000) points to ways in which a consideration of culture facilitates a pedagogy of evaluative teaching and hints at the possibility of postcolonial research as a practice of creative imagination. Thus, there are valuable lessons to be learned from culture in the pursuit of postcolonial-educational transformation. A relationship between postcolonial theory, culture, and education is intended to help teachers in societies with a history of oppression apprehend their practice in a historical context and begin to change it. What this means in practice is that teachers who teach with a critical historical and cultural awareness of their practice circumstances are able, in community with students and peers, to teach against ideas that continue to maintain practices of intellectual dependency, oppression, and social injustice. This brings me to consider the pedagogical force of culture as a methodological tool for postcolonial-educational research.

In the next section I will explore how a theory of postcolonialism could also provide a methodological approach for culturally ethical educational research in a postcolonial context. Within this context, it will become clear that the pedagogical work of culture, as argued by Giroux (2000, 2005) and Ramchand (2000), can inform critical cultural consciousness needed to shape the way in which the postcolonial teacher engages with and enters into educational research.

Postcolonial Thought: A Methodological Positioning

> Education is deeply implicated in the politics of culture...It is always part of a selective tradition, someone's selection, some group's vision of legitimate knowledge. It is produced out of the cultural, political and economic conflicts, tensions, and compromises that organise and disorganise a people (Apple 1996, 22).

The quotation from Apple's (1996) book *Cultural Politics and Education* is an appropriate opening for any discussion on the use of postcolonialism as a methodological means of carrying out culturally ethical educational research. It highlights an irrefutable connection between education and culture and points to tensions and compromises engaged within postcolonialism. It proposes that education is a historical product and that, what we teach (the curriculum) is a selection from that culture. It makes a political connection between education and culture through notions of "selection" and the "legitimacy" of what counts as knowledge (Apple 1996, 22). Like postcolonial thought, applied to educational analysis, it recognizes the aspirational/cultural function of education through the claim that the goals of education arise out of a culture's "vision" for itself (Apple 1996, 22). It reveals education as a field of political struggle (Young 1971), and the proposition is made that education is a tool of social control, a way of organizing groups of people into social sets.

Bell hooks (1991) in her book *Yearning: Race, Gender, and Cultural Politics*, endorses the argument that a critical-cultural analysis, of education, has the capacity to "disrupt and even deconstruct those cultural productions that were designed to promote and reinforce domination" (3). The critically and culturally aware teacher, enters postcolonial research with a strong respect for the history, agency, limitations, and complexity of the space and people she/he is about to work with. She/ he views the opportunity for research not as the opportunity to tell *the* story, rather, in telling *a part of a* story, and weighs the balance of the complexities of human existence. The aim of culturally ethical research should not be to produce a stable picture of the scenario, but to construct an incomplete web of the tensions and interrelations between people and objects of a particular culture. The opportunity offered in access to spaces and the people living within, is an occasion for openness to learning and reevaluating the value and appropriateness of assumptions. Postcolonial-educational research entered into with a respect for the layers of culture begins the process of research as a decolonizing methodology (Smith 1999).

As I conceptualize it, culturally ethical research is a research practice in which the researcher respects and considers the complexity of culture; the history that shaped that culture and the interrelationships of the people who live and work in that space. In this mode of research, the postcolonial-educational researcher continuously reflects upon the ways in which members of that culture make sense of and select the means through which their culture should be represented, reproduced, and transformed. Moreover, the researcher is continuously engaged in a reflection upon her or his impact upon the space and the tensions that emerge as a result of the encounter. Postcolonialism, as a theoretical and methodological framework for educational research, facilitates the teacher-researcher's ability to confront the psychosocial, cultural, and political struggles inherent within educational provisions and challenges the ways in which "we" come to know self and others. In doing so, the teacher-researcher is able to connect with teaching as a field of study in a manner that is culturally ethical.

Given the argument above, the position that I take is that for postcolonial-educational research, to be culturally ethical, it must be embedded in the cultural politics of the society. If it can be agreed that education is a selection from culture, and that the intention of education is to organize society, shape identities, and determine social roles, then it must also be granted that the study of education must be firmly placed in the study of those cultural and historical practices that shape it. In so doing, one realizes the cultural work of education and its inherent political position in relation to social reproduction and social transformation. To transform educational organizations is to deconstruct social structures and produce an alternative perspective to knowledge that is culturally and historically inherited. The use of a theory of postcolonialism as a methodological approach with which to engage in educational considerations operates from the premise that education is a space, a scape (Appadurai 1995), and a field of political struggle. The struggle engaged in is a contestation over whose knowledge should be given legitimacy, for what purpose, and how this knowledge should be transferred, at what phase in a person's life should the knowledge be transmitted, and how this knowledge should be interrogated.

As a method of inquiry, postcolonialism becomes an enabling tool (McLeod 2000) for the study and work of research in relation to its service to culture. As a part of the decolonizing project, postcolonialism positions educational research as a "site of significant struggle" (Smith 1999, 2) between the agendas of neoliberal market economics and privatization that are communicated through educational development policies and interpreted in practices of the classroom teacher. Postcolonialism as a site of ideological struggle facilitates the creation of a dialectic-scape within which the indigenous classroom teacher/researcher is able to analyze imperialism, and understand the "complex ways in which [knowledge] is deeply embedded in the multiple layers of imperial and colonial practices" (Smith 1999, 2).

Within this dialectical-scape teachers become aware of their reality, a reality where they are both conditioned by and are the creators of the educational culture in which they participate. Freire (1985) views this process of creating and conditioning as a historical one, and as such, teachers over time:

> Develop their own way of seeing and understanding the world, according to cultural patterns that are obviously marked by the ideology of dominant groups in their global society. Their ways of thinking, conditioned by their behaviour, which in turn conditions their thinking, have been developing and crystallizing over a long period of time (Freire1985, 31).

The cycle of creating and conditioning, within which the teacher is caught, is a mode of existence that, if unacknowledged, creates a "culture of silence" (Freire 1985, 31). A culture of silence is one where practices, policies, systems, and means of representation are accepted without any real examination. A culture of silence may exist because the opportunities are not created for the voices of teachers to be heard, or it may exist because the demands of teaching do not facilitate the time needed for reflective thinking and critical conversations within a professional community of practice. Disrupting a culture of silence then requires critical acts of cultural resistance. One such act is indigenous research that begins the process of cultural transformation by first acknowledging the presence of a culture of silence. Through indigenous research, teachers are able to foster the critical communities and networks through which their existence is given center stage, and in so doing, a culture of silence as a part of the educational culture gets disrupted. Postcolonial thought within specific contexts provides the teacher/researcher with the "methodological means" (Freire 1985, 31) of interrogating cultures of silence within education. It encourages the teacher/researcher to:

> Confront the biases that have shaped teaching practices in our society and create new ways of knowing different strategies for the sharing of knowledge. [To go] beyond the boundaries of what is acceptable, so that we can think and rethink, so that we can create new visions. [To] celebrate teaching that enables transgressions...It is that movement which makes education the practice of freedom (hooks 1994, 12).

Postcolonial thought as an analytical and methodological approach offers the teacher/researcher the opportunity to recognize teaching as a cultural performance, which, if interrogated and re-visioned, is able to begin the process of intellectual emancipation and cultural transformation. Postcolonialism offers educational research a methodology of critical ideology. Postcolonial methods then are shaped by the indigenous researcher's positional entry into educational research as one which revolves around concerns with representation, reproduction, and transformation.

Postcolonial Methods

For the purposes of this argument, postcolonial methods can be conceived as tools that are culturally appropriate to the context and educational problem being engaged. In the employment of these methods, it must be recognized that research-action concepts, such as investigation, examination, inquiry, and evaluation, while used in the writing of research can prove problematic as they resonate strongly with imperial modes of documentation (Smith 1999). This is because, as research concepts, they suggest a point of authority and legitimacy that falls outside the context being studied. In taking the position of outside, these actions construct a dualism of *them* and *us* and represent the researcher as essentially different from the participants of the research. In this manner, it confers a false authority onto the researcher, while rehearsing the internal contradiction of a theory of postcolonialism discussed earlier in this chapter.

The challenge of research-action concepts is that, as a postcolonial researcher, while I attempt to deconstruct the historical, cultural, and political parameters of my existence and practice as a teacher, I can only do so within the language available to me. Making me more a part of the "we" of the research requires that I shift the ways in which I think about research relationships as well as the way in which I use particular words related to research to describe the actions of the project. In so doing, I attempt to minimize the distance between myself, as the researcher, and the community with which I intend to connect. As such, the methods used in a research project should be used to engage with particular sets of experiences as told and interrogated by teachers/students, and as interpreted through postcolonial theory by me as a teacher-educator. The choice of methods in use in postcolonial educational research should be founded upon a sense of community and the ways that narratives are constructed to represent the cultural spaces in which teachers/students perform. A sense of community is required in order for participants and researchers to develop a "vigilant awareness of the work we must continually do to undermine all the socialization that leads us to behave in ways that perpetuate domination" (hooks 2003, 36). The narratives that emerge should in some way be represented as a part of the narrative tradition of the society. For the Caribbean, the narratives could emerge out of the oral traditions of storytelling, proverbs, speech-making, and singing through which the history and culture is passed on to the younger generation (Roberts 1997); the aims of which are sharing ideas, maintaining interest through humor, stimulating discussions that interrogate why things are the way they are and suggesting ways for transformation. The methods of choice become culturally appropriate because they begin from the historical and cultural place and position of the speaker, who as a protagonist, determines and constructs the experience to be shared. I find parallels of this within the work of life history as a narrative approach to research.

Referring to the impact of the life-history as a method of accessing the perceptions of individuals, Goodson and Sikes (2001) suggest that the stories we share in relation to ourselves are intended to shed light on the way in which individuals "understand the patterns of social relations, interactions and constructions in which the lives of women and men are embedded" (87–88). In reconstructing an experience for sharing, cognitive choices are made about what to share and why to share. Thus, what occurs is a new perspective on a past experience. In this way, the methods facilitate agency and social transformation through a community of telling and retelling.

Conclusion

In this chapter, I have argued that educational research in a postcolonial context needs to be of the kind that is culturally ethical and decolonizing. In so doing, the chapter provides the analytical and methodological perspective that guides the way in which educational research in postcolonial spaces can be reconceptualized along lines more comparable with postcolonial ambitions. In fulfilling this goal, such a perspective establishes a connection between culture, education, and postcolonial research. It shows how postcolonial thought as cultural and political contestation can serve as a theoretical and methodological tool for culturally ethical educational research. In the first case, education is considered to be a selection from culture, a culture that conditions the way teachers are represented, the roles they perform, and their capacity to reproduce or transform the culture in which they serve. In this chapter, it is acknowledged that the culture of teaching shapes the ways in which its teachers practice. Framed within postcolonial thought, the ethical and cultural implication of pedagogical and research practice suggests that culturally confident and conscious teachers are capable, through their practice, of transforming the culture within which they participate.

In the second case, once it has been accepted that what we teach is a selection from culture, then an interrogation of the practices of teaching cannot begin without a consideration of the ways in which former colonies account for the traditions and ideologies that exist and that determine the visions they have for themselves. The use of postcolonial theory to interrogate and analyze societal development can then determine the positionality that influences the way in which teaching and its practices are interrogated historically and re-envisioned to meet desires for intellectual emancipation. This reenergizes the transformative capacity of teaching. It also serves to provide the theoretical and methodological framework for interrogating educational research as culturally ethical practice that examines the intersection between the colonial residues of educational practices, the experiences of neoliberal globalization, and imperialism, and the challenges to these patterns of dominance.

References

Appadurai, Arjun. "Disjunction and Difference," In *The Post-Colonial Studies Reader*, edited by B. Ashcroft, G. Griffiths, and H. Tiffin, 468–472. London: Routledge, 1995.
Appadurai, A. "Grassroots Globalization and the Research Imagination." *Public Culture* 12, no. 1 (2000): 1–19.
Apple, M. W. *Cultural Politics and Education*. Buckingham: Open University Press, 1996.
Bhabha, Homi. *The Location of Culture*. London: Routledge, 1994.
Chandra, Sarika, and Neil Larsen. "Postcolonial Pedigrees-Postcolonialism: A Historical Introduction," *Cultural Critique* (winter 2006): 197–206.
Chowdhury, Kanishka. "Postcolonial Longings," *Modern Fiction Studies* 46, no. 2 (2000): 496–500.
Crossley, M., and L. Tikly. "Postcolonial Perspectives and Comparative and International Research in Education: A Critical Introduction." *Pedagogy, Culture, and Society* 40, no. 2 (2004): 147–156.
Fanon, Frantz. *Black Skin, White Masks*. London: Pluto Press, 1952.
Fanon, Frantz. *The Wretched of the Earth*. New York: Grove Press, 1963.
Fanon, Frantz. *Toward the African Revolution*. New York: Grove Press, 1964.
Farred, Grant. "A Thriving Postcolonialism: Toward an Anti-Postcolonial Discourse." *Nepantla: Views from South* 2, no. 2 (2001): 229–246.
Freire, Paulo. *The Politics of Education—Culture Power and Liberation*. London: Bergin and Garvey, 1985.
Freire, P. *Teachers as Cultural Workers: Letters to Those Who Dare Teach*. Colorado: Westview Press, 2005.
Fuchs, Barbara, and David Baker. "The Postcolonial Past." *Modern Language Quarterly* 65, no. 3 (2004): 329–340.
Gilroy, Paul. *The Black Atlantic: Modernity and Double Consciousness*. Cambridge: Harvard University Press, 1993.
Giroux, Henry. *Stealing Innocence: Corporate Culture's War on Children*. New York: Palgrave Macmillan, 2000.
Giroux, Henry. *The Abandoned Generation: Democracy Beyond the Culture of Fear*. New York: Palgrave MacMillan, 2003.
Giroux, Henry. "The Terror of Neoliberalism: Rethinking the Significance of Cultural Politics," *College Literature*, 32, no. 1 (2005): 1–19.
Goodson, Ivor, and Pat Sikes. *Life History Research in Educational Settings: Leaning from Lives*. Buckingham: Open University Press, 2001.
Harris, Wilson. "Creoleness: The Crossroads of Civilisation." In *Caribbean Creolization: Reflections on the Cultural Dynamics of Language, Literature, and Identity*, edited by Katherine M. Balutansky and Marie Agnes Sourieau,. Kingston: Press of the University of the West Indies, 1998, 23–35.
Hassan, Wail, and Rebecca Saunders. "Introduction, Part 1: The Project of Comparative (Post) Colonialisms." *Comparative Studies of South Asia and the Middle East*, 23, no. 1 and 2 (2003): 18–31.

Hickling-Hudson, A. "Towards Caribbean 'Knowledge Societies': Dismantling Neo-Colonial Barriers in the Age of Globalisation." *Compare: A Journal of Comparative and International Education* 34, no. 3 (2004): 293–300.

Hickling-Hudson, A. "Curriculum in Postcolonial Contexts." In *International Encyclopedia of Education,* 3rd ed., edited by P. Peterson, E. Baker, and B. McGraw, 299–306. Oxford: Elsevier, 2010.

hooks, bell. *Yearning: Race, Gender, and Cultural Politics*. London: Turnaround, 1991.

hooks, bell. *Teaching to Transgress: Education as the Practice of Freedom*. London: Routledge, 1994.

hooks, bell. *Teaching Community: A Pedagogy of Hope*. London: Routledge, 2003.

Jefferees, David, J. McGonegal, and S. Milz. "Introduction: The Politics of Postcoloniality." *Postcolonial Text* 2, no. 1 (2006): 1–8. doi:file://H:\Postcolonialism\Thepoliticsofposcoloniality_files\162.htm [Accessed 04 June 2007].

Kemmis, Stephen, and Peter Grootenboer. "Situating Practice: Practice Architectures and the Cultural, Social and Material Conditions for Practice." In *Enabling Practice: Challenges for Education,* edited by S. Kemmis and T. Smith, 36–59. Amsterdam: Sense, 2008.

Lamming, George. "The Occasion for Speaking." In *The Post-Colonial Reader,* edited by B. Ashcroft, G. Griffiths, and H. Tiffin, 14–18. London: Routledge, 1995.

Lavia, J. "Repositioning Pedagogies and Postcolonialism: Theories, Contradictions And Possibilities." *International Journal of Inclusive Education* 11, no. 3 (2007): 283–300. doi:10.1080/13603110701237548

McLeod, John. *Beginning Postcolonialism*. Manchester: Manchester University Press, 2000.

Majid, Anoua. "Can the Postcolonial Critic Speak? Orientalism and the Rushdie Affair." *Cultural Critique* 32 (winter 1996): 5–42.

Mishra, Vijay, and Bob Hodge. "What Was Postcolonialism?" *New Literary History* 36 (2005): 375–402.

Preece, J. O. M. Modise, and D. Mosweunyane. "Context Matters': Whose Concept of Growth And Development Are We Talking About?" *Compare: A Journal of Comparative and International Education* 38, no. 3 (2008): 267–280.

Ramchand, Kenneth. "The Lost Literature of the West Indies." In *Contending with Destiny: The Caribbean in the 21st Century,* Kenneth Hall and Dennis Benn, 513–529. Kingston: Ian Randle Publishers, 2000.

Rizvi, F. "Epistemic Virtues and Cosmopolitan Learning." Paper presented at the Radford Lecture, Adelaide, Australia, 2006.

Rizvi, F., B. Lingard, and J. Lavia. "Postcolonialism and Education: Negotiating a Contested Terrain." *Pedagogy, Culture and Society* 14, no. 3 (2006): 249–262.

Roberts, Peter. *From Oral Literature: Colonial Experience in the English West Indies*. Kingston: Press of the University of the West Indies, 1997.

Said, Edward. *Orientalism*. London: Routledge and Kegan Paul, 1978.
Said, Edward. "Resistance, Opposition, and Representation." In *The Post-Colonial Studies Reader,* edited by B. Ashcroft, G. Griffiths, and H. Tiffin, 95–98. London: Routledge, Taylor and Francis Group, 1995.
San Juan, Epifanio. *Beyond Postcolonial Theory*. New York: St. Martin's Press, 1999.
Shohat, Ella. "Notes on the 'Post-Colonial.'" *Social Text,* 31/32 (Third World and Post-Colonial Issues) (1992): 99–113.
Smith, Linda. *Decolonizing Methodologies: Research and Indigenous Peoples* London: Zed Books, 1999.
Tikly, L. "Education and the New Imperialism." *Comparative Education* 40, no. 2 (2004): 173–198.
Williams, E. *History of the People of Trinidad and Tobago*. Trinidad: PNM Publishing, 1962.
Wehrs, Donald. "Sartre's Legacy in Postcolonial Theory: or, Who's Afraid of Non-Western Historiography and Cultural Studies." *New Literary History* 34 (2004): 761–789.
Won Lee, Kyung. "Is the Glass Half-Empty or Half- Full? Rethinking the Problems of Postcolonial Revisionism." *Cultural Critique* 36 (Spring 1997): 89–117.
Young, Michael. "An Approach to the Study of Curricula as Socially Organised Knowledge." In *Knowledge and Control*, edited by Michael F. D. Young. London: Coulier-Macmillian, 1971, 19–46.

2

Validating Community Cultural Wealth: Toward Sustainable Empowering Learning Environments

Sechaba Mahlomaholo

Introduction

There was a man who was seated at the back of one of the relatively large auditoriums at the University of the Free State. It was late, around nine o'clock on the night of September 29, 2010. The hall was packed to capacity with academics from a wide spectrum of theoretical positions in South Africa and the world over. We were attending the annual conference of the Third Education Research Colloquium, a gathering that was convened to discuss emerging issues of social justice in education. There were also a few individuals representing organizations from civil society. We were about to conclude our three days of deliberations as members of the Anti-Racism Network in Higher Education as well as the international Apartheid Archives Projects, when a man at the back of the hall asked this gathering fundamental questions that stunned us all. The questions were simple and provocative. He said:

> *For the past three days, with due respect my professors, you have been telling many stories, mainly from the Truth and Reconciliation Commission. You have been analyzing all these big research ideas with the aim of fast tracking and facilitating national reconciliation, unity, social cohesion, and all. However, I still do not know what to do, because I am now 52 years old without any formal schooling*

> or qualification, and I am unemployed. I live on my mother's pension grant together with eight other members of our family. When I was of a school-going age, our farm school was closed down by the farm owner, who argued that there was no need for the education of kaffirs [a very rude and derogatory reference to people of African descent during the apartheid era, meaning an infidel without culture or manners], as she would always provide work and provisioning [sic] of a sack of maize meal, milk, and an occasional meat. Now, here I am with the whole of my youth, way past me. Now, how will these big ideas assist me? How will national reconciliation and that entire movement make up for all that I have lost? In fact, even the future of my children is still bleak, as I am not able to provide them with a decent education or any means of meaningful livelihood. It seems that the future of my generation is lost and more so of all of my subsequent generations.

These questions have haunted me ever since! I am writing this chapter in an attempt to formulate a response to some of these questions, and as a contribution to the ongoing discussions, which they invite. By way of initiating this conversation, I would argue that South Africa has not totally emerged from the stranglehold of apartheid ideology that discriminated against the majority black population. Indeed, examples of how its legacy continues to persist can be seen in all facets of life. The focus of this chapter will be on the challenges and opportunities of post-apartheid South African in relation to the educational system. This chapter argues for an alternative education, one that validates and capitalizes on the community cultural wealth of the hitherto excluded majority communities.

Vussy Lefalamang Moloi (2010), one of the people who spent years in exile in an attempt to help us achieve democracy in South Africa, cautioned me that advocating for "education for all," in an uncritical manner, as a response to the question of redressing past inequities, was not adequate, because statistics have shown that high levels of literacy and high academic and professional qualifications do not necessarily translate into improved economic and social well being of the people and the country. This advice is sound, because in post-apartheid South Africa, a national response to education reform has been fashioned by the global demands of the Education for All movement and the intention to meet the United Nations (UN) Millennium Development Goals (MDG). Both interrelated global initiatives, driven by representative arms of the United Nations, declare that access to basic education is a prerequisite to overcoming the social ills of poverty, injustice, and illiteracy. Indeed, I am reminded of the nexus between education and society where "education for all" may not be a panacea to all our social ills. In agreement with Harold Wolpe, I would argue that what is required in post-apartheid South Africa is an education of the people where, "the relationship between education and the social system is not a theoretical pre-given but it is contingent upon the concrete conditions of the social foundation including the education system itself" (1991, 79). Perhaps, Wolpe is alerting us to the fallacy that education is a neutral concept. Rather, I would concur that it "plays [a] fundamental role in the structuring and hence the restructuring of the system of social stratification" (1991, 77). For social transformation to take place, an appropriately retheorized education privileging and validating the aspirations of all, especially the underclass, together with significant changes in the material conditions of all seem to be the preconditions. Therefore, in attempting to respond to the questions of that 52-year-old man at the back of the auditorium, I agree with Wolpe that, "education is both functional for the system of domination and in contradiction to it" (1991, 79). What is therefore required is the impetus to reinvest it with the agency to create an alternative. However, it is to be noted that agency is important and valuable, but it is constrained and conditional.

Years of colonialism and racist apartheid have created in South Africa a situation where majority blacks (whether child or adult learners) are said to "underachieve" and are always at the bottom of any ladder or league table. Racism and apartheid have made differentiated performance based on race, natural and automatic. In elaborating this point, Francis, Hemson, Mphambukeli, and Quin (2003) have contended that sometimes blacks and the social category of the underclass are conditioned by the apartheid and colonial regime to the extent that they keep each other in check, lest one of them moves up the social ladder and escapes the oppression. This is what one may call peer pressure to keep one another down in a situation where racism placed them as the underclass. Even white people, who have by birth, been assigned superiority and position, always keep each other in check lest they open their ranks for infiltration from the lowly placed black. Familiar words like *kaffirboetie* (a derogatory term frequently used during the apartheid era to describe a white person who cared to improve the plight of the oppressed and marginalized blacks), are used to discourage this category of people to show appreciation and respect for people from excluded communities.

Consequently, the problem of "underachievement" by the majority of blacks is not necessarily a reflection of their individual or collective differences, but rather, it is a reflection of how much they are *owed* by the system that was designed to and continues to exclude and marginalize them. Gloria Ladson-Billings's (2006; 2008) observation is apposite, when in commenting on a similar situation regarding African Americans in the United States, she observes that their so-called academic underachievement in particular, is actually a misnomer. Her view is that the notion of underachievement, or the alleged achievement gap between blacks and (mainly) whites, shifts the blame to the individuals as though they are solely to blame for their lack of achievement. She argues that the problem is with the system and the distorted social arrangements that discriminate against some (mainly black), while privileging others (mainly white). We owe that 52-year-old man a mountain of debt that no Truth and Reconciliation Commission can ever hope to pay back. He has suffered injustices that may never be healed, and this backlog will continue to be experienced by his future generations for many more years to come. Irrespective of their efforts, it will not be easy to close down the racialized "gap" as their white compatriots are also not static, but are moving on in life. This social mobility to ever higher social categories is assured for the latter, while for the man at the back of the auditorium, the gap is forever widening.

In direct response to the questions posed from the back of the auditorium, I would argue that we need a counter-hegemonic kind of education that will unashamedly address the agenda for social justice. I agree with Wolpe that this approach requires:

> the kind of education that enables the oppressed to understand the evils of the apartheid system and prepares them for participation in a non-racial, democratic system; education that eliminates capitalist norms of competition, individualism and stunted intellectual development and one that encourages the collective input and active participation by all, as well as stimulating critical thinking and analysis; education that equips and trains all sectors of our people to participate actively and creatively to attain and concretize a non-racial South Africa. Education that enables workers to resist exploitation and oppression at the work place and that recognises that the immediate education and skilling of black people is itself a necessary part of the struggle towards a social just education and hence was part of the democratisation and national reconciliation agenda. (1991, 79–80).

In advancing this argument, I will discuss Yosso's "community cultural wealth" and its application to South African context as a basis for restructuring an education that is sustainable, empowering, and social just.

Some Challenges of Education in Post-Apartheid South Africa

One of the major challenges of post-apartheid South Africa is recovery from the Bantu Education Act of 1953. Described and experienced as one of the country's most racist laws, the act placed the previously autonomous practice of schooling under the mandates of the state. In this way, the state had full control of the operations and curricula. Central control by the state meant that the racist policy of the apartheid would become a feature of the education system where public funds were unequally distributed and schools segregated on the basis of race. More funding went to schools that catered to white students (Hartshorne 1992). In describing Bantu education, Baard and Schreiner state:

> In 1953 the government passed the Bantu Education Act, which the people didn't want. We didn't want this bad education for our children. This Bantu Education Act was to make sure that our children only learnt things that would make them good for what the government wanted: to work in the factories and so on; they must not learn properly at school like the white children. Our children were to go to school only three hours a day, two shifts of children every day, one in the morning and one in the afternoon, so that more children could get a little bit of learning without government having to spend more money. Hawu! It was a terrible thing that act. (Baard and Schreiner 1986, U.P.)

What Baard and Schreiner have described underscores the point made earlier about "underachievement" in the case of a large percent of blacks who "fail" to succeed at school and are limited in their social mobility. The problem is systemic and contrived; it is designed to treat the black population as less than human and to maintain white minority rule. These harsh, traumatic, violent, and unjust acts have had a cultural impact on all communities. For post-apartheid South Africa, the challenge of education for all has been and continues to be the development of policies and practices that will override the historical and contemporary circumstances that inhibit equity and social justice.

Educational legislative and policy imperatives, like the Higher Education Act (Department of Education—DoE–2003), the Education White Paper 3 (DoE 1997), the New Academic Policy (DoE 2002), the Higher Education Qualification Framework (DoE 2007), and the White Paper on Science and Technology (Department of Arts, Culture, Science, and Technology 1996) among others, put in place by the democratic South African government since 1994 are predicated on a yearning to create an education system, hence a society, based on the principles and practices of equity, social justice, freedom, peace, and hope. For example, the Education White Paper 3 in its preamble succinctly declares its intentions as being to:

> restructure and transform higher education programmes and institutions [so as] to respond better to the human resource, economic and development needs of the republic; redress past discrimination...and equal access; provide optimal opportunities for learning and the creation of knowledge; promote the values which underlie an open and democratic society based on human dignity, equality and freedom; respect freedom of religion, belief and opinion; respect and encourage democracy, academic freedom, freedom of speech and expression, creativity, scholarship and research; pursue excellence, promote the full realisation of the potential of every student and employee, tolerance of ideas and appreciation of diversity (1997, 7).

While the ideas expressed in this extract may seem to relate to higher education only, on closer scrutiny, all legislative and policy imperatives for Basic Education (grades R to 12, equivalent to the U.S. K to 12) are also grounded on the same themes of equity, social justice, freedom, peace, and hope. These imperatives ranging from the National Education Policy Act 27 (DoE, 1996a), the South African Schools Act 84 (DoE 1996b), Employment of Educators Act 76 (DoE, 1998), South African Council of Educators (DoE, 2000) and the Curriculum and Assessment Policy Statement (DoE, 2011) to mention a few, collectively and individually are geared toward:

> The advancement and protection of the fundamental rights of every person guaranteed in terms of Chapter 2 of the Constitution...thus enabling the education system to contribute to the full personal development of each student...in the advancement of democracy, human

rights and peaceful resolution of disputes, achieving equitable education opportunities and the redress of past inequality in education provision...(DoE, 1996, 4).

The intentions, as exemplified in this quotation, are laudable as they place, rightfully so, education at the center of social transformation, away from the unjust legacies of apartheid racism, sexism, and other forms of discrimination. Hopes for a better South Africa were raised, and as a nation, we were praised by the world. Unfortunately, sixteen years later, when people were expecting positive results, the findings of the *Report of the Ministerial Committee on Transformation and Social Cohesion and the Elimination of Discrimination in Public Higher Education Institutions* (DoE, 2008), popularly known as the Soudien Report, provided a devastating critique. It was a reminder that the ghosts of our horrific apartheid past were still here with us, and it would take a herculean task to even attempt to lay them to rest. To clarify the point, the Soudien Report makes this chilling observation that:

> It is clear from the overall assessment of the state of transformation in higher education, that discrimination, in particular with regard to racism and sexism, is pervasive in our institutions...that there is not sufficient institutional space to talk about race because people are scared it may get out of control. Staff needs space for open debate but race is difficult to talk about because it leads to misinformation and miscommunication. Students and staff (the latter included by me) are scared of victimisation. There is a culture of silence—people are threatened with dismissal if they speak out. A culture of silence exists and individual thinkers are a threat. If vocal they face the guillotine. One could be suspended. (DoE 2008, 112–113)

The findings of the Soudien Report were further confirmed by other studies pointing to the rampant racial exclusion of black people, among others, when it came to employment of academics and other professionals, especially at senior positions in higher education in South Africa. Data from the Higher Education Monitor (CHE 2007, 76) illustrate how unjust our social arrangements are where blacks are still excluded from meaningful employment in the higher education sector. This is the sector where knowledge is created, where leadership in all its facets is molded and high-level skills are cultivated and disseminated. The more prestigious the level of employment, hence responsibility, the less blacks feature. The people who constitute 80 percent of the South African population, only make up 11 percent of the professorial cohorts in our universities. This begs the question: whose knowledge is valorized, given these levels of exclusion? The CHE report goes further to show that:

> Postgraduate enrolments and graduations continue to be differentiated by race...Since 2004, there has been some fluctuation in the number of African students enrolling for postgraduate studies and overall the number has declined from 67,757 in 2004 to 57,198 in 2007, reflecting the overall decline in postgraduate enrolments. African students continue to be less successful in their postgraduate studies, compounding the difficulty of increasing black participation in research. The same pattern carries through to the doctoral level. Of the 1100 people who graduated with doctoral degrees in 2006, 618 (56%) were white and 331 (30%) were black. Considering that about 13% of doctoral graduates are foreigners and most of these are black, the system is producing very few black South African doctoral graduates. This not only limits the scope for increasing the participation of black researchers, but it also limits the potential for improving the racial profile of academic staff across the system (CHE 2007, 61).

The grim picture being painted by this study is made worse when one looks at the high levels of attrition by black learners at the school level (Bloch 2010). To emphasize the point, the Development Bank of Southern Africa's research reveals that:

> Where one in 10 white kids gets an A aggregate, only one in 1000 black kids do. Where 62.5% of grade 3 kids could do maths at appropriate levels a few years back in the Western Cape, only 0.1% of township kids could. More than 50% of white students go on to university; only 12% of black students do. Whites fare well at tertiary; black people struggle to find support. Such inequalities are unsustainable and unfair in a new democracy, where every child who is prepared to work, deserves the chance. (Bloch 2010, 1)

The various scenarios that have thus far been described are merely illustrative of a bigger problem encompassing the whole fabric of our social life. The fact of the matter is that it is still not easy for the majority of learners who are black to progress significantly in life (school, employment, upward social mobility, etc.) in spite of the demise of legal apartheid. A further question, therefore, arises from the statement made by the man from the back of the auditorium: Why do these seemingly racially biased and unjustly differentiated levels of performance and representation still persist throughout the education system in spite of the declared agenda of equity, social justice, freedom, peace, and hope as envisioned in the various educational, legislative, and policy directives, and what can be done to transform the situation?

Cultural Capital and Community Cultural Wealth

To respond to this broader question, I turn to the notions of cultural capital and community cultural wealth. Both these notions represent two ways of accounting for how we might interpret the lived experiences of communities. In the case of the former, it offers critical opportunities for understanding how social inequalities are organized and reproduced. According to Pierre Bourdieu (1993), cultural capital refers to the way in which the classification of distinctive attributes, knowledge, values, and ways of being are contrived to form social hierarchies. It provides an etiology of social-class formations; allows us to gain insights into the contested nature of social values; and offers a way of explaining the location of power and status in relation to education (see also Nan 1999; Jenkins 1992). Notwithstanding, its potential for offering oversight (at least) of the social relations, the usefulness of cultural capital as a conceptual device is limited in its attention to the notion of agency. When applied to the context of South Africa, it can be argued that there is a tendency to see the problem as being located in the "deficiencies" inherent in black learners and/or black academics. The argument is that they lack something, some competency or some level of quality that disqualifies them from moving through the system. Undoubtedly, the standards for progression are set, and theirs is to strive toward meeting them. However, although many of them struggle to do so, they are unable to live up to the expectations, mainly because they do not have the requisite *habitus,* or the disposition engendered by being born, and living in an environment that contains qualities similar to the ones required in academia (see Nan 1999; Jenkins, 1992; Bourdieu 1993; Sallaz and Zavisca 2007). Most black academics are the first-generation, and at most, second-generation university students or graduates. The history of participation, and hence, excellence, in higher education is still foreign to them compared to their white counterparts. They still do not have *the feel*—the acceptable language, demeanor, and accent that make their accessing, hence, participation, in the high-level academic discourses, smooth. The situation is similar for black learners who leave school early before completing even grade 12, for example. The problem is that they lack social and cultural capital, the required attributes for social exchange that are required to steer successfully the social structures that govern their everyday lives.

One of the challenges of education in post-apartheid South Africa is the implementation of programs that are publically acclaimed to encourage greater access to education to those communities that have been previously excluded and discriminated against. To date, we have many bridging courses and programs, mainly at universities and some schools, geared toward pumping knowledge into the heads of black learners who come from the "deprived" communities so that they can be rid of their cultural deficiencies and, thus, fit neatly into the prescribed dominant culture. Maphoka Liphapang's doctoral study describes this process of acculturation, where it is noted that good performance at school by black learners is based on the condition that they are assimilated into the dominant culture at former "whites-only model C" schools (2008). These public schools were fully funded out of the national budget of South Africa but admitted white learners only. The teaching staffs were also exclusively white. Despite these bridging courses, the reality is that many black learners still fail to make the grade. They continue to fail and leave school and university before obtaining the qualifications for which they enrolled.

An alternative way of interrogating the contemporary context is through the notion of "community cultural wealth." Yosso (2005) locates "community cultural wealth" within the theoretical framework of critical race theory (CRT) and advances its intention as challenging traditional notions of cultural capital. Yosso is critical of deficit models that describe marginalized and black communities from the position of disadvantage and deprivation. On the contrary, she argues that such communities indeed possess at least five forms of capital—aspirational, navigational, linguistic, familial, and resistant capital, as well as cultural capital and social capital (see Anzaldúa 1990; Delgado Bernal 1997, 2001; Auerbach 2001; Stanton-Salazar 2001; Solórzano and Delgado Bernal 2001; Faulstich Orellana 2003). These are unrecognizable to those who only chose to view communities and their capacity for social exchange through the lens of the white middle-class standard. Further, these interrelated forms of capital provide the basis for naming and claiming indigenous knowledge, skills, and practices that are so often expressed through everyday experiences within and outside these communities. It is important, therefore, to acknowledge that these communities "are places of multiple strengths" (Yosso 2005, 82).

In posing the question: Whose community has capital? Yosso places the issue of race as central to epistemological debate. Being maginalized and oppressed, indeed, being "pushed out" of the discourses of knowledge resonate with racialized policies of disenfranchisement that seek to reinforce cultures of silence. It is out of the struggles to survive and overcome that new ways of thinking and being emerge. I agree with Anzaldúa (1990), hooks (1990), Solórzano and Delgado Bernal (2001), and others that opportunities for social transformation lie within collective and individual performances of struggle, the aspirations for self-determination, and the envisioning of marginal spaces "as places empowered by transformative resistance" (Yosso 2005, 70). The role of education, therefore, within this milieu is to develop sustained learning environments that build on the indigenous knowledge of these communities.

Education as a social institution has always been at the heart of political struggles in South Africa. The notions of aspirational, navigational, linguistic, familial, resistant, social, and cultural capitals find practical application in the historical and contemporary contexts of the national education agenda. For example, the potent student demonstrations of the 1970s and 1980s were aimed at establishing an agenda for an alternative system of education called the People's Education for People's Power. Ntshoe states:

> Although education and schooling in South Africa was successfully employed to suppress particular communities, education simultaneously facilitated social change, political emancipation, and democracy. The creation of strong resistance movements that challenged the ruling party was one of the unplanned effects of Bantu Education. Hence, in South Africa, schools also played a major role in transforming the country from an apartheid to a democratic state. During the 1970s and 80s education became the center of political struggle in South Africa when fierce and often violent anti-apartheid protests were held in schools throughout South Africa. "Liberation before Education" was the protest mantra that became the battle call for the liberation movement. (2002, 64)

Post-apartheid South Africa has not been spared the uprising of students who continue to make public demands for free and democratic education for all at all levels of the system. The promises of a better life for all, which inspired the transformation of South Africa into its current democratic dispensation, continue to be the rallying points for the current demands. In reflecting on these students' demands, spearheaded by the South African Students Congress (SASCO), Saleem Badat made the following observations:

> Recently, the largest national student organization in South Africa, the South African Students Congress, organized a public demonstration in support of free higher education. In many quarters, this demand was considered outlandish. But is it? Are the ideas that health care should be available free of charge to all in need and that economic and social policies should prioritize full employment so that all can enjoy dignity to be scoffed at? Should we be shy of aspiring to live in societies that put human development and well-being first and prize highly educated, informed and critical citizenries? Is free higher education necessarily an undesirable *ideal*? (Badat 2011, 22)

The students' demands referred to above are part of a larger national discomfort with the current neoliberal policies that seem to betray the original objectives of the liberation struggle waged in South Africa (Mottiar and Bond 2011). These original objectives had been to create a more equitable society, where educational opportunities (among other services) were to be accessible to all, irrespective of one's social class, race, creed, or gender.

Community Cultural Wealth and Sustainable Learning Environments

Based on the above discussion, I argue that our work as researchers, academics, educationists, and educators should be shaped by our roles as organic intellectuals (Davidson 1977; Gramsci 1971). As organic intellectuals, our role is to create sustainable learning environments where we use our privileged position to create opportunities for learning and advancement for marginalized members of our communities. Our research thus becomes located in the experiences of the people we are conducting research with and/or teaching. Evidently, making significant dents at the macro-political levels of our unequal society is arduous; however, our awareness of the important role of the economic base of our society should enable us to have as our starting point the aim to increase their educational and social opportunities. As organic intellectuals, our target should be toward creating an alternative to the current hegemony and monopoly, which continue to distribute (inequitably) educational resources and opportunities and apportion them through considerations of race, gender, social, and class affiliations and ability. As organic intellectuals and researchers, we should see ourselves therefore as co-constructors and facilitators of learning who have to create sustainable learning environments everywhere education takes place. Gramsci has emphasised the importance of education and learning in any transformation process.

Sustainable learning environments can be defined as the development of a democratic agenda for social justice that is central to the form and content of contemporary schooling in South Africa. In a wider context, such environments relate to a people's education put into action through the efforts and on behalf of the majority who have been traditionally marginalized and excluded. Ntshoe (2002), in emphasizing that "education and schools have the propensity for redefining and maintain social change," elaborates:

> It is clear that schools need to re-socialize children into new roles so that they can play a part in the changed conditions. In the South African context, education and schooling should be employed to inculcate values that are consistent with building democracy. This includes tolerance, respect of individual cultures, languages, religion and traditions. (Ntshoe 2002, 66)

Conclusion

South Africa is chosen as a point of entry into the above discussion in an attempt to show how difficult it is to achieve national reconciliation when the material conditions of a significant section of society are still excluded and marginalized. In this chapter, it is suggested that one way of circumventing this problem is through discourses that recognize and validate all people irrespective of race, color, or social class. These discourses as argued above can best be created through education that brings the experiences, fears, and aspirations of vulnerable and excluded communities to the center of the national agenda. This chapter further argues that this objective will be fully achieved if these positive changes are linked to efforts to improve the material conditions of all the people as well. As researchers concerned with issues of social justice, our role as it is beginning to emerge, is pivotal in influencing policy agendas and developing programs, projects, and other strategies geared toward creating an alternative education system—one that is sustainable and recognizes the multiple strengths of traditionally marginalized and oppressed communities.

References

Badat, Saleem. "Free Higher Education in South Africa—Why Not?" *International Higher Education* 63 (2011): 22–23.
Bourdieu, Pierre. *The Field of Cultural Production: Essays on Art and Literature.* Cambridge: Polity, 1993.
Davidson, Alastair. *Antonio Gramsci: Towards an Intellectual Biography.* London: Merlin Press, 1977.
Flank, Lenny. *Hegemony and Counter-Hegemony: Marxism, Capitalism, and Their Relation to Sexism, Racism, Nationalism, and Authoritarianism.* St Petersburgh, FL: Red and Black, 2007.
Fowler, Bridget. *Pierre Bourdieu and Cultural Theory: Critical Investigations.* London: Sage Publications, 1997.
Francis, Dennis, Crispin Hemson, Thulisile Mphambukeli, and Jane Quin. "Who Are We? Naming Ourselves as Facilitators." *Journal of Education* 31 (2003): 136–150.
Gramsci, Antonio. *Selections from the Prison Notebooks.* New York: International Publishers, 1971.
Jenkins, Richard. *Pierre Bourdieu.* New York: Routledge, 1993.
Karakayali, Nedim. "Reading Bourdieu with Adorno: The Limits of Critical Theory and Reflexive Sociology." *Sociology* 38, no. 2 (2004): 351–368.
Lane, Jeremy. *Pierre Bourdieu: A Critical Introduction.* Sterling, VA: Pluto Press, 2000.
Ladson-Billings, Gloria. *Still_black@the_academy.edu.* Keynote address at the National Council of Teachers of English Midwinter Research Assembly, Chicago, IL, 2006.
Ladson-Billings, Gloria. "From the Achievement Gap to the Education Debt: Understanding Achievement in U.S. Schools." Presidential address at the American Educational Research Association Annual Meeting, San Francisco. *Educational Researcher* 35, no. 7 (2006): 3–12.
Ladson-Billings, Gloria. "It's Not the Culture of Poverty, It's the Poverty of Culture: The Problem with Teacher Education." *Anthropology and Education Quarterly* 37, no. 2 (2008): 104–109.
Lewis, William. *Louis Althusser and the Traditions of French Marxism.* New York: Lexington Books, 2005.
Liphapang, Maphoka Christien. "Inclusive Education in the South African Context: Analysis of How Cultural Diversity Can Be Accommodated in Former Model C Schools in Bloemfontein." Unpublished doctoral thesis, submitted to the Central University of Technology, Free State, South Africa, 2008.
Mahlomaholo, Sechaba M. G., T. Mamiala, V. Hongwane, S. Ngcongwane, K. Itlhopheng, J. Fosu-Amoah, R. H. Mahlomaholo, M. Kies, and M. Mokgotsi. *Attrition and African Learner Underrepresentation in the Grade 12 Top 20*

List of the North West Education Department. Potchefstroom, S. Africa: Platinum Press, 2010.
Moloi, Vussy Lefalamang. Interview of September 29, 2010.
Mottiar, Shauna, and Patrick Bond. *Social Protest in South Africa.* The Centre for Civil Society Social Protest Observatory, University of KwaZulu-Natal, 2011. Available at: http://ccs.ukzn.ac.za/default.asp?2, 27, 3, 1858)
Ntshoe, Isaac. "The Impact of Political Violence in South Africa: Past, Present and Future." *Current Issues in Comparative Education* 2 (2002): 62–69.
Reed-Danahay, Deborah. *Locating Bourdieu.* Bloomington: Indiana University Press, 2005.
Sallaz, J. J., and J. Zavisca. "Bourdieu in American Sociology, 1980–2004." *Annual Review of Sociology* 33 (2007): 21–41.
Spivak, Gayatri. "Can the Subaltern Speak," In *Marxism and the Interpretation of Culture,* edited by S. Nelson and L. Crossberg, 271–313. Basingstoke: Macmillan Education, 1988.
Vélez-Ibáñez, Carlos, and James Greenberg. "Formation and Transformation of Funds of Knowledge among U.S.–Mexican Households." *Anthropology and Education Quarterly* 23, no. 4 (1992): 313–335.
Villalpando, Octavio. "Self-Segregation or Self-Preservation? A Critical Race Theory and Latina/o Critical Theory Analysis of Findings from a Longitudinal Study of Chicana/o College Students." *International Journal of Qualitative Studies in Education* 16, no. 5 (2003): 619–646.
Villalpando, Octavio, and Daniel Solórzano. "The Role of Culture in College Preparation Programs: A Review of the Literature," In *Preparing for College: Nine Elements of Effective Outreach,* edited by (eds) William Tierney, Zoe Corwin, and Julia Colyar. Albany, NY: SUNY Press, 2005, 13–28.
Villenas, Sofia, and Donna Deyhle. "Critical Race Theory and Ethnographies Challenging the Stereotypes: Latino Families, Schooling, Resilience, and Resistance." *Curriculum Inquiry* 29, no. 4 (1999): 413–445.
Villenas, Sofia, and Melissa Moreno. "To *valerse por si misma* between Race, Capitalism, and Patriarchy: Latina Mother-Daughter Pedagogies in North Carolina." *International Journal of Qualitative Studies in Education* 14, no. 5 (2001): 671–688.
Wacquant Loïc. *Pierre Bourdieu and Democratic Politics.* Cambridge: Polity Press, 2005.
Yosso, T. J. "Whose Culture Has Capital? A Critical Race Theory Discussion of Community Cultural Wealth." *Race Ethnicity and Education* 8, no. 1 (2005): 69–91.

3

Rethinking Education in South Africa: Amplifying Liberation Pedagogy

Milton Molebatsi Nkoane and Jennifer Lavia

Introduction

The aim of this chapter is to explore how personal and collective experiences of an apartheid education system have caused disturbances in the thought and emotions of those who experience such a system. The central objective is to demonstrate how liberation pedagogy, that is, education as a practice of democracy and freedom, can engage its practitioners and beneficiaries. This engagement would of necessity seek to inspire an emancipatory consciousness and orientation and to maximize positive expression and capability, and to contribute to the growth and development of those communities that have and are experiencing discrimination, violence, oppression, and marginalization. Indeed, what we offer to the discourse around imagined futures is a critical analysis of practice and an understanding of dominant hegemonic ways of educating. This can be used to confront spaces of marginalization, such as those created by apartheid education in South Africa. The apartheid education system has deliberately contributed to pushing indigenous African masses to the periphery, and as such, *othering* the indigenous knowledge, thereby leaving a lasting impact on individuals' psyche, with emotions impaired.

Developing a sociological imagination requires a coming together of history and biography (Wright Mills 1959; Freire 1970). This unity is to be found in the application of a critical stance to understanding historical precedents, their continuities, discontinuities, and relevance to contemporary life. History and biography, therefore, take center stage in this chapter, which aims to examine the interrelatedness of teaching, learning, and researching as situated practice. Like Freire, "[we] hold that [our] own unity and identity, in regard to others and to the world, constitutes [our] essential and irrepeatable way of experiencing [our]self as a cultural, historical and unfinished being[s] in the world, simultaneously conscious of [our] unfinishedness" (1998, 51).

We write this chapter as postcolonial subjects; as black, activist teachers—one from the Caribbean and the other from South Africa, both of which signify a historical, epistemic melange inevitably laced with conflict, contestation, and resistance. As teachers of this ilk, the idea of being and becoming is pivotal in developing the self-confidence required to engage in a hopeful practice. Our intention is to advance an emancipatory agenda for the education of the teacher, being mindful that while we must, and choose to, assume responsibility for undertaking a radical agenda, there are no guarantees that such an agenda will indeed be interpreted and represented by those who may participate in it. Nonetheless, we are encouraged by the desire to challenge hegemonic thinking that neoliberal regimes in education are the only way to be, to do, or to learn. Indeed, in this era of globalization, the task of the postcolonial teacher takes on even greater significance, in our view, and it is our intention in this chapter to begin to unpack the complexities of practice through postcolonial lenses, paying particular attention to the context of South Africa in a post-apartheid era. We pay close and critical attention to the Freirean concept of teachers as cultural workers, agreeing that practice is implicated historically, socially, and culturally, and that such implications are constructed through intensions, interpretations, and relationships.

The burden of this discussion, therefore, is that European colonialism and the apartheid education system in South Africa deliberately constituted an organized philosophy and practice of education that perpetuated domination of Western knowledge at the direct expense of the African masses. The current education system still produces undeniably dangerous neocolonial and neoliberal tendencies, and the kind of education and knowledge that frustrates and threatens the total emancipation process. This chapter shows that liberation pedagogy has the effect of highlighting the need to critically reexamine traditional and dominant educational practices and provides a platform for anti-oppressive methods of teaching, learning, and research.

Neocolonial conditions are present in the South African education system (Subedi and Daza, 2008), therefore, an understanding of the past, not only in terms of a collective history, but also in relation to the lived experiences of the colonized in the past and present, acts as a salutary reminder of the persistence of hegemonic rule—always seeking to resuscitate and reestablish its power over mind and matter (see Bhabha 1994). From this perspective, we call for a counter-hegemonic offensive by providing insights into what might constitute critical practice, and postcolonial pedagogy, in postcolonial South Africa. This is an alternative that could contribute to the emancipation of subaltern groups. We will show that South Africans require a transformative approach to education reform in which a postcolonial agenda is made explicit.

Understanding Liberation Pedagogy

The concept of liberation pedagogy is inextricably linked to the work of Paulo Freire, wherein developing a philosophy of praxis he established the relationship between individual and collective learning and the desire to pursue an emancipatory agenda through community. Paulo Freire's evolution of liberation pedagogy as a practice of emancipation emanates from various education projects he undertook in Brazil in the late 1950s and early 1960s (see Freire 1970; Gadotti 1994), where he demonstrated the relationship between learning and teaching and the lived experiences of those who are the learners and teachers. For Freire, teachers are also learners! This has inspired and informed countless efforts to make life more humane for those oppressed by economic and ideological structures that denied them their dignity, human rights, and self-determination. Liberation pedagogy creates a platform for oppressed people to define for themselves their situations and to define actions that will promote their creativity to move toward self-determination. It is embedded in discourses of postcolonial theory. It is a way of thinking and knowledge production that takes an activist stance, that of influencing history rather than a passive stance of accepting the power of history. That is, it is orientated toward change and transformation rather than accepting things as they are. According to McLaren (2008), it is a way of thinking about, negotiating, and transforming teaching and learning, the production of knowledge, the social and material relations, and the social standing of the wider community, society, and nation.

A central tenet of liberation pedagogy is its intention to perceive education as transformative rather than merely reproductive. Moreover, education is seen as the cultural vehicle for enabling students, educators, and researchers to be agents who are actively engaged in promoting social change within and outside of the education system. It is in the interest of liberation pedagogy that clarity is maintained regarding whose interests are being served in any situation—those of the oppressed or oppressor. Bell hooks (1989) asserts that because those engaged in the production of knowledge are overwhelmingly white and middle class, their concerns often fail to address the circumstances of the poor or underprivileged groups. During the colonial era, which became crystallized in apartheid in South Africa, education was so rigid in the enforcement of absolute power in the classroom that questioning or resisting interpretations was never tolerated. Education imposed imperialist values upon social institutions, like schools and universities. Institutions of learning both modeled and taught imperialist values through curricula that served to reinforce the marginalized status of black South Africans rendering them as subhuman. This point is reinforced by Linda Tuhiwai Smith (1999), who states, in making reference to the historical conditions of indigenous people: "[They] were ranked above others in terms of such things as the belief that they were 'nearly human,' 'almost human' or 'sub-human.' This often depended on whether it was thought that the people concerned possessed a 'soul' and could therefore be 'offered' salvation and whether or not they were educable and could be offered schooling" (558). For Freire, the notion of our humanity is central to education as a cultural practice, and it cannot occur outside lived historical experiences and "the very social structures that we have created and to which we are conditioned" (1985, 113). Therefore, to fully appreciate the need for a liberatory pedagogy, there is need to be reminded of the historical conditions that have given rise to the post-apartheid problematic.

Education in South Africa

Apartheid was a legally enshrined racist policy that institutionalized the separation and categorization of the people of South Africa. Enacted in 1948 by the National Party that gained victory at the national election in that year, this overtly violent and oppressive system of colonial and neocolonial rule was extended into education policy, wherein 1953 the Bantu Education Act was established. Described as one of the most malevolent and offensive laws, the Bantu Education Act, enshrined the divine right of white supremist rulers to impose a racist curriculum upon a system that had previously enjoyed some level of autonomy. By taking away schools from the denominational missions that had had a long history of education by conversion and indoctrination, through the Bantu Education Act, the state assumed control of education. Based on a philosophy of purity of the races, the Act provided a mandate for unequal funding of schools, giving whites-only schools the lion's share.

In the apartheid years, government expenditures on education for the 1969–1970 financial year was R272.70 (South African rand) for every white child in school against R8.62 for every black child in school. This meant that for every R1, the government spent on the education for one black child between the age of 5 and 19, it spent R31.60, or 31.6 times as much, for each white child in the same age group. The long-term results of this inequity came out in the 1996 census figures (the first true census of all people in South Africa).

The apartheid government of South Africa during the early 1980s spent an average of $R1,211.00$ on education for each white child, and only $R146.00$ for each black child. The quality of the teaching staff also differed. For example, a third of all white teachers had a university degree, and the rest had all passed the grade-12 matriculation examination. While only 23 percent of black teachers had university degree, and 82 percent had not even reached the grade 12 matriculation (more than half had not reached grade 10) (SAIRR, 1983).

Evidently, during the period of apartheid, education as a practice was highly divisive and institutionalized the self-fulfilling prophecy of racial inequality, reproducing cycles of poverty, want, and dependence, racially ascribed as what the masses of South Africans deserved. The kind of education offered prepared and developed the minds of students to accept the dominant discourse. Students were indoctrinated into "otherness," "differences," "alienation," "disconnection," and "belonging" or "not belonging." Education, divided along racial lines, was designed to blind students to the differences between the centers of power and the periphery. The voices of the dominant were amplified and considered as the privileged voices—what was written or documented, what they said, how they thought, was given privileged status. Fundamental education change took place in South Africa in the early 1990s after years (more so in the 1970s and 1980s) of youth and other mass protests against the system of apartheid, including the annihilating effects of Bantu education. But what had already taken shape was an acculturation into Bantu that perpetuated the denigration of blacks; their history, culture, and identity (see Hartsone 1992, 41).

In further elaborating the point, we turn to the lived experience of apartheid education in which Milton narrates his experience by naming and claiming, "I am a product of an apartheid "Bantu education system." As mentioned earlier, Bantu education was designed for black South Africans and had three policy priorities. As Abid (2003) describes, the first was to create an abundance of skilled, but not highly educated, African labor needed for the country's rapid growth. Secondly, there was the need to quell the uprising of the masses of African people, who were gathering on the fringes of large metropolitan areas, preparing to claim their rights for full participation in civil society. Thirdly, there was need to lessen truancy by young people, which could have had the potential of radicalizing working-class people. In recalling his experience of schooling in apartheid South Africa, Milton Molibatsi Nkoane states:

> *My experience was that the curriculum was racist, Eurocentric, elitist, sexist, culturally biased, and racially selective* (see Clark and Worger 2004; Malberbe 1977; Harthhorne 1992; Nkomo 1992). *As a black South African learner, I was among many learners who were systematically disempowered and discriminated against. Our classrooms were overcrowded and school facilities were dilapidated, textbooks were missing or outdated, and our teachers were under-qualified and were technocratic and highly authoritarian. I went through this system of education from grade R–12.*
>
> *It was during my school days that I started to be conscious and understand fully the meaning of oppression and marginalization. It was through this kind of experience that the persistent urge grew in me for the alternatives and need for revolution. The apartheid education system was irrelevant to my world experiences and divorced from my social context. During the apartheid era in South Africa, as a black man, I was considered not human enough. Colonization crystallized in apartheid, dehumanized and objectified the indigenous African masses, and rendered me incapable of being human. I was hated, despised, detested, on the basis of my being or physical makeup. I was made to feel inferior and incapable of challenging the colonial order. I am now a free being in South Africa after 1994, and I am able to rediscover my own genius and reassume my life history.*
>
> *I am comforted by what hooks says:* "The engaged voice must never be fixed and absolute but always changing, always evolving in dialogue with a world beyond itself" (hooks 1994,11). *In this historical juncture*

in South Africa, we need to strive toward recognizing students as authorities on and authors of their own educational experiences and representations of those experiences.

The apartheid education system unconsciously, inculcated in me and in many black learners in South Africa the element of activism. Black schools in South Africa were turned into political sites, where political education was taught as a hidden curriculum. Many of the black schools in South Africa during the period of 1976–1980s were deeply involved in the struggle for justice. For example, in 1976, the all-black South African organization, under the leadership of Steven Bantu Biko, helped to unify students through the black consciousness movement. They demonstrated against discrimination and instruction in Afrikaans, the language perceived as the language of the oppressor, as it is the language of whites descended from the Dutch.

In addition, in the 1980s, hundreds of thousands of black South Africans who were banned from white controlled areas ignored the laws and infiltrated the forbidden regions in search of work and equality in educational opportunities. There was an increasing chorus of voices for an alternative education system or liberation pedagogy. The hidden (political) curriculum assisted in many ways to raise our consciousness about the devilish intents and policy priorities of the apartheid (Bantu) education system in South Africa.

According to Msila (2007), educational change in South Africa can be viewed within three distinctive phases; the first two being steeped in the divisive policy of apartheid and the last being the new and emerging post-apartheid context. In defining the South African context in this way, Msila undertakes a task that is not dissimilar to the tenets of this volume by interrogating the historical circumstances to exemplify the continuities in educational policy and practice during apartheid and post-apartheid. This raises the question: Can education compensate for the shortcomings of society? Can exploring the disparities in how different groups of learners have experienced education and addressing the threats and challenges of the contemporary context also do so? (Msila 2007, 147). Msila concludes, "The problem with colonial education and thus apartheid education in South Africa was that they spelt the end of traditional values learning in education. Currently, education faces these challenges in accommodating indigenous knowledge systems" (Msila 2007, 156).

The possibility of a complete overhaul of draconian rule could have only become a reality after the assumption of a democratic government and the election of the South Africa's first black president, which as Bredekamp has described was "the outcome of an intensified guerrilla and political struggle of three decades against the apartheid regime" (Bredekamp 2007, 1). This aspiration for self-determination was buoyed by public claims to reestablish and redefine what it meant to be African, acknowledging, resuscitating, and paying homage to indigenous peoples and extending a hand of conciliation at the same time. This turned out to be a program adopted by the Truth and Reconciliation Commission, given legal status by the Promotion of National Unity and Reconciliation Act, No. 34 of 1995, and sustained through legislative as well as other formal and informal platforms for dialogue and action to reimagine South Africa's cultural heritage and identity. Democratic South Africa had held out the promise of meaningful, sustained, and systemic change.

The democratic dispensation established in 1994 in South Africa set out "to transform educational provision to substantially improve access, quality, equality and redress for learners" (Pandor 2008, 17). In particular:

> The new democratic government was faced with the task of both rebuilding the system and redressing past inequalities. It has concentrated on creating a single unified national system, increasing access (especially to previously marginalised groups and the poor), decentralising school governance, revamping the curriculum, rationalising and reforming further and higher education and adopting pro-poor funding policies. (OECD 2008, 20)

Evidently, education was to be engineered as the cultural vehicle for realization of the Republican Constitution: to heal the divisions of the past and establish a society based on democratic values, social justice, and fundamental human rights; to improve the quality of life of all citizens and free the potential of each person; and to lay the foundations for a democratic and open society, in which government is based on the will of the people and every citizen is equally protected by law (RSA 1996). Therefore, education always has an agenda and in a Freirean sense; it is based on a politics of educating the "human person" (Freire 1998, 100). What is at stake here, in revisiting the past to glean understandings of the present and the future, is the imperative to elaborate a critical stance in relation to the reform rhetoric. By agreeing with Freire, we see education as an intervention in the world, actions that are thoughtful that refer "both to the aspiration for radical changes in society in such areas as economics, human relations and to health and to the reactionary position whose aim is to immobilize history and maintain an unjust socio-economic and cultural order" (1998, 99).

Postcolonial Praxis

Praxis refers to a cyclical, reflexive process of putting theory in practice. By *postcolonial praxis,* we refer to the application of that reflexive process in an examination of the postcolonial condition. The new dispensation in South Africa demanded a serious overhaul, restructuring, and transformation of the education system to redress the injustices of the past. In this process, government and education practitioners were confronted with a number of challenges, because apartheid in South Africa left the disastrous racial inequities in the education system; and there are deeply entrenched legacies of apartheid in education. These challenges can be found in policy development, the curriculum, and the experiences of learners. Our concern here is on the role of the teacher in light of the restorative project that is required. Interrogation of this role becomes even more central to discourses on education for democracy as expressed in post-apartheid educational policy.

For example, South Africans have tended to locate the National Qualification Framework (NQF) within South Africa's transition from authoritarianism to democracy. Formally established through the South African Qualifications Act (1995), the NQF unified the education system, redressing the separate policy of the apartheid regime by establishing a single educational system for all South Africans. It set out five objectives that were to be monitored, implemented, and evaluated through the South African Qualifications Authority. Conceived of as a unifying mechanism for a seamless education, the objectives of the NQF are expected to: create an integrated national framework for learning achievements; facilitate access to and mobility and progression within education, training, and career paths; enhance the quality of education and training; accelerate the redress of past unfair discrimination in education training and employment opportunities; and contribute to the full personal development of each learner and the social and economic development of the nation at large (see Allais 2007; DoE 2002). Evidently, the NQF is driven by goals of social justice, egalitarianism, redress, empowerment, flexibility, and mobility.

However, the extent to which the framework provides progress in policy and practice about educative practice can be questioned. We refer to the idea that South Africa introduced an outcomes-based approach to education, which is central to NQF. Support of outcomes-based education in anti-apartheid movements is derived from a belief in the importance of placing the learner at the center stage of education. However, South African education has tended to rigidly juxtapose outcomes-based education and knowledge-based education, with the latter being labeled as undemocratic and non-transformative, and reflects features of the apartheid education system, which was highly input-driven and pushed the ideological agenda of the apartheid government. In making this point, we do not want to lose sight of the tremendous advance that the NQF is in its aspiration to reposition education as a practice of democracy. Our concern, however, is twofold. In the first place, it does not go far enough in pushing against the legacies of colonialism and apartheid. Arguably, the post-apartheid education system in South Africa displays a considerable decline of radical perspectives and gradual accommodation of neoliberal perspectives. Educational policies in South Africa are informed and shaped by discourses popular in the United Kingdom and Australia, since the dawn of our democracy. These revolve around social constructivism, postmodernism, and progressive education, which underpin the conceptualization of major policies, such as National Qualification Framework and the outcomes-based approach to curriculum and related pedagogic approaches (see Jansen and Christie 1999; Young 2003). In South Africa today, there are tensions between commitment to equality and social transformation and the associated intention to replace old practices with new ones. In the process, South Africa is borrowing educational models developed in Western democratic countries without critical evaluation of their consequences.

The second concern relates to postcolonial praxis, which ought to highlight the need to critically reexamine traditional and dominant educational practices and provide a platform for anti-oppressive methods of teaching, learning, and research. In South Africa, for example, the skewed distribution of resources constantly reminds us of the verities of colonialism. The inequalities in the institutions of learning remind us that these are sites of struggle for equal rights and democratic practices. Neocolonial conditions are pervasive in the South African educational system (Subedi and Daza 2008).

The apparent decline of radical discourses in South Africa and the decline of the practice of critique, particularly with regard to state policy, are observed as subdued, subtle, and tamed voices on issues of social justice and human rights and uncontested neoliberal perspectives of what it means to educate. This is also extended to the persistence of hegemonic, positivistic research practices that still serve to objectify the research process. Our stance to advocate for critical pedagogy arises out of these conditions; the remnants of the colonial conditions have persisted and are resistant to change, and therefore, have not yet been eradicated. Bhabha (1994) asserts that postcolonialism is a salutary reminder of the persistent "neocolonial" relations within the "new" world, opening up the alternative spaces to reexamine the educational discourse, knowledge production of researching, teaching and learning in this country, to be able to respond to the challenges and claims that only some people are the custodians of knowledge.

But what is postcolonial discourse? Located within a contested terrain as Rizvi, Lingard, and Lavia (2006) have suggested, it can be said that postcolonial theories critique colonialism and the colonial aftermath. Further they claim:

> Postcolonialism draws our theoretical attention to the ways in which language works in the colonial formation of discursive and cultural practices. It shows how discourse and power are inextricably linked. Politically, it enables us to provide an account of the ways in which global inequalities are perpetuated not only through the distribution of resources, but also through colonial modes of representation, and in doing this it suggests ways of resisting colonial power in order to forge a more socially just world order. (Rizvi et al. 2006, 250)

Evidently, postcolonial discourse offers rich opportunities for researchers, teachers, and learners to engage with some of the key issues. It offers a space for challenging the given situation for social justice and social transformation, and enhances the principles of democracy. It further provides a way of focusing on ideological influences through the text and subtext(s) and highlights cultural and other differences as inflected in discourses, narratives, and social practices. Postcolonial discourses also cross some liminal spaces, making or revealing new fusions between the practices of knowledge production through research, teaching, and learning that allow engagement in dialogue and interrogate texts and subtext(s) (Wisker 2007).

Where is the place of educative practice and liberation pedagogy in postcolonial discourse? If the central focus of liberation pedagogy is to disrupt and dismantle the deeply entrenched legacies of colonialism and marginalization, it would be relevant for us in our teaching and practices in the classrooms to become conscious actors and agents of change, discouraging silence, marginalization, and disfranchising learners. It would further be relevant to challenge some of the social evils or social injustices that we are bound to encounter; for example, racism, homophobia, xenophobia, and others, thereby creating new and creative spaces for critical dialogue, reflection, and action. According to Frantz Fanon (1968; 1984), independence from colonialism does not mean liberation. He states that "national consciousness" often fails to achieve freedom, because its aspirations are primarily those of the colonized bourgeoisie, who simply replace the colonial rule with their own form of dominance and coercion over the majority of the people, often using the same vocabulary of power. Fanon contends that even after independence, the colonial subjects remain colonized psychologically. Their ways of understanding the world order are carried across into the desire for "whiteness" through a kind of metempsychosis: "Their desires have been transposed, though they have never, of course become white. They have a black skin, with white mask" (Young 2003).

When unpacking Fanon's stance on postcolonialism and theorizing liberation pedagogy, it is important to raise the challenges about issues of curriculum, pedagogy, and research, especially concerning Eurocentric versus Afrocentric knowledge biases. We need to interrogate how educational knowledge, particularly knowledge produced in Euro-American contexts, is complicit in reinforcing colonial notions of culture, power, and difference. Postcolonial discourse calls for the unlearning of "whiteness," and it questions how race and cultural differences have been framed within the field of education.

Decolonizing Practice: Exploring What Is Indigenous

We have argued that the education system in post-apartheid South Africa should reform and transform the former undemocratic, racist, Eurocentric, elitist, and sexist education system, however intense the tensions may seem. The educational structure is a bureaucratic one, which seems to subdue and tame voices and debates and force stakeholders to conform to official requirements. This has contributed to a lack of critical engagement and debate about pedagogical issues. However, we want to turn attention to the task of the postcolonial teacher to proffer how critical pedagogy can reorient the discourse by creating spaces for transgression against socially unjust practices. At the beginning of this chapter, we made the claim of writing from the perspective of postcolonial teachers. Taking such a stance entails struggling for the ethic of a hopeful practice; one in which the aspiration is to develop human capacities (Freire 1989). This involves developing a critical stance to context and content. More than the transfer of knowledge, we believe that the postcolonial teacher in adopting a decolonizing stance in relation to education and educative practice is involved in conscious, communicative action and moral agency. This practice is deliberate in choosing "to make possible the conditions in which learners, in their interaction with one another and with their teachers, engage in the experience of assuming themselves as social, historical, thinking, communicating, transformative, creative persons, dreamers of possible utopias, capable of being angry because of a capacity to love" (Freire 1998, 45). Therefore, what matters more than the official policy documents and frameworks are how teachers are prepared; what they do in and out of the classroom; and how they affect qualitative epistemic change.

One example of how indigenous practice is being advanced by South African educators and academics is the Creating Sustainable Empowering Learning Environments Project. This collaborative project involves the university, parents, students, and teachers. The focus of the project is to develop practices that are indigenous to South Africa in order to optimize educational opportunity and conditions for learning. In their preparation for teaching through the project, teachers are encouraged to use the everyday life stories and practices of schools and their communities to learn, to teach, and to research. The project gives priority to raising new and strong voices by stakeholders working together to: (1) eradicate extreme poverty and hunger; (2) achieve universal primary education; (3) promote gender equality and empower; and (4) rethink development and global partnership on our own terms (UNDP 2005, 2–3). These four elements constitute the priorities of the United Nations Millennium Development Goals (MDGs). However, the project is not restricted to merely responding to these global priorities, but rather, to allowing these priorities to become the platform for national and local dialogue and action for and with teachers and within the communities in which they work.

In this discussion, we are revisiting an agenda - for social justice and transformation. This agenda is informed by a recognition of oppression; the students' and teachers' capacity for critical consciousness; and recognition that students and teachers are subjects and actors in history (Weiler in Cook-Sather 2007). To add a caveat, we are cautious of the danger of totalizing, undifferentiated notions of and responses to oppression, marginalization, and disenfranchisement. In this argument and discussion of anti-oppressive education and educative practice, we are trying to avoid presumptions of singular, essential, authentic, and stable notions of the concepts of student and teacher and are sensitive to their identities, lived experiences, and culture.

Students' experiences and culture, like those of teachers, are precarious, contradictory, fluid, dynamic, never frozen, ever changing, and in process. Their voices are multiple and always in flux: "To simply encourage the expression of everyone's experiences, or voices, is in fact to encourage the more privileged voices, and often to contain the marginalized voices within the terms set by the most privileged" (Maher and Tetreault, in Cook-Sather 2007, 400). For us to engage voices of students and teachers in educational practice in South Africa, might create a space for oppressed, marginalized, and disenfranchised to share their own lived experiences as a means of reaching an understanding of their own power as knowers and creators of their own world and as potential transformers of their world. Through creating opportunities for dialogue and critical consciousness, this practice invites an engagement between teachers and students in a process of knowledge production. We agree with Freire that the danger of silence in a cultural and political sense is in the extent to which the status quo remains unchallenged, making us complicit in our own oppression. From our perspective, this cannot be an option for the postcolonial teacher.

We accept teaching as a political act expressed through cultural confidence—confident in our biography in relation to a wider collective history; confident in our subject matter; confident in our ability to communicate, negotiate, and mediate a curriculum; self-confident and confident in having high regard and respect for others. To do otherwise is to deny the dialectic that the voices of the muted and voiceless help in the interrogation of their social stations and their own experiences and in the process become conscious that this interrogation is a means by which to come to an understanding of their power to effect social transformation (Cook-Sather 2007).

Spivak (1988) asserts that the colonized, oppressed, and marginalized simply do not comply with the dominant discourses, but refashion and appropriate what is forced upon them. Postcolonial theories raise troubling questions about issues of curriculum, pedagogy, and research, especially concerning Eurocentric and American-centric knowledge biases. They question how knowledge produced in an Euro-American context by intellectual elites in both the so-called developed and developing countries is complicit in reinforcing colonial notions of culture, power, and differences. We want to turn our attention now to the specific project of liberation pedagogy in the context of South Africa and the imperatives for South African teachers in a period of democracy.

If we are to agree that critical pedagogy is also a practice of liberation, then we need to confront the complex issue of what is the epistemic basis of such liberation. Here we join Msila (2007) in interrogating the notion of indigenous knowledge systems that have located Africa at its philosophical and methodological center. In advocating for bringing African indigenous knowledge systems (AKIS) into the current system as an act of decolonizing the system, Msila identifies three viewpoints. The first are those who claim that the most appropriate strategy is to establish a parallel system to the conventional; the second perspective is a complete overhaul of the existing system by imposing the AIKS onto the existing system; and the third is "a system that is combined with the African context in which schools are situated. This is challenging and would require some form of retraining of educators for a transformative pedagogy that would be able to prepare learners for a new African identity" (Msila 2007, 155).

Our argument is focused on how African education also seeks to instill in its students an African consciousness and behavioural orientation that will optimize the positive expression of African students' fundamental humanity. In addition, we are concerned with its ability to contribute significantly to the total growth and development of the African community of which they are members. As a practice of education, such a focus is a process or vehicle for defining, interpreting, promoting, and transmitting African thought, philosophy, identity, and culture that of necessity will have to confront the colonial past of the African continent (Nkoane 2006). Afrocentric education cannot exist without recognizing its counter-discursive challenges and imperative to make Africans aware of the connections between history and biography in an individual and collective sense. The masses of South Africans have had a long tradition of survival and resistance, successfully countering oppression and creating liminal spaces where African people can reclaim their African critical consciousness, thereby facilitating a critical emancipatory approach in solving their problems. This process has also involved the interrogation of cultures that influenced African cultures with the purpose of identifying elements that need exclusion or incorporation (Nkoane 2006).

One of the challenges for critical pedagogy and teachers who are to be the architects of such practice is deconstruction and de-essentialising the term *Afrocentric education* as a fluid and dynamic concept. The appropriation of this concept means that within the context of the African renaissance, Afrocentric education is still in the making. Chinua Achebe spoke about the difficulties of defining an "African identity," saying that African identity is still in the making. There is no final identity of which one can say: "That is African." However, at the same time, there is an identity coming into existence, and Africa means something to some people (Makgoba 2005). Afrocentric education is then primarily defined by its dynamism. It is something developing and becoming; dynamic and vibrant, not fixed or static. It is not overdetermined by geopolitical, socioeconomic, ethnic, or cultural definition. Afrocentric education implies a position in discursive spaces and practices of knowledge and power relations that are fluid. The recognition of the fluidity of such a definition opens the way for Africans to take hold of their own destiny in order to shape it according to their own sociopolitical dynamics (Nkoane 2006).

Mahlomaholo (2004) asserts that African-ness is not biology or anatomy—these are nothing but markers that people have used to single out and target people for oppression, exclusion, and marginalization. African-ness, just like blackness, exists more in people's minds than in reality. The colonial system and apartheid had to find excuses that would justify the marginalization, disenfranchisement, oppression, exploitation, and social degradation of people, and they used negatively charged cultural constructions to achieve this goal. A decolonized approach to South African education is therefore required as part of a counter-discursive strategy. Decolonizing the education system is to acknowledge indigenous African knowledge that was excluded from the universal human knowledge. It means engaging in an act of recovery and restoration that which is particular and local in the context of African may be expressed in two ways. First, such a liberatory project can be seen as the recollection of past knowledge, which exists in Africans' imaginings of the ideal past before colonization, which has indeed survived despite efforts to deny, ignore, and eradicate its existence. Secondly, decolonizing education refers to ways of expressing an indigenous knowledge system and sees Afrocentric education as imagining the future beyond colonization, referring to these representations of Afrocentric education as the aspiration of self-determination and the experience of postcoloniality (Mahlomaholo 2004).

Conclusion

The success of an educative practice that includes decolonization, liberation pedagogy, and reclamation is urgent and unfinished business for South Africa. We have identified the importance of understanding the historical contexts to clarifying the challenges of the contemporary contexts. In this chapter, we have also located students and teachers as central agents in educational change and transformation, assuming their rightful place in knowledge production and knowledge dissemination. Further, we have argued that liberation pedagogy is a critical approach to the practice of education, and it has become even more relevant in postcolonial South Africa than ever before, because it is seen as a vehicle for empowerment for the powerless and the marginalized. Freire has reminded us of being aware of our unfinished business. As agents of social change, postcolonial teachers continuously experience themselves as "cultural, historical and unfinished beings in the world" (1998, 51). Post-apartheid South Africa requires teachers who must develop the courage to transgress in the face of unjust practices, pushing against old and new forms of colonialism. It requires intellectual curiosity; conscious action; openness to dialogue; a capacity to apprehend reality; critical reflection; moral agency; a commitment to developing indigenous learning systems; and a conviction that change is possible. This kind of education is nonprescriptive, relies on the imagination of the community, and affirms all people's rights to be and to become.

References

Abdi, A. 2003. "Apartheid and Education in South Africa: Select Historical Analyses." *Western Journal of Black Studies,* 27, (2): 89–97.

Allais, S. 2007. "The Rise and Fall of the NQF: A Critical Analysis of the South African National Qualifications Framework." Unpublished thesis, University of the Witwatersrand, Australia.

Bhabha, H. 1994. *The Location of Culture.* London: Routledge.

Bredekamp, H. 2007. "The Cultural Heritage of Democratic South Africa: An Overview." In *Libraries for the Future: Progress and Development of South African Libraries,* edited by T. J. D. Bothma, P. Underwood, and P. Ngulube, 1–12. Pretoria: LIASA.

Cook-Sather, A. 2007. "Resisting the Impositional Potential of Students Voice Work: Lesson for Liberatory Educational Research from Poststructuralist Feminist Critiques of Critical Pedagogy." *Journal of Discourse: Studies in the Cultural Politics of Education.* 28, no. 3 (September): 389–403.

Department of Education (DoE). 2002. *National Qualifications Framework*. Pretoria: Government Printers.
Fanon, F. 1968. *The Wretched of the Earth*. London: Penguin.
Fanon, F. 1984. *Black Skin, White Mask*. London: Pluto Press.
Freire, P. 1970. *Pedagogy of the Oppressed*. New York: Herder and Herder.
Freire, P. 1985. *The Politics of Education: Culture, Power, and Liberation*. South Hadley, MA: Bergin and Garvey.
Freire, P. 1998. *Pedagogy of Freedom: Ethics, Democracy and Civic Courage*. Lanham, MD: Rowman and Littlefield.
Gadotti, M. 1994. *Reading Paulo Freire: His Life and Work*. Albany, NY: SUNY Press.
Hartshorne, K. B. 1992. *Crisis and Challenge: Black Education, 1910–1990*. Cape Town: Oxford University Press.
hooks, b. 1989. "Black and Female: Reflections on Graduate School." *Talking Back: Thinking Feminist. Thinking Black*. Boston: South End.
hooks, b. 1994. "Embracing Change." *Teaching to Transgress: Education as the Practice of Freedom*. New York: Routledge.
Jansen, J. D. and Christie, P., Ed. 1999. *Changing Curriculum: Studies on Outcomes-Based Education in South Africa*. Cape Town: Juta and Company.
Mahlomaholo, M. G. 2004. "Empire Talks Back: Interrogating Indigenous Knowledge Systems in Postgraduate Curriculum." Unpublished Paper presented at postgraduate seminar 14 September 2004 at the Central University of Technology, Free State, South Africa.
Makgoba, M. W. 2005. *The African University: Meaning Penalties and Responsibilities; Towards African Scholarship*. Public Affairs and Corporate Communication. University of KwaZulu-Natal, South Africa.
McLaren, Peter. 2008. "Decolonizing Democratic Education: Marxian Ruminations." In Decolonizing Democratic Education: Trans-disciplinary Dialogues, edited by Ali A. Abdi and George Richardson, 47–55. Rotterdam: Sense.
Msila, V. 2007. "From Apartheid Education to the Revised National Curriculum Statement: Pedagogy for Identity Formation and Nation Building in South Africa." *Nordic Journal of African Studies* 16 (2): 146–160.
Nkoane, M. M. 2006. "The Africanisation of the University in Africa." *Journal of the Centre for the Study of Southern African Literature and Languages* (Alternation) 13, (1): 49–69.
Pandor, G. 2008. Preface, in *Reviews of National Policies for Education: South Africa*. Organisation for Economic Co-operation and Development, 20. Available at: http://www.education.gov.za/LinkClick.aspx?fileticket=sKsxhYorWOk%3D&tabid=452&mid=1034
Rizvi, F., B. Lingard, and J. Lavia. 2006. "Postcolonialism and Education: Negotiating a Contested Terrain." *Journal of Pedagogy, Culture and Society* 14, (3 (October): 249–262.
Sebedi, B. and S. L. Daza. 2008. "The Possibilities of Postcolonial Praxis in Education." *Journal of Race, Ethnicity and Education* 11, no. 1 (March): 1–10.

Smith, L. Tuhiwai. 1999. *Decolonizing Methodologies: Research and Indigenous Peoples*. New York: Zed Books.
South African Institute of Race Relations (SAIRR). 1984. *A Survey of Race Relations in South Africa, 1983*, vol. 37. Johannesburg: SAIRR.
Spivak, G. 1988. "Can the Subaltern Speak?" In *Marxism and Interpretation of Culture*, edited by C. Nelson and L. Grossberg. 271–313. Urbana, IL: University of Illinois Press.
The Republic of South Africa (RSA). 1995. *Act no. 58 of 1995: South African Qualifications Authority Act*. Pretoria: Government Printers.
The Republic of South Africa (RSA). 1996. *Act no. 108 of 1986: The Constitution*. Pretoria: Government Printers.
The Republic of South Africa (RSA). 1953. *The Bantu Education Act*. Pretoria: Government Printers.
The Republic of South Africa (RSA). 1995. *The Promotion of National Unity and Reconciliation Act*, no. 34. Pretoria: Government Printers.
United Nations Development Programme (UNDP). 2005. Millennium Development Goals. http://www.un.org/milleniumgoal.
Weiler, K. 1990. "Freire and a Feminist Pedagogy of Difference." *Harvard Educational Review* no. 61, 449–474.
Wisker, G. 2007. "Crossing Liminal Spaces: Teaching the Postcolonial Gothic." *Journal of Pedagogy: Critical Approaches to Teaching Literature, Language, Composition, and Culture* 7, no. 3 (2007): 401–425.
Wright Mills, C. 1959. *The Sociological Imagination*. Oxford: Oxford University Press.
Young, R. 2003. *Postcolonialism: A Very Short Introduction*. Oxford: Oxford University Press.

4

The Politics of Restrictive Language Policies: A Postcolonial Analysis of Language and Schooling

Antonia Darder and Miren Uriarte

> "Any meaningful analysis of the post-colonial situation in society requires an interpretation of the historically situated material, political, and cultural circumstances out of which policies of language use are produced."
>
> —*Themba Moyo (2009)*

Central to the history of colonization has been the use of restrictive language policies to ensure the exclusion of racialized populations from full participation within the economic and political landscape of the nation state. Hence, understanding the educational barriers of exclusion, along with the academic impact that such language policies produce, are the central questions that strike at the heart of this postcolonial analysis. More specifically, we examine the manner in which restrictive language policies were implemented over a four-year period within the public schools of Boston, Massachusetts, following the passage of Referendum Question 2 in 2002, a mandate to repeal the use of transitional bilingual education in favor of immersion programs. This story is particularly poignant in that Massachusetts was the first state in the nation to officially enact, in 1971, a transitional bilingual program to meet the needs of the state's growing Spanish-speaking student population. But that was the era of civil rights, when a myriad of educational efforts to address the long-standing historical inequalities faced by children in communities of color were being moved forward by civil-rights activists everywhere.

Today, however, it seems that previously held goals of educational equality and social concern for the most disenfranchised have fallen by the wayside, displaced by conservative solutions that assert the practicality and superiority of restrictive language policies in schools. Instead, neoliberal priorities have forcefully taken precedence over the goal of equality, despite educational rhetoric about the need to "narrow achievement gaps." Accordingly, business agendas and corporatist approaches prevailed, creating strong pressures for accountability structures and measures that have often trumped sound educational practices. Hence, complex testing schemes bind the work of teaching and learning, while punitive practices tied to high-stakes testing create inordinately stressful environments for both students and teachers. This is further exacerbated by privatizing initiatives that invite charter schools to compete with declining public-education funds. Similarly, accountability practices single out underperforming students and schools, which could result in positive outcomes were material and pedagogical resources mobilized to address the needs. Instead, such measures are being enacted precisely at the same time when the capacity of districts and schools to respond to the needs of English language learners has become ever more limited.

Over the last two decades, Massachusetts, as is true across the nation, has experienced a rapid increase in immigration, and with it, an increasing enrollment of speakers of languages other than English in its public schools. This phenomenon is now at work in most major urban centers, but it also has become increasingly an issue for large suburban and rural areas as well. The underlying cause of this unprecedented demographic shift is unquestionably the result of economic conditions that have given rise to job instabilities, not only in the United States, but globally. Hence, an examination of restrictive language policies and their implementation within the Boston schools serves as an excellent site of inquiry, in that it mimics many of the same conditions currently at work in the schooling of English learners across the nation.

Anchoring our "interpretation [within] the historically material, political, and cultural circumstances out of which policies of language use are produced," as Themba Moya suggests, is particularly salient here, given that the majority of English learners in Boston are from populations whose personal histories are deeply marked by the impact of colonization—Puerto Rico, Dominican Republic, Haiti, and Cape Verde, just to name a few. Hence, our analysis of the politics of language and schooling is enhanced by a postcolonial reading, which provides the analytical specificities to make sense of restrictive language policies across the larger national landscape, given the impact of these policies on the lives of (post)colonized students from impoverished working-class communities.

Our effort here is to engage concerns tied to language and inequalities front and center, shattering any illusions that languages others than English in the United States are genuinely welcomed and cultivated in public schools. Nothing could be further from the truth. Even in the light of research that specifically speaks to the cognitive advantages of bilingualism in sharpening intelligence and the capacity to engage more expansively within the world,[1] education in the United States has been and continues to be firmly grounded upon chauvinistic traditions of linguistic domination upheld by the colonizers who "culturally invaded," to use Paulo Freire's (1970) words, the Western hemisphere. Hence, just as colonial formations of slavery, land dispossession, and wealth extraction were enacted upon racialized subjects worldwide to ensure dominion, so were restrictive language practices, which, in many cases, resulted in linguistic genocide and cultural erosion (Darder and Torres 2004; Skatnubb-Kangas 2000; Freire and Macedo 1987).

Furthermore, restrictive language policies can formidably be traced to political economic exigencies of the nation-state, that seek to safeguard the control of its working populations, in order to ensure the quasistability of its ever increasing low-wage service sector—a labor market that requires a growing sector to be minimally educated. In fact, Jean Anyon (2005) asserts: "most job openings in the next ten years will not require either sophisticated skills or a college degree. Seventy-five percent of new and projected jobs will be low paying. Most will require on-the-job training only, and will not require college; most will be in service and retail, where poverty zone wages are the norm (370)." Simultaneously, more and more manufacturing and technical jobs continue to be outsourced to cheap centers of a now global workforce, increasing competition for access to the shrinking elite workforce of the knowledge economy, which is simply unable to absorb the growing population of U.S. workers—the largest number now coming from historically racialized communities.

This infusion of material conditions is significant to our analysis, in that, generally speaking, many advocates for bilingual education programs over the years have discussed questions of language and schooling in provincial or romanticized cultural terms, without linking the imperatives of culture, language, and identity to questions of collective sustainability, social agency, and class struggle. This is to say, that there has been a failure to consider the education of English-learners and their language rights with greater analytical depth, despite the manner in which workers are positioned within the U.S. political economy. Yet, it is only through such discussions can we begin to get at the core assumptions at work in the construction of educational language policies that impede the academic success of English learners in U.S. schools—who, contrary to public opinion, are overwhelmingly U.S. citizens and not exclusively undocumented immigrants, as the media and nativists would have us believe. Hence, we argue that current restrictive language policies for English-language learners must be critically interrogated in relationship not only to high-school dropout rates, poor academic performance, or college attrition rates, but also to the long-term consequences associated with lack of educational attainment. Typically, these consequences include housing segregation and labor (non)participation patterns, rising incarceration rates, and growing conditions of poverty—all intimately linked to the social arrangements responsible for the reproduction of racism and gross class inequalities.

Inseparability of Racism and Class Inequalities

> "Language conflicts...represent more than contending philosophies of assimilation and pluralism, disagreements about the rights and responsibilities of citizens or debates over the true meaning of 'Americanism.' Ultimately language politics are determined by material interests—that is, struggles for social and economic supremacy, which normally lurk beneath the surface of the public debate."
>
> —Crawford 2000, 10

Racism as an inherently political strategy of exclusion, domination, and exploitation cannot be extricated from its economic imperative, whether discussing questions of academic achievement or larger concerns tied to labor opportunities. Segregation, for example, as an outcome of racialization and class reproduction is firmly entrenched within the wider systematic necessity of a capitalist mode of production—which supports policies and practices within schools and the labor market that sustain the skewed economic interests of capital.

As such, inequalities resulting from restrictive language policies generally operate in sync with structures that perpetuate school segregation. Studies conducted in the last decade by the Civil Rights Project (Orfield 1999, 2001; Orfield and Lee 2007) found that although "progress toward school desegregation peaked in the late 1980s, as the court concluded that the goals of *Brown v Board of Education* had been largely achieved, 15 years later the trend has moved in the opposite direction" (Orfield 1999). Questions of segregation, therefore, still remain salient factors, particularly for working class Latino populations—now dubbed "the new face of segregation"—given that Latino students find themselves even more segregated today than their African America counterparts. This increase in Latino segregation has been particularly marked in western states, where more than 80 percent of Latinos students attend segregated schools, compared with 42 percent in 1968 (Dobbs 2004). In the northeast, 78 percent of Latino students attend schools with over 50 percent minority student population, and 46 percent attend schools with over 90 percent minority population (Orfield 1999). Similar patterns are quickly emerging in the South, where Latino population increases have been reported to exceed 300 percent in North Carolina, Arkansas, Georgia, and Tennessee. Thus, it should not be surprising to learn that 90 percent of neighborhood schools where English-language learners and children of color—most who are, in fact, citizens—attend are all located in areas of concentrated poverty. Moreover, students of color who are English-language learners are 11 times more likely to live in areas of concentrated poverty, than students of all ethnicities who attend predominantly "white" schools.

It is also significant to note that socioeconomic conditions, which are clear producers of gross racialized inequalities, such as lack of job security, insufficient income(s) to care for one's family, dwindling youth employment; the demise of "middle-class" union jobs, lack of health care; expanding poverty, and increasing incarceration of working-class man and women of color, are seldom raised as key factors in discussions of language and schooling. Yet, such conditions of political and economic disenfranchisement ensure greater incidence of residential segregation, as well, which has been found to be a significant factor in the English language development of children from language-minority communities. This is so, in that English learners, who are taught exclusively within English-only classrooms, are more likely to struggle with a home-school linguistic transition process that expects them to isolate and compartmentalize their language usage in ways that have been found to disrupt not only English language development, but academic achievement patterns

(Genesee 2006; Cummins 2000; Crawford 2000; Valenzuela 1999). Consequently, recent reports belie notions that sheltered English instruction will radically improve student performance. In fact, studies show no considerable improvement in rates of English acquisition (Thomas and Collier 2002). Moreover, what cannot be overlooked here is the loss of bilingual programs, which once afforded English language learners the opportunity to study academic content in their primary language, while learning English (Genesse 2006; Suarez-Orozco and Suarez-Orozco 2001; Portes 2001; Tollefson 2004; Cummins 2000; Skatnubb-Kangas 2000).

Complaints of cost have also been used by conservative forces to rally popular support against appropriate bilingual-education programs for English-language learners. Yet, absent from these discussion are the trillions of dollars being poured yearly into military spending, while public welfare concerns are redefined by neoliberal interests in such ways that essentially abdicate the State of its responsibility to adequately educate all children attending U.S. schools, including English learners. Instead, a sink-or-swim philosophy tied to the ethos of free-market enterprise has overwhelmingly penetrated the policy-making arena of educational language policies. As such, one-year English immersion programs have become the preferred mainstream intervention, despite overwhelming evidence collected over the last four decades that challenges the folly of an expedited English-only approach and exposes the negative academic consequences to the academic formation of English learners, safe for the small number who succeed and are then paraded as the exception of racialized populations, stereotypically perceived as less intelligent, less communicative, and less psychologically able to contend with mainstream expectations of schooling (Darder and Torres 2004).

Here, we want to note that although state laws may call for only a one-year immersion program for language support, most English language learners must remain in these programs a longer period of time. This is not surprising, in that studies consistently indicate that students require six years to learn English proficiently, even under conditions that provide them "cognitively complex curricula that develop thinking skills, through both their first and second languages" (Collier and Thomas 2010). However, both the use of English immersion strategies and the overwhelming intent of districts to mainstream these students quickly leads to conditions where English learners are not offered sufficient subject content in neither their mother tongue nor English, yet they are expected to perform adequately on tests that do not account for these debilitating academic conditions.

Even more disconcerting is the lack of adequate training and preparation that mainstream educators, including school psychologists, receive in both the area of appropriate teaching strategies and language assessment protocols for English-language learners. This, unfortunately, perpetuates false beliefs—again, despite research to the contrary—that teachers and allied personnel do not require any additional preparation to teach or assess English-language learners, given that innately "intelligent" children will surely excel no matter what type of educational program is offered them. Such fallacious conservative arguments allow school districts, if they choose, to relinquish any responsibility to provide professional development to mainstream educators, who are inexperienced in teaching or assessing English-language learners. One of the most striking consequences of this lack of knowledge is the statistically significant number of English-language learners, compared to their English proficient counterparts, who are referred to special-education programs for questionable intelligence, communicative disorders, and developmental delays (English Language Learners Sub-Committee 2009). Of course, given restrictive language policies implemented in most school districts and the lack of preparation in teacher-education programs, classroom teachers alone cannot be held responsible for this unfortunate institutional deficiency.

All this said, it is striking to note that, in the last two decades, as well-paying jobs in the United States began to disappear in the wake of the globalizing agenda of neoliberal interests and its shock-doctrine economics, exclusionary and restrictive language policies, along with mean-spirited anti-immigrant debates have surged. As a consequence, deep racialized resentments have been generated by job scarcity and subsequent competition across working-class and immigrant populations. Moreover, this misdirected resentment has not only been capitalized on by conservative forces to garner support from English-speaking working-class populations for English-only policies, but also to confuse parents of English-language learners into believing that English-only instruction is in the best interest of their children. Even more disturbing is the manner in which victim-blaming rhetoric, aimed at English-language learners and other students from racialized communities who fail to succeed in public schools, has been repeatedly used to obscure the deepening structures of economic inequality, inherent in U.S. capitalism.

Moreover, contradictory class-based attitudes are widespread, with respect to bilingualism in the United States. For example, while elite private schools place an increasing emphasis on the development of bilingual language skills for "global citizenship" and wealthy transnational corporations send high-ranking employees to Latin America, China, or other countries to learn a second language so they can compete more readily within the global marketplace, English-language learners in U.S. public schools—who most readily could develop bilingual skills—are being forced into English-only programs. Similarly, affluent public schools offer gifted language programs in Spanish, French, or Chinese, while these opportunities are almost nonexistent in low-income schools, where most English-language learners attend and where little effort is placed on expanding knowledge of their primary languages. Hence, access to genuine bilingual development and the cultural and global advantages it affords is only a prerogative of students from affluent classes. As such, racism and class inequalities fully converge in contradictory ways to perpetuate linguistic racialization.

The Process of Linguistic Racialization

> *"The cultural imperialism of the last century relegated the language of the colonized to a peripheral role by excluding it from institutions such as the education system—at issue are the role and status of language and its people."*
>
> —Paul Spooley 1993

In light of a colonial history of language imposition, a postcolonial lens is useful in forging an analysis of restrictive language policies and their impact on English-language learners, in that it historicizes conditions of language loss beyond that of individual choice or the practical inducement of English for academic and labor success. Moreover, views of language as "purely mechanical devices" (Nieto 2007) or solely signifiers of national allegiance can be decentered, as we engage with the powerful reality that language, political power, and economics are all inextricably tied to the ideological formations of the nation-state and, as such, language functions as a fundamental human resource for the construction of meaning and the establishment of relationships within both the private and public sphere. "In fact, the human being cannot exist without communicating; eliminating the possibility of communication from the human spirit entails removing its humanity" (Nieto 2007).

This is precisely the experience of many English-language learners when they enter a classroom where the supremacy of English functions not only against their academic well-being, but their democratic participation as well. Upon entering the English-only classroom, English-language learners are rendered voiceless in a foreign sound system and cultural milieu that does not afford them a place for self-expression or self-determination. And often, even when these students learn English, stereotypical perceptions of deficiency persist, which deny them meaningful opportunities to participate that English-proficient students readily enjoy in the process of their learning, considered critical to effective academic formation. Without these opportunities, the ability of English-language learners to succeed in school is overwhelmingly compromised, as they struggle not only to learn the grade-level content, but also grapple with traversing limited language comprehension, in a context that affords them little, if any, language support (Freire and Macedo 1987; Darder 2002; Valenzuela 1999).

Hence, it is no wonder that language constitutes such a deeply contested terrain of struggle in the education of English-language learners. Instructional language is, thus, implicated in significant ways, when considering the future possibilities and limitations students will experience, not only in the classroom, but out in the world as well. Similarly, community conditions that infuse life, meaning, and belonging into individual and collective life are also important factors in their academic achievement, given that education, economics, political voice, and democratic participation are significant to minority-language-community empowerment. This is to say, that when important human conditions, shaped by a long-standing history of oppression and marginalization are ignored, disregarded, or maligned within schools, the political empowerment and well-being of English-language learners and their families are also negatively affected (Olivos 2004; Darder 2002, 1991). This process can, unfortunately, leave language minority communities at the mercy of a hegemonic process that prevents them from naming their world and, hence, from participating in significant educational language-policy debates and decisions that will impact their children's destiny.

As a consequence, English-language learners, who enter the classroom with a primary language other than English, as mentioned earlier, are often (mis)assessed too quickly as intellectually deficient or developmentally delayed, as a consequence of assessment measures that do not take into account the dissonance experienced by otherwise intellectually capable children entering into a new language context.

Unfortunately, the linguistic forms of racialization at work in the schooling of English-language learners, or what Angela Valenzuela (1999) terms "subtractive schooling," disrupts the ability of both educators and policy makers to see beyond their shrouded projections of inferiority—a phenomenon that stifles the ability to recognize, assess, and employ the strengths and capacities these students already possess.

Thus, unexamined racialized perceptions of English-language learners often, unwittingly, render teachers blind to those cognitive resources that would normally provide the logical foundation for the new linguistic experience of learning English. Accordingly, the inability of mainstream teachers to engage the knowledge and skills that English language learners bring to the classroom is a key barrier to academic success; as is the absence of the primary language as the medium of instruction, which discourages not only the use of minority languages in the United States, but also disrupts the successful academic formation of marginalized students, who are further rendered vulnerable by restrictive language policies and practices.

In many ways, we can understand the task at hand, even today, to be one that requires us to decolonize our minds from debilitating beliefs that persistently racialize English-language learners, quickly judging them in need of remediation, yet unworthy of the expenditure of additional resources. In the logic of Race to the Top (RTT) and its predecessor, No Child Left Behind (NCLB), the goal of education is to create the global competitive edge that can ensure domination of the world's political economy—at the expense of children from the most vulnerable populations. As such, expenditures of educational resources are liberally being directed toward science, technology, engineering, and mathematics (STEM) in the government's frenzied attempt to meet its overarching goal. In the world of high-stakes accountability, STEM initiatives are pronounced the grand scheme for progress and global supremacy, while questions of democratic life have almost entirely been eclipsed.

In accordance, linguistic racialization here is implicated as part of a larger and more complex system of economic and political oppression that positions English-language learners and their families as disposable, second-class citizens (Darder and Torres 2004). This encompasses a process of racialization that often distorts the ability to see working-class minority language communities in the United States as worthy of full educational rights. The consequence is the perpetuation of a culture of failure and educational neglect that relegates these communities to a politically invisible nether land—aided by the politics of the labor market, ill-representations of the media, and the increasing incarceration of poor working-class men and women of color (Gilmore 2006).

Linguistic racialization within schools is further exacerbated by what Phillipson (2002) argues are the deleterious socioeconomic and cultural effects of the colonial language and the failure of elected leaders to implement a consistently democratic language policy. Indifference to the negative consequences of English-only instruction is particularly debilitating for working-class students who enter school as predominantly Spanish speakers. Unfortunately, as already discussed earlier, the failure of schools to engage the material conditions that these students and their families navigate daily circumvents accurate assessment and the development of public language policies and educational practices to support their effective academic development. And, despite the fact that Latino students can comprise 50–90 percent of the total student population in many districts, there has been a stubborn unwillingness to critically engage the manner in which the language needs of these children may differ. This is often reflected in the manner in which educators are trained to understand and thus, contend, if at all, with the needs of Spanish-speaking children as only individuals, rather than within a larger collective history of colonization, often taking place *within* their own lands. This is particularly the case for Puerto Ricans in the northeast and Chicanos in the Southwest, both groups whose racialized histories are indelibly fused with the African diaspora and indigenous populations, through processes often referred to as "miscegenation" and "*mestizaje*" (Anzaldua 1987; Rodriguez 2000; Valle and Torres 2000).

Central to this history is a Spanish-speaking population that overwhelmingly comprises the largest minority group in the United States. Los Angeles, for example, is second only to Mexico City as the city with the largest number of Spanish speakers. Other large Spanish-speaking populations are found in cities like New York, Miami, and Chicago, with Boston's Latino population having grown swiftly in the last two decades. This is to argue that the educational needs and politics of language conservation in these instances warrant greater collective reconsideration and community participation, given that "Spanish speakers represent 75 percent of the nation's English learners" (Collier and Thomas 2010), and in Boston, a full 25 percent of the student population is now considered English-language learners (Uriarte et al. 2010).

Yet, whenever there are efforts to engage more substantively with the significance of this phenomenon in the schooling of English learners, policy makers and district officials quickly retort that there are over 100 languages spoken in many of these districts, and how can teachers be expected to realistically meet the language needs of all these children. Rather than simply devolve into classically individualistic views of English learner students or essentialize all English learners into one neat population, it is imperative that the larger communal questions tied to language conservation and dual-language issues be recognized as quite a different affair, when considering the language needs of children who reside within very large language communities that existed in North America, even prior to the official establishment of the United States as a nation-state.

Hence, theories and assessment of language needs, as well as educational policy considerations tied to language of instruction must contend with this significant linguistic history, along with its pedagogical meaning for cultivating community empowerment and democratic participation—both processes which are, unfortunately, at odds with powerful nativist interests in the United States today. As a consequence, mean-spirited public debates have ensued, resulting in two decades of initiatives and referendums that have simultaneously worked to eliminate language rights, immigrant rights, and worker rights in states like California and Arizona. As would be expected, these political debates have led to increased policing of the United States–Mexico border, arguments against "political correctness," and a politically disabling national culture that seems to have lost its former ties to the long-held democratic principle of social justice for all.

Nativist Preoccupations

"There is no room in this country for hyphenated Americanism."

—Theodore Roosevelt, 1915

We have argued here that educational language issues associated with English learners must be understood within historical and material conditions that inextricably link racism and class inequalities in powerful ways. Yet, this view, now more than ever, has become contentious ground, in that it goes counter-current to both conservative and neoliberal ideologies that support English-only policies, individual rights over collective rights, exclusive nation-state allegiance, unified national identity, and schools as economic engines for the advancement of the U.S. free-market economy—all touted as the only guarantee for the progress and prosperity of the nation. These, of course, are at the heart of the many arguments launched against bilingual education and, most recently, against ethnic-studies high-school programs in Arizona, where the state passed legislation opposing courses that focused on teaching the history of U.S. minority groups. Proponents of such policies claim that programs such as bilingual education and ethnic studies promote divisiveness and weaken the fabric of national identity.

In concert with colonial roots, there has been a long history of nativist attitudes, policies, and practices in the United States. In the late 1700s, refugees from France and Ireland prompted the passage of the U.S. Alien and Sedition Acts of 1798. Then again in the mid-1800s, another wave of immigration from Europe caused contentious political debate. In the late 1800s, debates against Chinese workers intensified and led to the passage of the Chinese Exclusion Act of 1882. Then the Gentlemen's Agreement of 1907, an informal agreement, was aimed at controlling Japanese populations. During much of the twentieth century, schools in the Southwest were driven by a strong assimilative Americanization curriculum that segregated Mexican children, with the expressed intent to civilize them to an American identity (Sanchez 1951). In the civil-rights era, many efforts were launched to ameliorate the impact of racialization processes at work in the schooling of African American and other children of color. The political and legal challenges to racism in U.S. schools ultimately led to the successful ruling in Brown v. Board of Education (1954), which opened the door for a multitude of educational efforts, giving rise to both the multicultural education and bilingual education movements.

In the last two decades, many of the gains of the civil-rights era have been successfully eroded by nativist forces. A strong conservative wave in California led to the successful passage of anti-immigrant (Proposition 209 in 1996) and antibilingual (Proposition 227 in 1998) initiatives in the state. These conservative campaigns led to the dismantling of the Lau v. Nichols decision, which guaranteed the rights of bilingual children to be educated in their primary language. Following the 1998 passage of Proposition 227 (or "English for the Children") in California, Arizona immediately followed suit. Then in 2002, the voters of Massachusetts overwhelmingly approved Question 2, a similar initiative that ended transitional bilingual education for English learners. In each of these cases, bilingual programs that utilized the primary language as the medium of instruction were replaced by one year of sheltered English instruction.

As a consequence, educational issues rooted in the cultural and linguistic needs of minority-language students now find little room for discussion, leaving minority-language-rights advocates to weather serious political attacks. In the process, conservative anti-immigrant supporters seek to extinguish the strength and vitality of Spanish-speaking communities. The growing Spanish-speaking immigrant population, in particular, along with their culture and language are deemed a threat to the integrity of the nation. These xenophobic attitudes expressed by the English-only movement are also heard in the vociferous anti-immigrant attacks of the newly formed ultra-right, populist Tea Party and the nativist discourse of many conservative public intellectuals, political figures, and media broadcasters. Bilingual education, ethnic studies, and, especially, Latino immigration are all blamed for not only a crisis in national identity and the economic decline, but a growing national-security risk, which they insist is leading the nation into insurmountable political and economic turmoil.

From the standpoint of nativist groups, anti-immigrant sentiments and English-only proposals are justified on the grounds that Spanish-speaking immigrants are an expense to the government; isolate within their own communities; refuse to learn English; steal jobs from native citizens; disrupt patriotic ideals; cause a burden upon social services; overpopulate; and are a growing threat to the stability of "American culture." These claims underscore fierce opposition to bilingualism in schools, ignoring the truth that most English-language learners are either legal residents or American citizens. Moreover, despite the fact that English is clearly the top contending hegemonic language of globalization, nativist organizations such as U.S. English "believe that English is threatened by other languages in the U.S., mainly Spanish. This organization advocated for the implementation of different language policies to secure that English is threatened no more as the common language in the United States" (Nieto 2009, 236).

Hence, nativists often scapegoat Latino populations (immigrant or not) and are content to sacrifice the language needs of Spanish-speaking children, in order to conserve the economic and political interests of elites who have consistently bankrolled both anti-immigrant and anti-bilingual campaigns across the country (Gandera 2000; Crawford

1992). Hence, restrictive language policies in public schools are clearly marked by a larger set of conservative and neoliberal goals associated with protecting white Anglo-Saxon Protestant (WASP) dominance, in which the supremacy of English has become a significant political battleground.

Impact of Restrictive Language Policies on English Learners: A Boston Study

"[Restrictive language] policies and educational practices are <u>always</u> situated in relation to wider issues of power, access, opportunity, inequality, and, at times discrimination and disadvantage."

—Stephen May and Nancy Hornberger, 2008

As might be expected, political goals tied to the conservation of English as the official language of schooling for all children in the United States has seldom reaped positive consequences for language minority children and their communities, who are forced to navigate the negative outcomes of English-immersion strategies. Such strategies forsake the linguistic strength of the primary language, and in its place, resurrect former assimilative assumptions and practices of the pre-civil-rights era, namely, "that children learn English best by being immersed in an English-only classroom environment" (Uriarte et al. 2010). Yet, despite little empirical evidence to support this contention, many school districts across the country have switched in the last decade from more comprehensive bilingual approaches to the use of sheltered English immersion programs as the preferred mode of language support.

At this juncture, it is worth noting that a variety of leading language researchers in the field, including James Crawford (2004), Jim Cummins (2000), Wayne Thomas and Virginia Collier (2002), and Stephen Krashen (2003), argue that the mainstreaming of English-language learners into English-only classrooms blatantly disregards ongoing research that repeatedly illustrates the importance of an additive approach, rather than one that subtracts the students' primary language from their academic learning experience. Moreover, an English-immersion mandate is generally based upon purely instrumentalized and fragmented notions of language, divorced of language as a human right and the significance of culture, identity, and community interaction to the effective development of both the first and second language (Skattnub-Kangas 2000).

Rather than accelerate English acquisition, the subtraction of native language development deprives children of the numerous benefits conferred by bilingualism. While affirming the importance of English-language acquisition, most recent studies on effective models of immigrant adaptation point to the importance of children retaining the ability to function in their original culture, even as they attain a new one. Portes and Rumbaut (2001) refer to this ability to manage both cultures as "selective acculturation," the most advantageous way for children to undergo an adaptive integration into the new context. In this framework, children are typically fluent in both languages, minimizing intergenerational conflict, and preserving parental rights over their children. "Dissonant acculturation" emerges when there is a loss or a rupture with the culture of origin, including limited bilingualism, or the loss of the primary language, thereby rupturing family ties and causing intergenerational conflict (Portes and Rumbaut 2001, 52). This process has been positively associated with all significant indicators of high-school academic performance—including math and reading levels, as well as overall grade-point average (Portes and Rumbaut 2001).

This knowledge, however, did not make much of a difference, as the English for the Children campaign, liberally financed by California's conservative businessman Ron Unz, made its way through the Massachusetts electorate in the fall of 2002. Similar referenda sponsored by the right-wing organization, U.S. English Only, had been successful in California (Proposition 227 in 1998) and in Arizona (Proposition 203 in 2000). Following this lead, Massachusetts's Question 2 was passed overwhelmingly by 68 percent of the voters. The referendum, similar to its predecessors, stipulated that "with limited exceptions, all public school children must be taught English by being taught all subjects in English and being placed in English language classrooms," replacing both transitional and maintenance bilingual programs that had been available to English-language learners with sheltered English-immersion programs.[2]

From afar, Massachusetts was an unlikely candidate for this change, being a state that historically prided itself in its liberal and innovative approaches to social policy, including education. But perhaps the most jarring aspect of this shift in political direction was the fact that Massachusetts had led the nation in 1971, when the state legislature mandated transitional bilingual education for English-language learners. Hence, it is not surprising that, once U.S. English Only forces began taking Question 2 to the streets, many teachers were vocal in their opposition to the measure, as were immigrant and language-minority communities. But most educational leaders, although they seem to understand that this was not a sound educational initiative, remained silent.

The Context of Language-Restrictive Policies in Massachusetts

Unlikely as it may seem, the roots of this dramatic change were actually not too far under the surface. For one, the 1971 legislative mandate for bilingual education resulted from the lack of implementation of the 1967 Bilingual Education Amendment to Title VII of the Elementary and Secondary Education Act of 1965, which instituted a federal commitment to the implementation of bilingual education. By 1970, little headway had been made in the establishment of bilingual programs. In Boston, for example, despite documentation of the lack of matriculation of Puerto Rican children,[3] the Boston Public Schools insisted that there was no evidence of need. This forced the community to prove a need existed. And this, the community did, obligating the School Committee to begin funding limited bilingual programs, until 1971, when the state legislature finally mandated bilingual programs for all English-language learners and assigned community organizations the responsibility for their implementation.

It was the Latino community's direct participation in the education of their children that led to a strong preference for maintenance bilingual education. With this model, students were assisted to maintain and develop in the capacity to use their first language, even as they acquired English as a second. However, there was strong resistance at that time to the implementation of maintenance programs by those who advocated for immersion, as a recipe for quick assimilation for the city's new (im)migrants. Transitional bilingual education, as legislated in 1971, represented a compromise between these two poles—and, as a likely result, neither side was satisfied with the outcome, as Latino parents and community leaders continued to advocate for more comprehensive bilingual programs, while conservative proponents of immersion pushed in the opposite direction. Nevertheless, school districts developed a wide array of approaches, ranging from programs that emphasized the use of the native language to those that minimized it. Moreover, as new immigrant groups arrived, new language programs were offered.

For thirty years, this remained Massachusetts's framework for the implementation of bilingual education; however, throughout most of this period, bilingual programs largely languished. For example, in Boston with the largest number of English-language learners, the well-documented process of desegregation of the Boston Public Schools coincided, and largely submerged, the implementation of bilingual programs. Nevertheless, parents organized in the Master Parent Advisory Council (Master PAC) were arduous advocates for district bilingual accountability. They negotiated a voluntary Lau Compliance Plan with the Boston School Committee in 1979, to comply with the U.S. Office of Civil Rights' Lau Remedies, which followed the Supreme Court's ruling in Lau v. Nichols in 1974 (Boston Public Schools 1999, 14), and then amended this plan in 1981, 1985, and 1992. Parents also sued the district successfully to obtain equitable services for bilingual students (Boston Public Schools, 1999, 13). This consistently strong advocacy on the part of parents was the bane of superintendents, leading one to complain that the district was nurturing the organization of parents so that they could, in turn, sue the district (Tung et al. 2009).

Bilingual programs in Boston and elsewhere in the state evolved in the shadow of parents' activism, with strong support from teachers and others directly involved in their development. Advocates demonstrated many successes, including the involvement of most districts with more than 20 students requiring language support; the development of new programs to support the education of students of dozens of languages; and the development of exemplary dual language programs. But in spite of these successes, there was no consistent documentation or evaluation of the progress of English-language acquisition for English-language learners, despite the fact that districts reported this information to the Massachusetts Department of Education on a yearly basis (DeJong, Gort, and Cobb 2005, 597–598) and, as a consequence, bilingual programs lingered, largely from state neglect.

Two additional factors greatly influenced the outcome of this story. The first is the state's shift to a high-stakes environment, as part of the implementation of its 1993 Educational Reform initiative. At the onset, this broad initiative increased spending in education and distributed funding more equitably between urban and suburban districts, offering new resources to the education of language-minority students. The initiative proposed higher standards for all students and schools and new curriculum standards and requirements in core academic areas, which were to guide the development of local curricula, increase time-on-task for students, and tighten standards for new teacher certification and teacher education, as well as retraining established teachers, including special training in multicultural education and teaching strategies for English-language learners. This all seemed a welcome step toward alleviating the devastating results of the cultural clash between minority students and the mostly white teaching force. The reform also introduced measures to hold districts accountable for identifying students, schools, and districts in need of assistance, in an effort to guarantee improved school performance. Alongside, multiple measures of student achievement were to be integrated into the process of aligning local curricula to the statewide "frameworks," as a way of establishing student competence in those areas (Uriarte 2002).

No group stood to gain more from these proposed changes than Latinos, whose children had the lowest levels of achievement of any group in the Commonwealth of Massachusetts.[4] Latino enrollment in the state's public schools, which had been growing for three decades, had skyrocketed, particularly, in urban districts. At the time, more than 66,000 Latino children were enrolled in Massachusetts schools, a 20 percent increase in just five years. In Boston, for example, 20 percent of the students were Latinos, and in smaller towns such as Lawrence and Holyoke, they made up almost 70 percent of students enrolled (MDOE 1992). As far back as 1976, reports by Latino community agencies and state task forces pointed to high grade retention and high school dropout rates. In 1986, the Education Task Force of the Massachusetts Commission on Hispanic Affairs, a commission sponsored by the Massachusetts legislature, concluded, "the Massachusetts public education system is failing to carry out its mission and its responsibility to the Hispanic community" (Massachusetts Commission on Hispanic Affairs 1986, 5). In the opinion of the task force, this was due to underfunding of school systems where Latino students predominated, as well as the absence of culturally sensitive curricula and classroom practices. In 1989 and 1990, protests reached a crescendo in a series of contentious meetings with the leadership of the Boston Public Schools, when it was reported that the annual Latino dropout rate had reached 30 percent in some Boston high schools, forcing the city to recognize its failure in educating Latino students.[5] Hence, when the Massachusetts legislature passed the Educational Reform Law in 1993, many Latinos supported the initiative.

But conditions changed swiftly as the political leadership of the state moved to the right. Under great pressure from the business sector, the composition of the State Board of Education changed, as did the orientation of the reforms. Most notable and controversial was the board's decision to adopt a series of standardized tests, administered in several grades as the primary measure of student achievement; and to require that students pass the 10th-grade version of the standardized test, in order to graduate from high school. With the Massachusetts Comprehensive Assessment System (MCAS), Massachusetts began the implementation of high-stakes testing as the sole measure for graduation.[6]

The implementation of this 10th-grade graduation requirement had a devastating effect on the graduation rate of Latino students. In the first two years of its implementation, more than half of Latino 10th graders taking the Math and English Language Arts (ELA) tests failed one or both exams, and therefore, did not graduate from high school (Uriarte and Lavan 2006). In cities like Lawrence and Holyoke, the failure rates reached more than 70 percent. By 2008, 23 percent of Latino students were still failing either in Math, ELA, or both and, therefore, did not graduate from high school (Uriarte and Agusti 2009). Although this appears to show improvement, the data is called into question by a high dropout rate among Latino students, a rate that has remain almost 30 percent for more than a decade. Hence, those students taking the MCAS test in grade 10 excludes the most vulnerable Latino students, most of whom now drop out prior to the 10th grade. Consequently, high dropout rates and the high-stakes environment have resulted in Latinos attaining the lowest graduation rates in the state. This consistent failure by schools to deliver a minimum level of education has had devastating effects on the lives of Latino students and on their communities.

The context for the shift in the focus of the state's education reform is in concert with the earlier analysis of recent transformations in the political economy of public education in the United States. The competitive advantage of Massachusetts, vis-à-vis other states, centers on the education of its workforce as the state reinvents its economic base to stay at the forefront of innovation. Massachusetts, the poster child of the knowledge economy with its plethora of high-ranking educational institutions, has an economy that is in its fourth transformation since the 1950s—from manufacturing to high-technology manufacturing, to software and finance, to biotechnology and life sciences—with each change requiring a workforce with higher levels of education.

But, these industries represent a growing, but limited number of jobs. Supporting this economy is a vast array of service employment, with less stringent educational requirements (although in Massachusetts, some service employment still demand a significant level of education) and increasingly becoming a niche for black, Latino, and immigrant workers (Sum et al. 2006; Borges-Méndez et al. 2008). As would be expected, Latinos, because of their poor level of educational attainment, do not fare well in this economy. Among all groups, Latinos have the highest proportion of its population working in the service sector, with 52 percent of Latinos employed in service occupations, compared to 40 percent of the general population. Moreover, Latinos occupy the lower-wage niches of this sector; and, although their participation in the labor force is high (many working more than one job), the median income of Latino households is only 48 percent of that of the general population, in addition to having the highest poverty rate of all groups in Massachusetts (Borges-Mendez et al. 2006; Uriarte et al. 2006).

Meanwhile, the state remains committed to its neoliberal reform agenda, in great measure because, in the eyes of most educational policy leaders, the strategy of high standards and strong accountability is considered a success, given that Massachusetts has shown the highest performance of all states for National Assessment of Educational Progress (NAEP), for close to a decade. What is not so readily disclosed is that Massachusetts also ranks among the five states with the widest gap in achievement between white and Latino students in both NAEP Math and Reading (NAEP, n.d.). This achievement gap particularly affects students from racialized working-class communities but, according to a 2010 report from the Massachusetts Board of Elementary and Secondary Education's Proficiency Gap Task Force, the widest gap is between English-language learners and English-proficient students (Proficiency Gap Task Force 2010).

The other factor that influenced the success of the referendum was the reemergence of anti-immigrant sentiments in the state. Although Massachusetts does not have an immigrant population that is comparable to that of southern or western states, there had been rapid growth of the immigrant population in the previous three decades and a not-so-subtle change in the origin of these immigrants. Historically, Massachusetts had been a port of entry for immigrants from Canada and Europe, and the state is home to large populations of French Canadians, Portuguese, Irish, Italians, and Greeks. At the beginning of the twentieth century, about 30 percent of the population of the state was foreign born, a proportion that declined steadily until it reached less than 9 percent in 1970. But between 1970 and 2000, the immigrant population in the state began to rise again, reaching almost 13 percent. By 2000, the composition of immigrants had changed, and instead of the largely Canadian and European stock of the earlier era, 65 percent of the state's foreign born hailed from Latin America (30 percent), Asia (25 percent), and Africa (7 percent) (Sum and Fogg 1999).

Despite these changes, the state continued to support social programs for immigrants, even in light of federal restrictions by the 1996 Personal Responsibility and Work Opportunity Reconciliation Act (PRWORA). However, anti-immigrant sentiments flared following September 11, 2001, radically shifting attitudes in the state. Researchers who polled voters during the November 2002 election concluded that the approval of the referendum against bilingual education reflected a reemergence of negative attitudes toward immigrants, due to their increasing population. Capetillo-Ponce and Kramer (2006) also found a general lack of information among voters about bilingual education and the implications of the proposed changes. Furthermore, they argue that, in the absence of objective information, voters were easily swayed by other factors. Looming large among these was the belief that high levels of immigration were tolerable only as long as "the newcomers pay their own way, don't get special breaks (such as bilingual education), and assimilate at a relatively rapid rate" (17). As such, nativist arguments anchored in traditional assimilationist notions and bolstered by neoliberal imperatives led Massachusetts voters to undo 30 years of educational practice, radically changing the educational conditions of English-language learners across the state.

The Impact of Question 2

In the academic year 2002–2003, the year Question 2 was approved by Massachusetts voters, 141,408 students enrolled in Massachusetts public schools were native speakers of a language other than English, representing over 14 percent of all Massachusetts public-school enrollments, and of these, 51,622 were designated as of limited English proficiency (LEP), or 5.2 percent of all enrollments (MDOE 2003). The referendum became law as Chapter 386 of the Acts of 2002 in December and was implemented across the state in the fall of 2003, replacing a wide-ranging set of bilingual programs with Sheltered English Immersion (SEI). Unlike transitional bilingual education, which relied on the English learners' own language to facilitate the learning of academic subjects as they mastered English, the SEI model is based on the concept that the English language is acquired quickly (1 year) and relies on the use of simple English in the classroom to impart academic content. For this reason, the law has the goal that English-language learners be in SEI programs for no longer than one year and then transition into mainstream classrooms, as discussed earlier. Parents can seek to "waive" the placement of their children in SEI programs and request to have their children placed in General Education or in a limited number of available bilingual education programs.

The changes instituted by the new law had broad implications for the education of English-language learners. It prohibited the use of the native language in instruction, favoring the placement of students from various language backgrounds in the same classroom to force the use of English as the sole language for communication. The law stipulates that students can be provided some nominal assistance in their first language, but this is seldom available or implemented. The use of instructional materials and books in the primary language of English-language learners is prohibited—a fact that was interpreted by some districts in ways that led to the disappearance of all books in languages other than English. The organization of programs changed, with many districts interpreting this not only as the end to bilingual instruction, but as the "end of programs" for English learners. There is evidence that the implementation of the changes required by Question 2 varied substantially across the state (DeJong, Gort, and Cobb 2005) and that the professional development of teachers, overall, fell woefully behind the need (Rennie Center 2007), resulting in many English-language learners being placed in classrooms with teachers who were not adequately prepared to teach them.

Yet, despite the grave implications of this policy change and the number of children affected, the state has yet to conduct a thorough evaluation of the impact of the law. Immigrant communities and education advocates, confused about the implementation of the law and aware of the soaring incidence of high-school dropout rates among English-language learners, finally forced the first assessments of the law's impact, focused first in Boston and then across the state (Tung, et al. 2009; Uriarte et al. 2009; Uriarte and Karp 2009; English

Language Learners Sub-Committee 2009). Below we summarize the key findings of these initial assessments:

1. *Increasing enrollments.* The enrollment of English language learners increased 27 percent statewide, since 2001 (Uriarte and Karp 2009). Boston has the highest number of English-language learners enrolled in the state's public schools (Tung et al. 2009).
2. *Gross Mis-Assessments.* Although the state showed growth in enrollments, some districts experienced sharp declines. In Boston, for example, both the identification of students of limited English proficiency and their participation in programs for English-language learners declined significantly, due to problems with assessment and the information provided to parents about the choices of programs for their children. The problems with gross mis-assessment were consistent and increasing through time, so that by 2009, almost half of the English-language learners requiring services were not receiving them. This disregard for the needs of vulnerable children prompted a review by the U.S. Department of Justice and the Office of Civil Rights of the U.S. Department of Education, which is ongoing (Vaznis 2009).
3. *Over-Enrollment in Special Education.* The over-enrollment of students of limited English proficiency in special education (SPED) programs is, of course, tied to mistakes in assessments of students. Between 2004 and 2009, the statewide assignment of English-language learners to SPED programs increased from 12.7 percent to 16.0 percent and, in some Massachusetts districts, reached 40 percent (in Holyoke) and 30 percent (in Springfield) in 2009 (Uriarte and Karp 2009; English Language Learners Sub-Committee 2009, 10). The sharp differences between the districts suggests that determinations of the need for SPED programs may have resulted from judgments made by district staff with varying levels of professional competence in determining appropriate placements. Informal reports suggest that in some districts, assessments are conducted by monolingual English-speaking staff through the use of translators or by professionals who are not qualified to assess and evaluate English-language learners for special-education needs. This is particularly problematic, given that the assessment of disability relies heavily in direct communication between the child and the examiner, which may explain why the three high-incidence disabilities among English-language learners are communications, intellectual disabilities, and developmental delays—all sensitive to the efficacy of this communication (English Language Learners Sub-Committee 2009).
4. *Problems with the Measurement and Reporting of Performance.* Most reported measurements of achievement for English-language learners do not take into account that they are the result of the aggregation of the performance of children at various levels of language proficiency.

The measurement in itself projects an expectation that students at all levels of English proficiency should perform comparably to English-proficient students on standardized tests in English, when, in fact, this should only be expected of students who have reached the highest levels of English proficiency. For example, in Massachusetts, the pass rates for the English Language Arts test of the Massachusetts Comprehensive Assessment System (MCAS) of English-proficient students and all English-language learners show wide disparities (over 30 percentage points) between the groups, a disparity which is expected, given that it includes children at very low levels of English-language proficiency. However, when the English Language Learners Sub-Committee of the Proficiency Gap Task Force of the Board of Elementary and Secondary Education disaggregated the outcomes of English-language learners by level of language proficiency, one conclusion from their 2009 report was particularly striking. Although, as expected, the lowest pass rates were among the students with the lowest levels of English proficiency, English-language learners who had attained the highest levels of English proficiency actually out- performed English-proficient students in Massachusetts. Hence, the narrative of failure that shadows these students throughout their schooling is largely a result of the way districts measure and report their performance.

5. *Premature Imposition of Testing Regime.* The problem in Massachusetts, then, is not that English-language learners are not capable of scoring well on the MCAS, but rather that they are prematurely thrown into the accountability regime, before they have been taught English well enough to do so. English-language learners are tested after just one year in Massachusetts schools, even though it is well-known that it is highly unlikely that these students will attain the level of English-language performance required to pass the MCAS in only one year. In fact, only a relatively low proportion of English-language learners at all grade levels had attained full English proficiency, even after five years in Massachusetts schools (MDESE2009, 6). Hence, this imposition of testing regiments, with full knowledge that these students are unable to perform adequately, inserts them into a "meant to fail" situation that represents an educational injustice and a deleterious environment for the academic development of these children.

6. *Academic Content Taught in English.* Recent studies using random assignment of students have found that students in both sheltered English-immersion and transitional bilingual programs show similar advances in learning to read English (Zeher 2010). At issue is the time the process of language acquisition takes under both models and the impact of each to academic content. This is certainly the quandary facing Massachusetts educators. Due to changes in instruction mandated by Question 2, all academic content must be taught in English, including

all books and materials. Given that it takes several years for students, particularly older students, to attain the level of proficiency in English that would allow them to obtain grade-level understanding of academic content taught only in English, this represents a major concern. As would be expected, for 8th and 10th graders, large gaps exist between English-proficient students and those at the highest levels of language performance (English Language Learners Sub-Committee 2009). This is surely tied to the "watering down" of the curriculum of English-language learners, which is inevitable under conditions where students are forced to learn in a language they do not fully comprehend. The gaps between these two groups in science—a content dependent on language for its delivery—are even more salient, reaching a more than 30-point difference among 8th-grade students (English Language Learners Sub-Committee 2009). The lower levels of performance in math and science, even for students at the highest levels of language proficiency, indicates, both, that students with newly acquired English language skills may not have enough command of the language to access academic content and that this content may not have been successfully delivered through the scaffolding of content, as required in sheltered English-immersion instruction. And although the logical conclusion would be that these students should be provided content in their own language as they learn English, by law, school systems cannot provide this instruction in the student's primary language. The restrictive language policies that are today law in Massachusetts bind teachers, schools, and districts to the implementation of educational practices that set students up to fail, leaving them defenseless to the difficult materials struggles that they are likely to face as they enter adulthood.

7. *Academic Disengagement and a Rise in Dropout Rates.* Sheltered English immersion, even when taught well by teachers who are professionally trained to deliver it, scaffolds the academic content to match the level of English proficiency of the students. This means that English-language learners entering a Massachusetts school in 9th grade and with an English proficiency at levels 1 or 2, are receiving academic content at a very basic level. This not only leads to lower levels of achievement, but also to students disengaging from school altogether and dropping out. Perhaps the most salient effect of the change from transitional bilingual education to sheltered English immersion has been the rise in the dropout rates for English-language learners, while the dropout rates for English-proficient students remains relatively stable. The trend for both groups in the five years following the implementation of Question 2 is shown in Figure 6.1.

Analysis of dropout data from specific districts supports the findings of the state trends and adds some important dimensions. Studies of

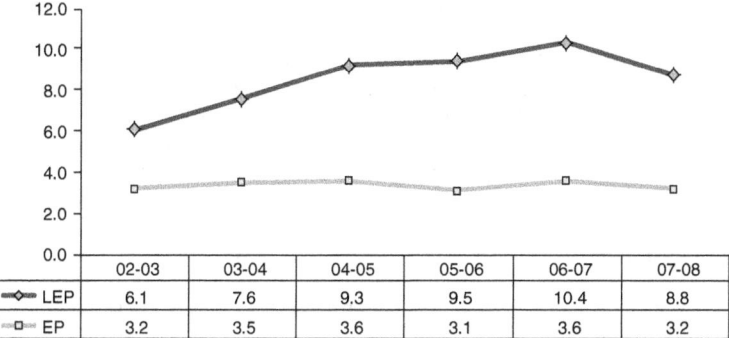

Figure 4.1 Annual high-school dropout rate, comparing EP[1] and LEP[2] in Massachusetts from the 2002/2003 to the 2007/2008 academic years.

[1] EP = English proficient
[2] LEP = limited English proficiency

Source: Data provided by MDESE to the Gastón Institute, University of Massachusetts, Boston, on May 20, 2009.

outcomes for Boston English-language learner, for example, show that their annual high-school dropout rate nearly doubled from 2003 to 2006 (6.3 percent to 12.1 percent). It is also noteworthy, that students in transitional bilingual programs for the year 2002–2003 showed a dropout rate lower than that of native English speakers (8.7percent for native speakers vs. 6.3 percent for those in ELL programs). However, by 2006 the dropout rate for English-language learners (at 12.1 percent) had surpassed that of native speakers (at 11.7 percent) (Tung et al. 2009). The Boston data show the effect of the dismantling of bilingual-education programs, which in many cases provided a nurturing environment for students and promoted their academic engagement.

8. *Lack of Teacher and School Preparedness.* Evidence of both the lack of preparedness of students emerging from sheltered English immersion programs and the failure of general-education high schools to welcome these students comes from Worcester. Data compiled by the Sub-Committee on English Language Learners show that the highest dropout rate (67 percent in 2009) is found among students at the higher levels of English proficiency, that is, those English-language learners transitioning into general-education programs. The lack of an engaging curriculum at the students' grade and intellectual level (not just their level of English proficiency), together with the scant preparation of these students to address content in general-education high schools

are critical factors affecting their disengagement, once they transition. Hence, the unchallenging and/or inhospitable environment created by teachers and schools unprepared to address the needs of these students is of major concern, given that lower levels of educational attainment is more likely to ensure that English-language learners will have a poorer quality of life than their educated peers; and, hence, fewer opportunities for full democratic participation in the larger society.

Conclusion

> "Democracy is severely limited when people cannot use their own languages."
>
> —Nettles and Romaine (2000)

In this chapter, we have provided a postcolonial discussion of language and schooling as it pertains to English-language learners, followed by the story of the impact of language-restrictive policies in the state of Massachusetts, which expelled the use of primary-language instruction in the schooling of English-language learners and replaced it with sheltered English-immersion programs. The Massachusetts case well illustrates and echoes, through an examination of the historical context and discussion of empirical data, the most salient points of the preceding theoretical analysis. One significant question that remains, of course, is in what ways parents of English-language learners and their communities grapple with the negative impact of restrictive language policies upon their children, particularly with respect to questions of democratic participation and their efforts to transform the negative material conditions that shape their lives. This is a particularly salient point, given that Latinos, for example, despite their huge numbers in many regions, still contend with political invisibility and lack of decision-making power within mainstream educational institutions.

Yet, despite many of the problems at work in Boston, what cannot be overlooked is that it was principally Latino parents and community leaders who historically placed pressure upon the Boston school district and the Commonwealth of Massachusetts to be responsive to the needs of their children; and it was parents and community advocates who demanded transparency in assessing the effects of the implementation of the restrictive language policies mandated by Question 2. As such, the social agency enacted by Latino parents and community leaders was directly responsible for challenging violations to the educational rights of their children and, with that, review of Boston schools by both the Department of Justice and the Department of Education's Office for Civil Rights. This is, by no means, a powerless community of victims. Nevertheless, we are well aware that in the current political climate, public institutions seem more and more immune to community advocacy efforts, as neoliberal agendas function, wittingly or unwittingly, to perpetuate a culture of failure and educational neglect. Unfortunately, these conditions often render community efforts not only less effective, but far more difficult to sustain.

There is no question that "for many Latinos in Massachusetts, the vote on Q. 2 was probably an uneasy introduction to the American political system, especially if they understood the vote for English-only as an assault on their language and parental rights (Capetillo-Ponce 2003). Hence, all this speaks to the need for greater consolidation of community strength and the importance of cultivating greater knowledge of educational institutions and the political processes tied to policy decisions that impact the schooling of language-minority children. We know that in Boston, as in other parts of the nation, community political efforts that utilized the powers of federal intervention and the protections still afforded by civil-rights laws, were successful in creating new avenues for reform and in democratizing the education of English-language learners" (Beck and Allexsaht-Snider 2002).

However, given current neoliberal policy restraints, where only a small number of English-language learners are receiving the educational preparation they require to academically succeed, we are left with a daunting task to struggle together, as political allies, educators, parents, and members of language-minority communities, in an effort to, once again, transform racialized inequalities connected to restrictive language policies in U.S. public schools. This discussion truly reminds us, as Edward Said and other postcolonial theorists have so rightly insisted, *democracy is never guaranteed*. It is a contested political field of social relations, which requires us to return, time and time again, to the struggle for social justice and self-determination. It signifies *a revolution in the living*, rather than an objective and absolute utopia to which we will someday arrive.

Notes

1. *BBC News*, "Research to Find Effects in Brain of Bilingualism," reports on the research of Virginia Gathercole at Bangor University, who is exploring the benefits of being bilingual. She stated in the article, "The very act of

being able to speak, listen, and think in two languages and of using two languages on a daily basis appears to sharpen people's abilities to pay close attention to aspects of tasks relevant to good performance."
2. Following the protest of parents and education advocates, two-way bilingual programs were retained.
3. Hubie Jones, then director of the Roxbury Multiservice Center and chairperson of the Task Force of Children Out of School, years later would explain that in "The Way We Go to School," a 1969 report of children not in school, "We estimated that there may have been 10,000 kids not attending school who had a right to do so because of the exclusionary policies and practices, primarily practices, of the school system. The largest group of those people that we estimated were Latinos." At that time, the vast majority of Latinos in Boston were Puerto Rican.
4. See Hispanic Office of Planning and Evaluation (1978), for attendance, dropout and retention rates in the late 1970s; Wheelock (1990) for dropout and truancy rates through the 1980s; Uriarte and Chaez (2000) for dropout rates through the 1990s.
5. Boston Public Schools (1989a and 1989b) and D. Ribadeniera (1989, 45)
6. For a full description of the initial impact of high-stakes testing on Latino students, see Uriarte 2002; Uriarte and Chavez 2000.
7. The full name of the Gastón Institute is the Mauricio Gastón Institute for Latino Community Development and Public Policy, University of Massachusetts, Boston.

References

Anyon, J. (2005). "The Political Economy of Race, Urban Education, and Educational Policy." In *Race, Identity, and Representation in Education*, 2nd edition, edited by Cameron McCarthy, et. al. New York: Routledge.

Anzaldua, G. (1987). *Borderlands La Frontera: The New Mestiza*. San Francisco: Aunt Lute Books.

Beck, S. A., and M. Allexsaht-Snider. (2002). *Recent Language Minority Education Policy in Georgia: Appropriation, Assimilation, and Americanization*. In Education in the *New Latino Diaspora: Policy and the Politics of Identity*, edited by S. Wortham, et. al. Westport, CT: Ablex Publishing.

Borges-Méndez, R., J. Jennings, D. Haig-Friedman, M. Hutson, and T. Eliot Roberts. (May 2008). *Immigrant Workers in the Massachusetts Health Care Industry*. Malden, MA: The Immigrant Learning Center.

Borges-Mendez, R., N. Lavan, and C. Jones. (August 2006). *Latinos in Massachusetts: Selected Economic Indicators*. Boston: Gastón Institute.[7]

Boston Public Schools. (January 1999). *The Bilingual Education Task Force, Report to the Boston School Committee*. Boston: Boston Public Schools.

Boston Public Schools. (May 1989a). *Brief Report on Dropout Statistics for Hispanic Students in the Boston Public Schools: Focus on High Schools and Neighborhoods*, Exhibit 2, Office of Research and Development, Boston.

Boston Public Schools. (May 1989b). *Hispanic Dropout Program*, Office of Equal Opportunity, Boston.

Capetillo-Ponce, J., and R. Kramer. 2006. "Politics, Ethnicity, and Bilingual Education in Massachusetts." In *Latinos in New England*, edited by A. Torres. Philadelphia: Temple University Press.

Collier, V. P., and W. P. Thomas. (2010). "Helping Your English Learners in Spite of No Child Left Behind." *Teachers College Record* (March 11). Accessed May 11, 2010. doi:http://www.tcrecord.org ID Number: 15937.

Collier, V. P., and W. P. Thomas. (2009). *Educating English Learners for a Transformed World*. Albuquerque: Fuente Press, Dual Language Education of New Mexico.

Commonwealth of Massachusetts, Secretary of State. (n.d.). *Question 2: Law Proposed by Initiative Petition: English Language Education in Public Schools. Information for Voters, the 2002 Ballot Questions*. Accessed June 11, 2010. doi:http://www.sec.state.ma.us/ele/ele02/elebq02/bq022.htm

Crawford, J. (2000). *At War with Diversity: U.S. Language Policy in an Age of Anxiety*. Clevedon, UK: Multilingual Matters.

Crawford, J., ed. (1992). *Language Loyalties: A Source Book on the Official English Controversy*. Chicago: University of Chicago Press.

Cummins, J. (2000). *Language, Power, and Pedagogy*. Clevedon, UK: Multilingual Matters.

Darder, A. (1991). *Culture and Power in the Classroom*. New York: Bergin and Garvey.

Darder, A. (2002). *Reinventing Paulo Freire: A Pedagogy of Love*. Boulder, CO: Westview Press.

Darder, A. and R. D. Torres. (2004). *After Race: Racism After Multiculturalism*. New York: New York University Press.

DeJong. E., M. Gort, and C. Cobb. (2005). "Bilingual Education within the Context of English-Only Policies: Three Districts' Response to Question 2." *Massachusetts. Educational Policy*. 19 (4): 595–620.

Dobbs, Michael. (2004). "U.S. Segregation Now at '69 Level: Study Shows 15-Year Decline; Hispanics Less Integrated than African Americans." *Washington Post*, January 18, A10.

English Language Learners Sub-Committee. (December 2009). *Halting the Race to the Bottom: Urgent Interventions for the Improvement of the Education of English Language Learners in Massachusetts and Selected Districts*. Final Report to the Massachusetts Board of Elementary and Secondary Education's Committee on the Proficiency Gap. doi:http://www.massmabe.org/Portals/0/2009_HaltingRace%20Full.pdf

Freire, P. (1993). *Education for Critical Consciousness*. New York: Continuum.

Freire, P. (1970). *Pedagogy of the Oppressed*. New York: Continuum.

Freire, P., and D. Macedo. (1987). *Literacy: Reading the Word and the World*. New York: Routledge.

Gandara, P. (2000). "In the Aftermath of the Storm: English Learners in the Post 227 Era." *Bilingual Research Journal* 24, no.1 and 2 (winter and spring): 1–13.

Genesee, F., ed. (1999). *Program Alternatives for Linguistically Diverse Students*. Washington, D.C.: U.S. Department of Education, Center for Research on Education, Diversity, and Excellence.

Genesee, F., K. Lindholm-Leary, W. M. Saunders, and D. Christian. (2006). *Educating English Language Learners: A Synthesis of Research Evidence*. New York: Cambridge University Press.

Gilmore, R. (2006). *The Golden Gulag*. Los Angeles: University of California Press.

Hispanic Office of Planning and Evaluation. (December 1978)., *Puerto Ricans in Boston: Current Conditions in Education and Employment*. Boston.

Krashen, S. (2003). *Explorations in Language Acquisition and Use*. Portsmouth, NH: Heinemann.

Massachusetts Department of Education (MDOE). (October 1992). School District Profiles. doi:http://www.doe.mass.edu/pic.www/profmain.htm.

Massachusetts Department of Education (MDOE). (August 2003). *Questions and Answers Regarding Chapter 71a: English Language Education in Public Schools*. www.doe.mass.edu/ell/chapter71A_faq.pdf

Massachusetts Commission on Hispanic Affairs. (1986). *Report of the Education Task Force*. Massachusetts Statehouse, Boston.

Massachusetts Department of Elementary and Secondary Education (MDESE). (2009). *Massachusetts English Proficiency Assessment (MEPA) Statewide Results: Spring 2009*, p. 6. doi:http://www.doe.mass.edu/mcas/mepa/2009/results/09state.pdf.

May, S., and N. Hornberger. (2008). *Encyclopedia of Language and Education*, vol. 1, 2nd ed. *Language Policy and Political Issues in Education*, v. Heidelberg: Springer Science-Business Media.

Moyo, T. (2009). *Linguistic Diversity and Development: The Language Question and Social Justice in Southern Africa*. Urbana, IL: Forum on Public Policy.

National Assessment of Educational Progress (NAEP). (n.d.). *State Comparisons*. National Center for Education Statistics, U.S. Department of Education. doi:http://nces.ed.gov/nationsreportcard/nde/statecomp/

Nettles, D., and S. Romaine. (2000). *Vanishing Voices: The Extinction of the World's Languages*. London: Oxford University Press.

Nieto, D. G. (2007). "The Emperor's New Words: Language and Colonization in Human Architecture." *Journal of the Sociology of Self-Knowledge*. Special issue, (Summer): 231–237.

Olivos, E. (2006). *The Power of Parents: A Critical Perspective of Parent Involvement in Schools*. New York: Peter Lang.

Orfield, Gary. (1999). "New Study Finds Increasing Segregation." The Civil Rights Project, Harvard Graduate School of Education, Boston, June 8.

Orfield, G. (2001). *Schools More Separate: Consequences of a Decade Resegregation*. Report of the Civil Rights Project, Harvard Graduate School of Education, Boston

Orfield, G. and C. Lee (2007). *Historical Reversals, Accelerating Resegregation, and the Need for New Integration Strategies*. A Report of the Civil Rights Project/ *Proyecto Derechos Civiles*. Los Angeles, University of California at Los Angeles.

Phillipson, [Au: first initial?]. (2006). *Rights to Language: Equity, Power, and Education.* New York: Routledge.

Portes, A., and R. Rumbaut. (2001). *Legacies: The Story f the Immigrant Second Generation.* Berkeley, CA: University of California Press.

Proficiency Gap Task Force. (2010). *A Roadmap to Closing the Proficiency Gap.* Report presented at the May 24, 2010 meeting of the Massachusetts Board of Elementary and Secondary Education (MBESE).

Ramanathan, V., and B. Morgan. (2007). "TESOL and Policy Enactments: Perspectives from Practice." *TESOL Quarterly* 41, no. 3 (September).

Ribadeniera, D. (1989). "Wilson, Hispanics Agree on School Plan." *The Boston Globe,* November 16, 45.

Rodriguez, C. (2000). *Changing Race: Latinos, the Census, and the History of Ethnicity.* New York: New York University Press.

Sanchez, G. (1951). *Concerning Segregation of Spanish-Speaking Children in the Public Schools.* Austin, TX: Inter-American Occasional Papers.

Skutnabb-Kangas, T. (2000). *Linguistic Genocide in Education—or Worldwide Diversity and Human Rights?* Mahwah, NJ: Lawrence Erlbaum.

Spooley, P. (1993). *Racism and Ethnicity.* Aukland: Oxford University Press.

Suarez-Orozco, C., and M. Suarez-Orozco. (2001). *Children of Immigration.* Cambridge, MA: Harvard University Press.

Sum, A., I. Khatiwada, S. Palma, and P. Tobar. (October 2006). *Immigration's Impact on the Workforce Research Brief.* Boston: Commonwealth Corporation.

Sum, Andrew, and Neal Fogg. (1999). *The Changing Workforce: Immigrants and the New Economy of Massachusetts.* Boston: MassINC and Citizens Bank. doi:http://www.massinc.org/handler.cfm?type=2andtarget=Changing Workforce/index.html

Task Force of Children Out of School. (1969). *The Way We Go to School.* Boston: Massachusetts Advocates for Children.

Thomas, W. P. and V. P. Collier. (2002). *A National Study of School Effectiveness for Language Minority Students' Long-Term Academic Achievement.* Santa Cruz, CA: Center for Research on Education, Diversity, and Excellence.

Tollefson, J. W. (2004). *Medium of Instruction Policies: Which Agenda? Whose Agenda?* Mahwah, NJ: Lawrence Erlbaum.

Tung, R., M. Uriarte, V. Diez, N. Lavan, N. Agusti, F. Karp, and T. Meschede. (2009). *English Learners in Boston Public Schools: Enrollment, Engagement and Academic Outcomes, AY2003–AY2006.* Final report. Boston: Gastón Institute. doi:http://www.gaston.umb.edu/articles/2009%20Final%20 ELL%20Report_online.pdf.

Uriarte, M, R. Tung, N. Lavan, and V. Diez. (2010). "Impact of Restrictive Language Policies on Engagement and Academic Achievement of Boston Public School Students in Programs for English Learners." In *Forbidden Language,* edited by Patricia Gandara and Megan Hopkins. New York: Columbia University Teacher's College Press.

Uriarte, M., and F. Karp. (October 2009). *English Language Learners in Massachusetts: Trends in Enrollments and Outcomes.*Boston: Gastón Institute. doi:http://www.gaston.umb.edu/UserFiles/09ELLsinMA%20brief.pdf.

Uriarte, M., and N. Agusti. (May 2009). *Latino Students in Massachusetts Public Schools: 2009 Status Report.* Prepared for the Governor's Latino-American Advisory Commission.
Uriarte, M., N. Lavan, N. Agusti, M. Kala, F. Karp, P. Kiang, L. Lo, R. Tung, and C. Villari. (2009). *English Learners in Boston Public Schools: Enrollment, Engagement, and Academic Outcomes of Native Speakers of Cape Verdean Creole, Chinese Dialects, Haitian Creole, Spanish, and Vietnamese.* Boston: Gastón Institute. doi:http://www.gaston.umb.edu/articles/2009%20Language%20Groups%20Report_online.pdf.
Uriarte, M., P. Granberry, and M. Halloran. (2006). "Immigration Status, Employment, and Eligibility for Public Benefits among Latin American Immigrants in Massachusetts." In *Latinos in New England,* edited by Andrés Torres. Philadelphia: Temple University Press.
Uriarte, M., and N. Lavan. (September 2006). *Trends in Enrollments and Outcomes for Latino Children in Massachusetts Public Schools.* Boston: Gastón Institute.
Uriarte, M. (2002). "The High Stakes of High Stakes Testing." In *The Power of Culture: Teaching Across Language Differences,* edited by Zeynep Beykont. Cambridge, MA: Harvard Education Publishing Group.
Uriarte, M., and L. Chavez (2000). *Latino Students and the Massachusetts Public Schools.* Boston: Gastón Institute.
Valenzuela, A. (1999). *Subtractive Schooling: U.S. Mexico Youth and the Politics of Caring.* New York: State University of New York Press.
Valle, V., and R. D. Torres. (2000). *Latino Metropolis.* Minneapolis: University of Minnesota Press.
Vaznis, J. (August 26, 2009). "U.S. Inspects Boston's Language Instruction." *Boston Globe,* A1.
Wheelock. A. (1990). *The Status of Latino Students in Massachusetts Public Schools: Direction for Policy research in the 1990's.* Boston: Gastón Institute.
Zeher, Mary A. (April 9, 2010). "Bilingual Ed., Immersion Found to Work Equally Well." *Edweek.* doi:http://www.edweek.org/ew/articles/2010/04/09/29bilingual_ep.h29.html)

5

Súil Eile: A Different Perspective on Migration, Language Acquisition, Belonging, and Multicultural Society

Simon Warren

Introduction: *Súil Eile*

Súil Eile is the on-air identity of Teilifís na Gaeilge (TG4) the Irish-language television station in the Republic of Ireland.[1] The current television advertisement under the logo of Súil Eile involves a series of clips, all taken within the same traditional-looking Irish bar. However, the advertisement plays on the translation of *Súil Eile* into the English, which literally means "another view." Each version of the advertisement draws the viewer's attention to a hidden aspect of the bar scene, relating each of these to a particular type of programming output, whether in drama, sports, news, history, or music. But it also has the effect of disrupting the well-worn image of the Irish drinking-hole with its nostalgic feel. In a sense, the advertisement works by being self-conscious of the potential for Irish-language media to engage in a culture of nostalgia rather than a medium for engaging with the contemporary moment. This tension between the cultural politics of language and identity as a form of cultural conservationism and as identity-making is at the heart of this chapter.

TG4, established in 1996, is a public-service broadcasting that is mainly, though not exclusively, in Irish. TG4, as with the national Irish-language radio station Raidió na Gaeltachta, emerged out of grass-roots campaigning by Irish-speaking communities, and in particular, political organizations, such as Cearta Sibhialta na Gaeltachta (Gaeltacht Civil Rights Movement) (Delap 2008). It has been argued that there would be no Irish-language media had it not been for this language movement from below, willing to engage in a kind of civil disobedience in order to achieve some degree of parity with the English-speaking majority. Indeed, this issue of the articulation of linguistic politics through the medium of civil or minority rights is a central issue explored in this chapter. Súil Eile, then, invokes the image of a popular cultural politics of language and identity, perhaps even an example of struggles for cultural confidence.

This particular concern, the cultural politics of the Irish language, is a specific case of a more general and global issue—that of the fate of threatened or endangered languages (Nettle and Romaine 2000). It also sits within a concern within Europe for the health of regional and minority languages and the increasing dominance of English as the political lingua franca of the European Union (see Barbour and Carmichael 2000; Mumford 2007; Phillipson 2003; Trenz 2007). Mainstream literature on language and identity predominantly deals with the relations between dominant and subordinate languages where the minority language is that of migrant groups (Race 2011) or contestation between competing dominant languages as in Canada (Kymlicka 1989) or Belgium (Blommaert and Verschueren 1998). Less is written about the relations between minoritized languages and their relations with powerful, often colonial, languages, where these powerful languages become the common vernacular. Irish is an interesting case in that English, as the previous colonial language, has become the dominant language in the sense that it is widely used and is most prevalent in public and private lives. Therefore, the cultural politics of the Irish cannot simply organize itself around an opposition between the language of the people against the language of the colonial power. It has to deal with the reality of English as the common vernacular of most Irish people. Therefore, how does it construct a popular cultural politics in this context? The political resources drawn upon in the cultural politics of Irish, as evidenced in one local case study, is the focus for this chapter. In particular, as I outline below, I explore the potential for different kinds of political language to build a cultural politics of Irish, and specifically, the limitations of a minority-rights perspective.

The Empirical Case

In June 2009, a case was brought to the High Court in the Republic of Ireland by a group of parents, acting for their children, against the language policy adopted by the Board of Management of the community secondary school in Dingle,[2] on the West Kerry peninsula, in southwest Ireland. The central issue at stake in this case, as claimed by the parents' group, was that the civil and human rights of their children to education were being denied because of the school's policy of Irish-medium education. This referred to the policy of the school, in line with its statutory duties under the Education Act no. 51 of 1998, and by virtue of its location in one of the officially designated Irish-speaking regions of Ireland, Gaeltacht, that the medium of education and the business of the school would be conducted through Irish. The parents' group maintained that the opportunity to succeed educationally, and therefore, economically, was denied their children by being required to undertake their secondary-school education through the medium of Irish rather than English. The community school was formed as a new coeducational-community secondary school, amalgamating the previous boys' and girls' schools in the town.

This is the only post-primary school in the area, and it serves both the Irish-speaking and English-speaking communities on the peninsula. The new school opened in 2007 and was immediately confronted with a group calling itself the Concerned Parents of Corca Dhuibhne campaigning against the school's language policy. Within the first months of the new school year, the Concerned Parents group organized two public meetings, a petition, and a student strike; campaigned for the Department of Education to conduct a parent and student survey; and initiated court proceedings. At both public meetings, those speaking in Irish were heckled and jeered. At the first meeting, one of the key protagonists likened the school's policy, and that of Irish language activists generally, to the genocidal actions of Adolf Hitler (Creedon 2007). At the second meeting, a key member of the group reportedly referred to the school's policy as "ethnic cleansing." This was followed by an editorial in one of the national newspapers, the *Irish Examiner,* comparing the schools' language policy with Islamic extremism and the London bombings in July of that year (Editorial 2007). This campaign has caused bitter divisions between people in the area and has become an issue of national importance. The parents who took their case to court and the school eventually made an out-of-court settlement. This settlement has maintained Irish as the language of instruction and business, but in addition, extra supports have been put in place for those students whose competence in Irish might restrict their access to the curriculum and achievement. Elsewhere I have discussed how the cultural politics around the school's language policy can be characterised in terms of a conflict between the group rights of the Irish-speaking community and the individual rights of those seeking English-medium education (Warren 2011). I have also discussed in some detail the history of the cultural politics of language and its links to national state formation (Warren 2012).

This series of events, the emergence of a strident cultural politics of language, and the national focus on a local affair occurred at the height of Ireland's economic success. Until recently, Ireland traded under the brand name of the Celtic Tiger, an economic miracle that rivaled the preceding successes of the Asian Tiger economies. Ireland moved from being one of the poorest nations in Europe with a largely agriculturally based economy to being at the top of Europe's economic league, boasting the fastest rate of growth as measured by gross domestic product (GDP).[3] A cornerstone of this economic miracle was Ireland's success in attracting inward foreign investment, particularly in the areas of pharmaceuticals and information technology. The names of companies making Ireland their European base include Pfizer, Intel, Dell, and Google. Another significant feature of the Celtic Tiger was that Ireland transformed from being a country of emigration to one of immigration. Not only were Irish people returning to Ireland, but Ireland became an attractive destination for many migrants seeking social and economic security. Migration flows peaked in 2006–2007 at well over 100,000 immigrants per year following the expansion of the European Union and the Irish government's decision, along with Sweden and the United Kingdom, to allow citizens from the "accession eight" (A8)[4] former Eastern European countries that joined the European Union (EU) in May 2004 to work in the country immediately. This decision, and the level of inward migration from the EU, particularly from Poland, was the most significant factor in transforming Ireland into a migration state (Government of Ireland 2008; Joyce 2008; Ruhs 2005). The attractiveness of Ireland as a destination for migration and foreign investment is, in part, provided by Ireland being the only English-speaking country in the Eurozone.

In the shadow of the Celtic Tiger, however, was another Ireland—Irish-speaking Ireland. Although Irish is the first official language of the state, it has not been the common vernacular for over 250 years. Currently, only 3 percent of the resident population speaks Irish as their first language, though approximately 12 percent claim to use it on a daily basis (Government of Ireland, Central Statistics Office 2007). The social geography of Irish presents a rather anomalous picture. The language is in decline in its traditional heartlands on the rural western seaboard, while it appeared to be growing in urban areas (Ó Giollagáin et al. 2007; Ó Riagáin 1997). The class composition of Irish-speakers has also undergone a transformation with an increasing number of middle-class speakers. The urban Irish speaker, however, is characterized simultaneously by being geographically dispersed across urban areas and concentrated around Irish-medium education schools. What they lack is the normal set of economic and social networks that sustain intergenerational transmission of the language. Therefore, the traditional Irish-speaking regions remain highly important in maintaining the language as a common community vernacular (see also Williams 2000 for a similar analysis of the linguistic geography of Wales). But, these are also the most economically and socially vulnerable regions. The Celtic Tiger was marked by an uneven development; the traditional Irish-speaking areas received the least benefit from the country's economic success and suffered relatively high levels of rural poverty (Whelan and Maître 2006).

The Problem with Culture

The central question examined by this book is: Can education contribute to the cultural confidence of peoples and communities who have endured centuries of oppression and marginalization? But the central concept around which this book is organized—cultural confidence—is problematic. To engage with *culture* is to engage with *the problem of culture*. There is not space here to discuss this fully. Instead, I will set out the understanding of culture that underpins my discussion. I approach the problem of culture from a perspective that understands that although we have to engage with the concept because the term is so powerful and ubiquitous, it is a dangerous notion. It is a dangerous concept because it can suggest that culture and cultures are fixed, homogeneous, and tied to biology. Instead, I take the view that what we call culture, which can range from descriptions and analysis of intimate or little lives, such as cafe culture, through anthropological examinations of the cultural organization of human activity, to the power and role of symbolic systems, is not something out there already intact waiting for us to examine, but instead is something that is historically formed and continuously produced (Jenkins 1997; May 2001).

Culture is something that requires explaining rather than being used to explain other phenomena. This is the central argument put forward by Rogers Brubacker (Brubaker 1996; 2004) in his analysis of identity and ethnic mobilization. Brubaker argues that we need to view groupness (or cultural identity) as events, things that happen, as practices of group identification. As such, we do not need to reject group identifications, such as ethnicity, nation, or linguistic community as no more than social constructs, but instead. our job is to take account of the practices that constitute groupness in particular ways and to explain the conditions under which identities become reified, that is, understand them as categories of practice. Culture and identity then are performative rather than substantive. Culture and identity are enacted. We engage in processes of identification rather than having or being defined by cultural categories.

Ethics, Politics, and Positionality

My interest in the cultural politics of place and language is simultaneously political, academic, and personal. A reader might ask why an academic from a British institution is writing about the Irish language and be concerned as to whether this constitutes a form of cultural imperialism, an appropriation of the issues that animate the "Other," ripping it from the visceral context of its politics. In this chapter, I explore the constitution of a cultural politics of place and language that has been mobilized around the Irish-medium education policy of a community secondary school in an Irish-speaking region of Ireland, Gaeltacht. I have a personal interest in this because my own children attend this school, and so, the "choice" of the medium of educational instruction was one I could not avoid. While my family lives in the region and my children attend the secondary school, we are not from there. Like many others, we have been able to draw upon our reasonable resources as a middle-class professional family to make a lifestyle choice and relocate to rural Ireland. We actually live outside the Gaeltacht, which meant that my children's primary school education was not through the medium of Irish. Like the majority of children in Ireland, they received one hour's teaching of Irish a day. As a family, we did not have Irish, and consequently, Irish was not the medium of communication at home, although my own family in the area are Irish speakers. The idea of transition to secondary school was, initially, unproblematic. Committed to the principle of comprehensive education, we assumed that the children would attend the local secondary school. Therefore, we were prepared, so we thought, for the children moving to a school where the medium of education was Irish. Being good middle-class parents, this preparation involved buying in extra Irish lessons for the children and taking a keen interest in learning the language ourselves. The anticipated smooth transition to secondary school (though we knew that the initial phase would be problematic because of the linguistic dimension) turned out to be one of high anxiety and political sensitivity. Details of the dispute over the school's language policy have been briefly reviewed above. Of significance at this point is that the events around the school transformed a private sentiment into a public position. Above I have placed quotation marks around the word *choice* because, although the decisions to move to Ireland and which secondary school the children would attend did involve elements of rational choice, of cost-benefit analysis, and were not abstract but instead were ethically imbued. The kind of middle-class lifestyle choice we were engaged in, like many others, involved specific kinds of cultural and political investment.

We were not moving to a "lifestyle" space, but rather, to a specific location, a deliberate reversal of the expulsion of Ireland's youth during the 1950s when my parents emigrated, and especially of the flight of Ireland's young women that my mother was part of (Ryan 2003). We were taking the combined cultural, economic, and symbolic capitals accrued in Britain as part of the Irish diaspora and investing it "back home," facilitated by the economic conditions represented by the Celtic Tiger years. There is a whole set of cultural issues here related to the returning diaspora that I do not have space to discuss. Suffice to say that "coming back home" is highly problematic. Therefore, there was no real choice between different rural locations or even between different parts of Ireland. There was only ever one place to go back to. Consequently, as a family, we were positively disposed toward aspects of the cultural landscape. We also brought with us a lifetime's commitment to the antiracist struggle in Britain. We had been involved in campaigns against the National Front in the 1970s, worked around antiracist education, and we were involved in organizations such as the Campaign Against Racism and Fascism as well as various anti-deportation campaigns through the 1980s and 1990s. My own academic work had involved me in collaborations with schools, local education authorities, and government departments around antiracist education (e.g., Warren 2006; Warren and Gillborn 2003). When the dispute around the school arose, I was already sensitized to issues of difference, diversity, and bilingualism. However, the models of diversity and bilingualism that had structured my professional and political activity in

Britain did not necessarily equip me with the means to analyze the situation in which I found myself. These models were predominantly constructed around an evaluation of a host country's response to in-migration (arriving immigrants). Instead, I was confronting a politics of language-shift reversal, a set of analyses and policy responses that I was unfamiliar with.

Taking a public stance in relation to the secondary school's language policy was not a battle I took on willingly but felt compelled to do so. As I outline below, the public discourse of the dispute was configured around an apparent opposition between bilingualism (the right to choose English as the medium of education) and a politics of cultural restoration (Irish-medium education). Although Irish had been my mother's "mother tongue," it was not particularly present in my upbringing. However, on reflection, it was always there. There was always some sense that although all my family, whether in Britain, America, Australia, or Ireland, spoke English as a matter of course. However, the variety of English was strongly inflected by the idioms and structures of Irish. I knew, in an almost preconscious way, that there was this other language. At about the age of 13, I received a package from my relatives in Dingle that included a children's magazine in Irish. I was fascinated, and my interest in the language can be traced back to that moment. But, up to my move back to Ireland, my view had been that while an attachment to Irish had cultural and sentimental value, Irish was essentially a dead language, and the political and economic future of Ireland did not lie in a politics of cultural restoration (see Calvet 1998 for an interesting discussion of "dead" languages). In defining Irish as a dead language, I was of course unable to explain who these ghosts were that continued to speak Irish, and indeed, conduct much of their lives through this supposedly dead language. Missing from my analysis was any sense of the relation between Ireland's experience of British colonialism and the dominance of English.

Consequently, the cultural politics around the school's language policy disrupted many of my habituated responses to diversity. Yet, the fate of the language was clearly related to the ongoing processes of colonial rule. While the situation was not directly analogous to the situations I had encountered in Britain, I could construct a tentative ethical-political position by defining the position of Irish in terms of minority rights. I found myself, therefore, not just sending my children to the community school but taking an active and public position in support of the school's policy. My journey into viewing these personal and political activities from an academic perspective was driven by a need to better understand the complexities and nuances of the cultural politics of Irish. While my initial position was defined in terms of minority rights, I felt uncomfortable with this. But I lacked an analytical language and epistemic foundation on which to construct a more sophisticated understanding of the issues and whether I had, in fact, stood on the right side of the barricades.

Main Argument and Chapter Outline

In this chapter, I argue that the struggle around the school's language policy represents a tension at the heart of liberal conceptions of belonging, or citizenship, in particular, the tension between individual and group rights. Related to this I question is the sustainability of pursuing a cultural politics of language based on the assertion of minority rights. I develop my argument by first briefly outlining the historical formation of language policy in Ireland in terms of a shift from a nationalizing politics of language revival to a more muted, individualizing approach. I follow this historical background by reconstructing the empirical case in terms of a tension between individual rights, privileged in liberal theories of citizenship, and the increasing demand for recognition of particular, or group, rights. This reconstruction involves a critical engagement with one important formulation of multicultural citizenship, which offered by Will Kymlicka. I discuss the limitations of Kymlicka's formulation as applied to the empirical case. I conclude by drawing on Andrea Baumeister's critique of Kymlicka and suggesting that Chantal Mouffe's conception of politics provides a more sustainable foundation for building a cultural politics of language formulated in terms of notions of solidarity rather than democracy as procedure and formal equality.

Recovering Language: From Nationalizing Project to Minority Rights

In this section, I explore the emergence of education as the key domain where revival of Irish was located in the newly independent Irish state. In particular, I trace how the dominant paradigm of language shift-reversal moved from group rights within a nationalizing project to an increasing emphasis on minority group rights, defined geographically, within an overarching framework organized around the relationship between the individual citizen and the state.

Language Revival, Nationalism, and Institutionalization of the Gaeltacht

The shift from Irish to English as the common vernacular is a product of Ireland's experience of English colonial domination, where Irish increasingly became confined to the economically peripheral western seaboard. It came to be associated with poverty, marginalization, and emigration. It was in this context that people increasingly adopted English as the language of progress and modernization. It is against this background that the Irish nationalist movements of the nineteenth and twentieth centurys sought to invoke the idea of a collective and unitary Irish people, bearing the symbolic right to nationhood and sharing a similar descent and cultural identity. In particular, the Irish nationalist movement articulated the nineteenth-century belief in the congruence between nation, state, and linguistic homogeneity (Mac Giolla Chríost 2005; May 2001; Ó Riagáin 1997). Ó Croidheáin (2006), for instance, locates the Irish cultural revivalist movement in a wider nationalist sentiment, in particular, the association of the Irish language with an unbroken Gaelic heritage in the form of the Irish rural population, especially that located in the Gaeltacht regions. Similarly, Nuala Johnson (Johnson 1998, 174) has noted how the Gaeltacht regions emerged as "the archive of Irish identity" within a wider European nationalist ferment. Following independence of 26 of Ireland's 32 counties in 1922, the new Irish state set about a project of language revival. If the nationalist movement was constitutive of a "charting of cultural territory" (Said 1993, 252) that enabled a new way of imagining Ireland as being a form of "state-seeking" nationalism, the new state could be conceived as a form of "nationalizing" nationalism (Brubaker 1996, 2004).

Education carried the main burden of creating an Irish-speaking Ireland. More than any other area of language policy, the place of the Irish language in education was a focus for political and cultural struggle from the beginning (Kelly 2002). The rationale for the strategy was that Irish in the Gaeltacht regions would be sustained through Irish-medium education, while the language would grow in the predominantly English-speaking areas, initially through immersion education, and latterly, through the teaching of Irish as a subject. This was partly predicated on a strategy of Irish-language use spreading increasingly from the traditional Irish-speaking areas to the adjoining bilingual areas. The geographical concentration of Irish speakers largely on the western seaboard, a direct result of colonial rule, was formalized as an administrative entity, the Gaeltacht. This institutionalization of the Gaeltacht partly involved the creation of the Gaeltacht as an archive of the nation, as the symbolic representation of Irish-speaking Ireland. But it also involved attempts to redress the long-term economic and social decline in these areas. Economic regeneration in the Gaeltacht regions aimed to stem the out-migration (leaving Ireland) of Irish-speakers, thereby, strengthening the Gaeltacht as the heart of Irish-speaking Ireland.

Toward Minority Rights

Iarfhlaith Watson (2008) argues that Irish state policy toward Irish has contained a contradiction between a notion in practice of reviving the language because of its symbolic importance while "disregarding its revival" (71). This contradiction presents itself in the continued popular support for the language in opinion polls while failing to see intergenerational transmission of Irish in the home, hence, the reliance on the education system. Watson makes the point that from the 1950s onward, as nationalist discourses came in for sustained critique within Ireland, Irish became regarded by the state as the language of a linguistic minority, an issue of minority rights rather than national obligation. In particular, in the current context of globalization, speaking Irish is constructed within rational choice terms, the privatized choice of individuals. Mac Giolla Chríost (1998) and Ó Riagáin (1997) have both traced the shift toward a more privatized notion of Irish. Prime responsibility for this shift is attributed to the state. Mac Giolla Chríost discusses the period between the 1950s and the 1970s as involving continuity and change. For instance, during this period, the standardization of Irish, begun in 1922, was completed and the process of institutionalizing the Gaeltacht continued with greater emphasis placed on economic development. But this standardization had seen the geographical boundaries reduced in size. This was also the period in which key symbolic areas that gave Irish functional importance were diminished. Prior to 1973, in order to pass the end of the compulsory schooling exam, it was necessary to achieve a pass in Irish language. This requirement was removed. In 1974 the requirement for proficiency in Irish for entry to and promotion in the civil service was also removed.

Ó Riagáin (1997, 22) argues that this reflects a weakening in political commitment to the development of effective measures to promote and sustain Irish, and a shift toward using the guise of "public opinion" to justify an emptying out language policy. Significantly, this period saw a decline in the number of primary schools operating a policy of *lán-Ghaeilge,* or bilingualism, and shifting over to the dominance of English. Up to the 1950s, over half of primary schools were either operating a system of *lán-Ghaeilge,* or bilingual education. There was even some evidence of a growth in Irish in previously non-Irish-speaking areas that could be attributable to Irish-medium education. However, the government appeared to view public opinion in the 1960s as hostile to the number of all-Irish schools, and therefore, the number declined so that in 1980–1981 only 3 percent of children were being taught through Irish (inclusive of the Gaeltacht areas). The argument that this decline simply represented a shift in public opinion, in other words, people voted with their tongues, is hard to sustain when it is considered that, as the state withdrew its support for *polasaí lán-Ghaeilge,* there was a revival of all-Irish schools funded by parents rather than the state (Ó Riagáin 1997).

This shift toward the increasing privatization of Irish was closely related to integration of Ireland into the world capitalist economy and the particular mode this took in Ireland. The economic crisis of the 1950s and the emergence of mass outward migration prompted a reconsideration of policy across the board. Gearóid Ó Thuathaigh (2008,33) notes that "By the early 1960s the state's principal objectives were being articulated in new terms, strongly focused on economic performance and improved living standards, in the interests of economic growth and population retention." The nationalizing politics of the newly formed state in 1922 was replaced with a policy that sought to replace nationalism and protectionism of all sorts with an openness that manifested itself in the membership of the European common market'. The nationalizing project associated with the early years of the new state, especially with the administrations led by Éamonn De Valera and the Fianna Fáil party, conceived of economic and cultural development as mutually constitutive, of economic development and Gaelic revival as complementary political projects. A key feature of the shift in political imagination post-1950s is the increasing dominance of a model of economic development based on a separation of the economic from the cultural (Kirby 2002). It is not difficult to see how the Irish language is changed from a public virtue to a private interest in these circumstances.

Some have argued that there is some continuity in political logic from the 1950s through to the Celtic Tiger (Peillon 2002) in this regard. A key feature of the Celtic Tiger years was the increase in conspicuous wealth, specifically, property and cars. Michael Cronin (2002, 61–62), in the same edited collection as Peadar Kirby and Michael Peillon, discusses the way a new economic elite emerged. One of the emblematic figures of this elite was that of the urban, often Dublin-based, bourgeoisie who could travel in style in their new cars along the new motorways to their holiday homes in rural idylls, such as Dingle, Galway, or West Cork. The Celtic Tiger years saw an increase in wealth polarization that also mapped itself onto an East-West, urban-rural divide (Kirby 2010; O'Hearn 2003). These macro-level shifts can be seen to be experienced as generational changes in the socioeconomic structure of places, such as Dingle. The decline of the language within the Gaeltacht region is linked to the changing economic base that produced the particular social relations that sustained the cultural hegemony of Irish in the region; in particular, structural changes in farming, fishing, and land ownership, leading to the continued decline in the economic viability of the Gaeltacht regions (Crowley 2006). The Dingle peninsula area saw its economic base shift from fishing and farming to one dominated by the service sector. At the same time, while the rural areas surrounding the town of Dingle declined in population, Dingle itself grew as a result of non-Irish-speaking inward migration from other parts of Ireland as well as from other countries (Ó Riagáin 1992; Ó Riagáin 1997). The areas of the strongest Irish-speakers on the peninsula were most affected by out-migration. This process has continued. What we see, then, is a parallel change in the economic, social, and linguistic structure of the region. Conchúr Ó Giollagáin and Seasamh Mac Donnacha (2008) have noted the changing demographics of the Gaeltacht regions, especially the impact of in-migration, and that research shows that "English-speaking in-migrants form a large proportion of Gaeltacht-based parents, a fact which has serious implications for future sociolinguistic trends in the Gaeltacht" (110). It is important to note that the largest ethnic groups to migrate into areas such as Dingle are either British-born or Irish. Multiculturalism, therefore, takes on a particular character. The usual binary of dominant (imagined) national culture in relation to *minority-migrant* culture does not work. Irish-speaking Ireland is a minority subset within an imagined national community. The inward migration of Irish and British-born English speakers can be understood as the inward migration of a culturally privileged population (as English speakers) into an area of cultural vulnerability. Education becomes the territory on which tensions between these communities is enacted, the territory on which culture (as group-making) is performed.

My argument is that these structural changes have made it possible for a more stridently individualist notion of rights to challenge a more collectivist one. As more mobile non-Irish-speaking populations, less rooted in the area than traditional Irish-speaking households, move into the area, so there emerges an increasing demand for "choice." Irish-medium education may not be viewed by this group of parents as a useful "positional good" (see Ball 1996; Bowe 1994 for a critique of "choice" discourses in the British context). English as a "world language" might be seen as offering more value as a mobile commodity (Pennycook 1994; Phillipson 2009). Of importance here is the way this discourse of choice leads to a cultural politics of language and identity constructed around a conflict between individual and group rights.

Contested Rights and the Limits of Linguistic Conservation?

This formulation of the particular constitution of multiculturalism in Dingle (and other Irish-speaking areas) confounds dominant models of multiculturalism. Irish-speaking Ireland is neither an "ethnic minority" nor a "national minority," nor are they, in Will Kymlicka's terms, a "lifestyle" group (Kymlicka 1995). The national majority are not, as in Canada, settler communities; nor are they, as in France, a regional language suppressed in an attempt to forge a unitary polity (Grillo 1989; Judge 2000); or, as in Spain, a distinct national or regional entity as with Catalonia (Woolard 1989). English-speaking individuals moving into the Gaeltacht do not constitute an ethnic or linguistic minority within the national polity, requiring accommodation through some form of minority rights. Instead, their claims are based on the assumed privileging of individual rights within a liberal nation state.

This conflict between group and individual rights can be seen as central to the dispute around the community school's policy. The language policy of the school and the status of the school as a Gaeltacht school are asserted by many defenders of the school's policy, because of the role of education in the intergenerational transmission of Irish, and of education being central to sustaining the Gaeltacht as a particular linguistic region. Therefore, Irish-medium education can be viewed as a public, and not just a private, good. The right to Irish-medium education is seen to accrue to a linguistic community, the right being attached to them as a group and not just as individuals. Against this perspective is asserted the prioritizing of individual rights of those seeking an English-medium education. It is not that Irish-medium education is not granted legitimacy, but its status as the medium of instruction of education as a public good is disputed. In other words, Irish is defined as primarily a cultural and, therefore, a private matter. This is at the heart of liberal arguments against multiculturalism generally and linguistic rights specifically (Barry 2001). Group rights claims, it is argued, should not, in a liberal democracy, supersede individual rights. In other words, the majority community, in this case English-speakers, should not carry a disproportionate cost for the support of a minority community. The accommodation of group rights, in this case of Irish speakers, has been a feature of the Irish national project since 1922. I argue that this has seen the constitution of a "stranger within." In particular, this has been achieved through the institutionalization of Irish-speaking Ireland in the form of the Gaeltacht. That is, Irish-speaking Ireland was fixed spatially, separating it increasingly from the majority English-speaking Ireland. As neoliberal economic models of modernity took hold over the Irish political imagination, the tension between group and individual rights was bound to intensify. The defense of group rights becomes even more difficult to sustain when there are a significant number of those within the Irish-speaking community who dissent from the demand for group claims and do not necessarily identify with a group defined linguistically.

Beyond Rights?

The conflict around group and individual rights and Irish as a normative public language can be construed as a contest between different conceptions of citizenship. Will Kymlicka, the highly influential theorist of liberal multiculturalism, has argued forcefully and persuasively for forms of differentiated citizenship that accommodate group claims within a liberal democracy (Kymlicka 1989; 1995). In *Multicultural Citizenship,* Kymlica (1995) proposes a descriptive and normative model of differentiated citizenship. He makes a primary distinction between two categories of cultural identity upon which his model is based—national minorities and ethnic minorities that may attract different kinds of group rights, self-governing, and polyethnic rights, respectively. Kymlica then maps on two kinds of nation-state on to this primary distinction: multinational states and polyethnic states. Canada, with its federal arrangements to accommodate the different self-governing rights of Canada's indigenous peoples (First Nations), and anglophone and francophone Canada, provides the archetype for his model of multinational state and differentiated citizenship. For Kymlica, the only legitimate basis for group rights within a liberal democracy is that of national minorities. Language, by which he means national language, is a defining characteristic of a national culture that provides a national minority with its coherence. Ethnic minorities, on the other hand, should not enjoy the right to self-governance, since their presence within a national territory is voluntary. The institutionalization of Irish-speaking Ireland in the spatial territory of the Gaeltacht and other protections for Irish can be understood as forms of group-based rights as advocated by Kymlica.

In this rights-based approach, we are still left with the problem of how to deal with two sets of competing rights claims, the success of one entailing the apparent negation of the other. I suggest that liberal multiculturalism can only take us so far in resolving this. I agree with Joseph Carens' (1997) critique of Kymlicka that the hierarchical differentiation between national and ethnic minorities is unhelpful. Joseph Carens (1997) and Iris Marion Young (1997) attempt to apply Kymlicka's model to a range of empirical situations beyond the simple binary he sets up. They conclude that his model is not robust and it fails to deal with the majority of real multicultural situations. Certainly, if we were to apply his model to the Irish context, and specifically, to that relating to the school's language policy, we soon find ourselves in conceptual trouble. Irish-born, English-speaking citizens relocating to the Gaeltacht are neither "national" minorities nor "ethnic" minorities. So, are they eligible for self-governing or polyethnic rights? They are citizens of a state where Irish and English are official languages, but they reside in a geographic territory where Irish is accorded special privilege. They can be seen to have moved voluntarily, in Kymlicka's view, and therefore, would not automatically attract privileges—other than being speakers of a socially powerful language, whose power does not decline as a consequence of promoting Irish.

A rights-based approach appears then to have severe limitations. Group claims will always be confronted with limitations imposed by individual liberty. How do we overcome this?

Conclusion: Cultural Confidence or Social Solidarity?

In a similar tone to Carens and Young, Andrea Baumeister (1999; 2000) notes that, in the face of increasing demands from national and ethnic minorities, liberal democratic states struggle to work out the best way of accommodating demands for group recognition without undermining individual liberty.

The tensions surrounding the school's policy bring to the fore liberal democracy's problematic relation with diversity. As Baumeister (2000) clearly argues, if at the heart of a liberal understanding of citizenship (belonging) is the idea of the abstract, undifferentiated, autonomous individual, who can attract rights on the basis of formal equality, then anything that has the appearance of particularity is excluded from the public domain and relegated to the private and the cultural. Within liberal democratic theory, all individuals enjoy equal moral value. Matters of difference, be they religious faith, sexual orientation, or ethnicity, are consequently regarded as private matters and should not be the providence of public political concern. This is the basis for the separation of church and state in many liberal democracies. Therefore, in the face of increasing particularist demands, liberal democracies, such as Ireland, have sought to accommodate these demands so long as they do not undermine individual liberty. This is why liberal multiculturalists, such as Kymlicka, have developed the idea of individuals as rooted in cultural communities as a basis for accommodating particular kinds of group rights within a liberal democratic framework. Because liberalism relies on politics being translated into contractlike procedures (forms of social contract between individuals and the state), Kymlicka has formulated a set of formal categories of rights, with "national" groups being privileged within his framework.

The basis of rights claimed by different actors in the local setting is quite distinct. The claims made by the Concerned Parents group are classically liberal. They assert the right of their children to have an education in English so as not to disadvantage them in the wider world. The right to access to education as a public good and the right to the benefits of that education without discrimination are classic liberal demands. They are not claimed on the basis of any particular characteristic of individuals as members of a group. In contrast, the rights claimed by those supporting the school's policy are, by and large, based on group identification. The group nature of the claims is, first, based on the assertion of the cultural particularity of the Gaeltacht as defined principally by language. Associated with this is the presumption that Irish should, therefore, be given legal protection as a normative public language, in this instance, as the medium of education. The idea of legal protection arises out of the fact that English is the dominant cultural form of nearly all forms of social life. Consequently, without deliberate privileging of Irish, it is feared that English would become the default language in a weakly defined bilingualism. Secondly, Irish is invoked as the national language enshrined in the Irish Constitution. Therefore, as citizens of the state, parents have the right, in the liberal sense, to demand Irish-medium education. However, this second basis of for demanding rights is not as strongly articulated as the first. The right to Irish-medium education is, therefore, claimed primarily on the basis of the asserted characteristics of a cultural group—Gaeltacht parents.

Baumeister (Baumeister 1999; 2000) is concerned that the promotion of group rights in the political sphere is at odds with the notion of identity as contingent and performative. Instead, group claims imply fixity of identity and that individuals are either in one group or another. Carens and Young charge Kymlicka with the same fallacy (Carens 1997; Young 1997). A key concern for Baumeister is that such rights claimed on the basis of group identity privilege the uniqueness of group experience at the possible expense of solidarity. This is why Baumeister turns to the political theory of Chantal Mouffe to provide an alternative to a rights-based approach. I have drawn on Chantal Mouffe's work elsewhere to think through the potential for a nonessentialist popular politics of place and identity (Warren 2011; 2012). As with the notion of culture and identity outlined in the introduction here, for Mouffe, identity is always formed relationally, constructed in terms of "us" and "them" and is organized around different world views or articulations of the public good, and so on. Further to this, the "we" (as Irish or English speakers) is not already given or preexisting but constituted through political struggle itself. In a very real sense, two communities of interest were formed out of the contestation of the school's policy. They had to be formed through the political work of persuasion and mobilization. Consequently, the terms on which politics is formed are always contingent and up for renegotiation. From this perspective, Irish-speaking and English-speaking Ireland are not two entities locked in a zero-sum game. Therefore, the reliance on democracy as procedure, as required in a liberal theory of rights, is untenable. Instead, by privileging political contestation, and building a defense for *polasaí lán-Ghaeilge* around arguments for different "ways of life," of how we live in and with diversity, issues of culture have to be located in the public domain and articulated as forms of social solidarity, rather than cultural confidence.

Notes

1. To see the advertisement, go to: http://www.youtube.com/watch?v=x9EdIbxZAyE&feature=related
2. An Daingean was the official Irish language name for the town under the Official Languages Act of 2007. Subsequently, a local campaign persuaded the Irish government to amend the place names order so that the town would be officially known by a bilingual version *Dingle/Daingean Uí Chúis*. The town is more popularly known through its English name of Dingle. For the purposes of this article, I will use the English language version, in part because the Irish-language version is disputed.
3. For a discussion of the inadequacy of gross domestic product (GDP) as a measure of economic health in Ireland see P. Kirby, *The Celtic Tiger in Collapse: Explaining the Weaknesses of the Irish Model* (Basingstoke, UK: Palgrave Macmillan, 2010).
4. The A8 countries are Czech Republic, Estonia, Hungary, Latvia, Lithuania, Poland, Slovakia, and Slovenia.

References

Ball, S., R. Bowe, and S. Gewirtz. (1996). "School Choice, Social Class and Distinction: The Realization of Social Advantage in Education." *Journal of Educational Policy* 11 (1): 89–112.

Barbour, S., and Carmichael, C., ed. (2000). *Language and Nationalism in Europe*. Oxford: Oxford University Press.

Barry, B. (2001). *Culture and Equality: An Egalitarian Critique of Multiculturalism*. Cambridge, MA: Harvard University Press.

Baumeister, A. T. (1999). "Multicultural Citizenship, Identity and Conflict." In *Toleration, Identity and Difference*, edited by J. Horton and S. Medus. Basingstoke, UK: Palgrave Macmillan.

Baumeister, A. T. (2000). *Liberalism and the "Politics of Difference."* Edinburgh: Edinburgh University Press.

Blommaert, J., and J. Verschueren. (1998). *Debating Diversity: Analysing the Rhetoric of Tolerance*. London: Routledge.

Bowe, R., S. Ball, and S. Gewirtz. (1994). "'Parental Choice', Consumption and Social Theory: The Operation of Micro-Markets in Education." *British Journal of Educational Studies* 32 (1): 38–52.

Brubaker, R. (1996). *Nationalism Reframed: Nationhood and the National Question in the New Europe.* Cambridge: Cambridge University Press.

Brubaker, R. (2004). *Ethnicity Without Groups.* Cambridge, MA.: Harvard University Press.

Calvet, L. J. (1998). *Language Wars and Linguistic Politics.* Oxford: Oxford University Press.

Carens, J. H. (1997). "Symposium on Multicultural Citizenship by *Will Kymlicka*: Liberalism and Culture." *Constellations* 4 (1): 35–47.

Creedon, T. (2007). "Parent's Row Breaks Out Over School's Irish Language Policy." *The Kerryman,* September 12, 2007, Tralee.

Cronin, M. (2002). "Speed Limits: Ireland, Globalisation, and the War against Time." In *Reinventing Ireland: Culture, Society and Global Economy,* edited by P. Kirby, L. Gibbons and M. Cronin. London: Pluto Press.

Crowley, E. (2006). *Land Matters: Power Struggles in Rural Ireland.* Dublin: Lilliput Press.

Editorial. (2007). "Language Barriers—Irish at the expense of education?" *Irish Examiner,* October 17, 2007, Cork.

Government of Ireland. Office of the Minister for Integration. (2008). *Migration Nation: Statement on Integration Strategy and Diversity Management.* Dublin: Stationery Office.

Government of Ireland. Central Statistics Office. (2007). *Census 2006.* vol. 9, *Irish Language.* Dublin: Stationary Office.

Grillo, R. (1989). *Dominant Languages: Language and Hierarchy in Britain and France.* Cambridge: Cambridge University Press.

Jenkins, R. (1997). *Rethinking Ethnicity: Arguments and Explorations.* London: Sage.

Johnson, N. C. (1998). "Making Space: Gaeltacht Policy and the Politics of Identity." in *In Search of Ireland: A Cultural Geography,* edited by B. Graham. London: Routledge.

Joyce, C. (2008). "Annual Policy Report on Migration and Asylum 2007: Ireland." Dublin: ESRI.

Judge, A. (2000). "France: One State, One nation, One Language?" In *Language and Nationalism in Europe,* edited by S. Barbour and C. Carmichael. Oxford: Oxford University Press.

Kelly, A. (2002). *Compulsory Irish: Language and Education in Ireland, 1870s–1970s.* Dublin: Irish Academic Press.

Kirby, P. (2002). "Contested Pedigree of the Celtic Tiger." In *Reinventing Ireland: Culture, Society and Global Economy,* edited by P. Kirby, L. Gibbons and M. Cronin. London: Pluto Press.

Kirby, P. (2010). *The Celtic Tiger in Collapse: Explaining the Weaknesses of the Irish Model* Basingstoke, UK: Palgrave Macmillan.

Kymlicka, W. (1989). *Liberalism, Community and Culture.* Oxford: Clarendon Press.

Kymlicka, W. (1995). *Multicultural Citizenship: A Liberal Theory of Minority Rights.* Oxford: Clarendon Press.

Mac Giolla Chríost, D. (2005). *The Irish Language in Ireland: From Goídel to Globalisation.* London: Routledge.
May, S. (2001). *Language and Minority Rights: Ethnicity, Nationalism and the Politics of Language.* Harlow, UK: Longman.
Mumford, C., ed. (2007). *Cosmopolitanism and Europe.* Liverpool: Liverpool University Press.
Nettle, D., and S. Romaine. (2000). *Vanishing Voices: The Extinction of the World's Languages.* Oxford: Oxford University Press.
O'Hearn, D. (2003). "Macroeconomic Policy in the Celtic Tiger: A Critical Assessment." In *The End of Irish History? Critical Reflections on the Celtic Tiger,* edited by C. Coulter and S. Coleman. Manchester: Manchester University Press.
Ó Croidheáin, C. (2006). *Language from Below: The Irish Language, Ideology and Power in 20th-Century Ireland.* Oxford: Peter Lang.
Ó Giollagáin, C., and S. M. Donnacha. (2008). "The Gaeltacht Today." In *A New View of the Irish Language,* edited by C. Nic Pháidín and S. Ó. Cearnaigh. Dublin: Cois Life.
Ó Giollagáin, C. R., S. M. Donnacha, F. N. Chualáin, A. N., Shéaghdha, and M. O'Brien. (2007). *Comprehensive Linguistic Study of the Use of Irish in the Gaeltacht: Principal Findings and Recommendations 2007/ Staidéar Cuimsitheach Teangeolaíoch ar Úsáid na Gaeilge sa Ghaeltacht; Príomhthátal agus Moltaí.* Dublin: Stationery Office.
Ó Riagáin, P. (1992). *Language Maintenance and Language Shift as Strategies of Social Reproduction: Irish in the Corca Dhuibhne Gaeltacht, 1926–1986.* Dublin: Linguistic Institute of Ireland (ITE).
Ó Riagáin, P. (1997). *Language Policy and Social Reproduction.* Oxford: Clarendon Press.
Ó Tuathaigh, G. (2008). "The State and the Irish Language: An Historical Perspective." In *A New View of the Irish Language,* edited by C. N. Pháidín and S. Ó. Cearnaigh. Dublin: Cois Life.
Peillon, M. (2002). "Culture and State in Ireland's New Economy." In *Reinventing Ireland: Culture, Society and Global Economy,* edited by P. Kirby, L. Gibbons and M. Cronin. London: Pluto Press.
Pennycook, A. (1994). *The Cultural Politics of English as an International Language.* Harlow: Longman.
Phillipson, R. (2003). *English-only Europe?: Challenging Language Policy.* London: Routledge.
Phillipson, R. (2009). *Linguistic Imperialism Continued.* New York: Routledge.
Race, R. (2011). *Multiculturalism and Education.* London: Continuum.
Ruhs, M. (2005). *Emerging Trends and Patterns in the Immigration and Employment of Non-EU Nationals in Ireland,* Blue Paper 19, Dublin, The Policy Institute, Trinity College, Dublin.
Ryan, L. (2003). "Moving Spaces and Changing Places: Irish Women's Memories of Emigration to Britain in the 1930s." *Journal of Ethnic and Migration Studies* 29 (1): 67–82.
Said, E. (1993). *Culture and Imperialism.* London: Chatto and Windus.
Trenz, H. J. (2007). "Reconciling Diversity and Unity: Language Minorities and European Integration." *Ethnicities* 7 (2): 157–185.

Warren, S. (2006). "Integration of New Migrants: Education." In *Refugees and Other New Migrants: A Review of the Evidence on Successful Approaches to Integration*, edited by S. Spence. Oxford Centre on Migration, Policy, and Society, University of Oxford.

Warren, S. (2011). "Against Cosmopolitanism? A Theoretical Exploration of the Tensions between Irish-Speaking Ireland and Post-Nationalist Multicultural Ireland." In *Polish-Irish Encounters*, edited by Sabine Eggar. and John McDonagh Frankfurt: Peter Lang.

Warren, S. (2012 forthcoming). "The Making of Irish-Speaking Ireland—Belonging, Diversity, and Power." *Ethnicities*.

Warren, S. and D. Gillborn. (2003). "Race Equality and Education in Birmingham." Birmingham, Equalities Division, Birmingham City Council and Birmingham Race Action Partnership, United Kingdom.

Watson, I. (2008). "The Irish Language and Identity." In *A New View of the Irish Language*, edited by C. Nic Pháidín and S. Ó. Cearnaigh. Dublin: Cois Life.

Whelan, C. T., and B. Maître. (2006). *Levels and Patterns of Material Deprivation in Ireland: After The "Celtic Tiger."* Working paper no. 171. Dublin: ESRI.

Williams, C. H. (2000). "On Recognition, Resolution and Revitalisation." In: *Language Revitalization: Policy and Planning in Wales*, edited by C. H. Williams. Cardiff: University of Wales Press).

Woolard, K. A. (1989). *Double Talk: Bilingualism and the Politics of Ethnicity in Catalonia*. Stanford, CA: Stanford University Press.

Young, I. M. (1997). "Symposium on Multicultural Citizenship by Will Kymlicka: A Multicultural Continuum; A Critique of Will Kymlicka's Ethnic-Nation Dichotomy." *Constellations*, 4 (1): 48–53.

6

Reimagining Lines of Flight in Schooling for Indigenous Students in Australia[1]

Bob Lingard, Greg Vass, and Elizabeth Mackinlay

Introduction

The challenge for education and educational research to ensure the cultural confidence of peoples and communities who have experienced protracted oppression and marginalization remains to be satisfactorily negotiated. Educational research has traditionally been framed by the ontological and epistemological assumptions of global north theory and theorists (Appadurai 2001), rather than by what might be seen as southern theory (Connell 2008), that is, knowledge produced outside the global north hegemony in what is typically seen as the margins. Indeed, Linda Tuhiwai Smith, a well-known Maori academic, has argued that the word *research* "is probably one of the dirtiest words in the indigenous world's vocabulary" (1999, 1). As research academics positioned by such northern theory as well as indigenous perceptions of the historical linkages between research and colonization, research and the othering of indigenous peoples, we recognize, the significance of our positionalities to the work we attempt reflexively to do. We return to this matter later in the chapter. While this is dangerous terrain for us, it is a necessary discomfort, a form of intellectual displacement in Edward Said's (2000) terms, which might assist in contributing to advancing knowledge and debates.

Just as we need, as researchers, to be reflexively aware of our positioning, so too do we need to be aware of the effects and assumptions of school curricula (and testing) that underpin the schooling of indigenous students in contemporary Australia. This is in recognition that the epistemologies and ontologies underpinning global north theory and research are also found within education policy and practices and also in school curricula and pedagogies in the Anglo American nations of the global north. The conditions of schooling that will foster cultural confidence for indigenous students and communities will need to reconcile these tensions through actively encouraging listening, learning, and the leavening of knowledge developed outside the traditional global north forms (e.g., within Australian indigenous communities), as well as confronting issues to do with the place of these dominant systems of knowledge in indigenous schooling. The two prominent indigenous educators we deal with in this paper, Noel Pearson and Chris Sarra, explicitly recognize the need to reconcile these tensions.

In this chapter, we accept that there are layers of diversity within localized communities across the globe as well as in the Australian context. Indeed, one of the issues we seek to address and challenge in this chapter is the essentializing of both indigenous peoples and communities within contemporary social and education policy amidst such diversity, and we would add, their white other (see Luke et al. 1993). As we will demonstrate, the "closing the gap" focus of contemporary indigenous policy in Australia, while well intended, almost "whitewashes" the structural and historical bases of the current (diverse) indigenous condition and neglects the colonial past and its residues in the colonial present (Gregory 2004) that continue to have real material effects in the everyday/ every-night lives of indigenous Australians. The focus on closing the gap negates the need as well to consider what Gloria Ladson-Billings (2006) calls the "education debt" in relation to oppressed peoples; with closing the gap, there is almost an inbuilt amnesia about colonization and deep structural inequalities. A closing-the-gap strategy also denies what Fraser (1997) has called a politics of recognition, that is, it denies the veracity of indigenous knowledges and epistemologies in its implicit goal for indigenous Australians to perform as well in schooling as middle-class nonindigenous Australians on a curriculum framed by dominant knowledges. These educational concerns are heightened in the current national schooling reform context in Australia, especially in respect of the impact of high-stakes literacy and numeracy testing, which works with a politics of sameness, eliding difference.

Part of what we seek to do in this chapter will entail exploring how prominent contemporary indigenous voices, such as Noel Pearson and Chris Sarra, are positioned and how they are deployed within the discourse of closing the gap, which in turn frames contemporary indigenous policy. Here the subaltern is speaking (Spivak, 1996), but how are these voices taken up in the global north paradigm of what Gillborn (2008) calls "gap talk" in contemporary schooling policy?

Our argument proceeds as follows: First, we consider the intractable and treacherous terrains of contemporary indigenous education policy. Next we examine three positions within this field, namely, Noel Pearson's "radical vision" for contemporary schooling for Indigenous students; then we focus on Chris Sarra's "strong and smart" strategy, and finally, we address the broader "closing-the-gap" Australian and Queensland state policies. In considering possible conclusions, we interrogate whether a postcolonial stance, aligned with Young (2003) and as aspirational as anything else, is appropriate to underpinning contemporary indigenous education in Australia. We conclude the chapter by offering a tentative response to the meta-question that frames this edited collection: "Can education contribute to the cultural confidence of peoples and communities who have endured centuries of oppression and marginalization?"

Locating Indigenous Students in the Australian Educational Landscape

Intractable Terrain

The education of indigenous students has been a political, policy, academic, social, and sore point of consideration since coming to national attention in Australia during the 1960s. It was in this period that globalization discourses created conditions that supported the ideological construction of what is now known as "indigenous education," a process grounded in the historical specificities of the Australian context (Rizvi 2007). In this sense, the creation of indigenous education occurred at this time in association with broader sociopolitical forces as a strategy for distinguishing this group from the dominant one, enabling targeted policy and resource allocation that worked with an essentialized category of Indigenous students. Prior to this, the different state education systems could be described as having in common education policy approaches that have been characterized as those of exclusion or assimilation with respect to indigenous students and also in relation to migrant students (Beresford 2003). Since this time, however, there appears scant evidence to suggest that the sustained or widespread engagement and improvement in outcomes of indigenous students within education is evident (Gray and Beresford 2008). From this, indigenous education could be described as located within intractable terrain. Two contributing factors are discussed here that help explain why this is the case.

First, up to until the 1960s, a paucity of available, cohesive, and relevant data ensured that a concern with the outcomes and engagement of indigenous students in education remained largely hidden (Malin and Maidment 2003, 87). This was a result of the fact that until the Referendum of 1967, indigenous Australians were not recognized in the Australian census; thus, no reliable data were available. In many respects, this continued even after 1967, with issues connected to the collection and availability of data being an ongoing concern identified by Mellor and Corrigan (2004) in their review of indigenous education. These authors suggested that (national) testing may help redress "gaps" in understanding and accountability in the provision of education to indigenous students. A move that was subsequently taken up in 2007, with the introduction of the National Assessment Program for Literacy and Numeracy (known as NAPLAN), leading to the construction of data that in turn were used to justify and map out subsequent education policy. Of note here, NAPLAN data were directly linked with the development of Closing the Gap on Indigenous Disadvantage: the Challenge for Australia (2009, 7), a federal policy that stresses the importance of "accountability and reporting" as linked with "measurable targets" and the commitment to improve "statistical collection services that are currently not sufficient." While acknowledging that access to relevant and suitable data can be a valuable tool that can assist in the redistribution of education resources to target specific concerns, our worry arises from the data being presented and utilized as if it were politically neutral, rather than recognizing the politics and semiotic work involved in categorization that underpins policy as numbers and evidence-based policy (Lingard, Creagh, and Vass, 2011). It appears that there is little questioning or debate about who decides, how they decide, and what the specific educational concerns are that warrant attention or why. Hence, there is the potential for maldistribution of educational resources (Power and Frandji 2010) in ways that may maintain indigenous education within this intractable terrain.

The second contributing factor that helps explain why indigenous education is located within an intractable terrain, derives from prevailing assumptions about authority and the ability of the state to frame and assert the education agenda upon communities irrespective of localized needs or interests. Within Australia, similarly to many other colonized settings, indigenous education is framed within a deficit paradigm, with the intent of ameliorating the "disadvantage" associated with being indigenous, often touted as motivating the initiative. Chris Sarra's approach, which we consider later in this chapter, is to confront that deficit view of indigenous identity head-on through his "stronger and smarter" philosophy. However, the continuance of such a deficit approach can be seen in the title of the Closing the Gap on indigenous Disadvantage policy mentioned above. Beresford explains this approach as a:

> perspective [that] has its foundation in a conservative worldview that Aboriginal people lack the cognitive capacity or environmental stimulation to succeed at school. Although discredited for several decades...the view persists among some conservative teachers who continue to believe that a lack of adequate preparation for schooling in the home, poor language and literacy skills, and problems of attendance, health and nutrition explain the failure of many Aboriginal children to thrive in school. (2003, 27)

From this, continued deficit thinking is linked with the maintenance of low expectations of indigenous students academically and behaviorally in the classroom, education policies that avoid systemic critique, and education research that is limited by being positioned within this paradigm. Additionally, this thinking gives rise to compensatory strategies that view the education system as already adequate for the task, and therefore, as capable of compensating for the perceived deficiencies of the students. In seeking to compensate for deficiencies, initiatives have largely continued to benefit teachers, retaining "transmission" style or scripted pedagogy that aims to inculcate rules, values, and knowledge of relevance to the dominant "white" society (Ah Sam and Ackland 2005, 185). While education policy, research, and practice continue to evade casting a critical gaze at the self and at the system, it seems unlikely that shifting indigenous education out of this intractable terrain will occur.

Treacherous Terrain

A concern with indigenous education is in some senses, by its very nature, a complex prospect to consider in a holistic sense. Geographic distances, political structures, and localized histories and cultures are some of the issues that undermine the utility of federal or state education policy designed to meet universally the needs of indigenous students spread as far and wide as Alice Springs, the Gold Coast, and inner-city Redfern in Sydney. Adding further complexity to this, while Australia is viewed as a global-north setting, in many respects, current approaches to indigenous education could be described as seeking to surmount challenges typically associated with global south contexts, indeed so-called Fourth World contexts in remote parts of Australia. This situation enables indigenous education to be regarded as a highly politicized and socially contested education policy context; in this sense it is located within treacherous terrain. As such, the position and perspective of those who contribute to education debates that are focused on this treacherous terrain warrant consideration. The need to cast a reflexive gaze that helps locate us, the authors of this chapter, on this treacherous terrain weighs heavily on our minds, because we are not indigenous and recognize Tuhiwai Smith's point about research and the colonization of indigenous peoples.

In some respects, we share much in common. We are all white, university trained, have lived much of our lives in Brisbane (the capital of Queensland), have professional and research interests in education, and more than this, we share similar concerns about social justice in education in relation to indigenous students. There are, however, important points of distinction. Bob, now a widely recognized and respected educational researcher, began his academic career working under the powerful and influential academic Professor Betty Watts in what was arguably groundbreaking research that focused on this terrain in the 1970s, including an Evaluation of the Aboriginal Secondary Grant Scheme done for the Whitlam Labor government. However, in the intervening years, he has not had this focus as a research priority, but he has retained a strong commitment to reconciliation with indigenous Australians, and addressing indigenous disadvantage, and overcoming the education debt to indigenous Australians, a stance adopted by all three of us. Liz began her academic career in ethnomusicology, working within a remote indigenous setting, Burrulula, and she has subsequently maintained close professional and personal relationships with people from this area through her marriage to a Yanyuwa man. She has in recent years become increasingly focused on education with a specific focus on indigenous schooling. She is also an editor of the *Australian Journal of Indigenous Education*. Greg is currently a full-time doctoral candidate who recently took leave from full-time teaching in the hope of developing a greater understanding of the relationship between the education system and indigenous students. His honors research looked at indigenous art, and he currently volunteers as a tutor for Aboriginal secondary students.

While we hope that the varied backgrounds and experiences of the three of us will come together to offer something of merit to debates on indigenous education, this chapter is written in recognition that we occupy an uncomfortable position within the treacherous terrain. We have approached writing this chapter ever mindful that we are not indigenous, we are positioned as global north researchers, and that ultimately, we cannot lay claim to speak for or with the authority of having experienced the lived perspective of being indigenous and attending school in this country. Yet, our view is that our experiences, research, and understandings enable us to reflect upon indigenous education at this moment in contemporary Australia on the grounds that the indigenous situation in Australia is one that all citizens should have concerns about, while also not wanting to restrict the voices that can speak in indigenous policy debates. Gayatri Spivak (1990), the postcolonial critic, has expressed a similar stance in a more abstract way, as the need to reject a reductionist biodeterminism about who has the right to speak in relation to debates around difference. At the same time, we are mindful that our voices are not indigenous ones and offer our perspective in an open and respectful spirit toward the conversation about moving indigenous education forward in Australia.

Our pro-indigenous perspective here can perhaps be compared with male pro-feminism, a stance that recognizes that feminist desired changes in the gender order also require changes in the construction and practices of masculinity (see Lingard and Douglas 1999). Likewise, we recognize that improvement of the indigenous position in Australia demands a changed stance from other Australians. Nonetheless, this is difficult terrain for us. We acknowledge Linda Tuhiwai Smith's point about research not having a good standing among indigenous peoples, given historical memories of what was done to indigenous peoples in its name.

Education Policy Reform Responses in Queensland

A Pedagogy of Hope in a Time of Suffering: Pearson's "Radical" View of Education and Equality in Australia

In this section we deal with the work on indigenous schooling of the well-known Aboriginal leader Noel Pearson. Pearson is a widely recognized figure in Australia, with regular columns in the national newspaper, *The Australian*, dealing with his stance on the way forward for indigenous schooling. In our account here, we are drawing mainly on Pearson's recent essay, *Radical Hope* (2009). Pearson's discussion of this way forward begins with an overview of the predicament that many indigenous communities faced over one hundred years ago, and that many are facing right now, in terms of how Aboriginal and Torres Strait Islander communities sustain and transmit indigenous ways of being, doing, and knowing in a globalized world amid the upheaval and destruction wrought by colonization. He suggests that indigenous peoples' capacity to maintain their languages, traditions, and knowledges is directly related to the serious regard in which these very things are held. "Are we Aborigines a serious people? Do we have serious leaders? Do we have the seriousness necessary to maintain the hard places we call home?," he asks (11). For those of us who have worked in and have close relationships with the kinds of remote indigenous Deed of Grant in Trust (DOGIT) communities to which Pearson implicitly refers, we know exactly how hard it is to live in such places. Deed of Grant in Trust, or DOGIT, communities were established in the mid-1980s in Queensland as a system of community-level land trust to administer former reserves and missions. Governed by local representatives elected every three years, the trusts became known as Incorporated Aboriginal Councils, and there are more than 30 DOGIT communities in Queensland. Hopevale, in the heart of Pearson's own traditional country of Cape York in northern Queensland, was the first Aboriginal community to receive a DOGIT in 1986. However, in recent years, he has been increasingly critical of DOGIT communities for failing to enact the seriousness required to live up to the promise of self-determination. Pearson attributes the lack of success to alcohol, unemployment, and welfare dependency, mixed uneasily with and feeding insidiously into a flailing capacity to sustain indigenous cultural practices and laws in the modern world.

In many ways, Pearson's radical vision for the education of indigenous Australian children is inherently linked to his professional, political, philosophical, and personal experiences of living and working in DOGIT communities and fighting for a better life for his people. He acknowledges that indigenous communities in Australia have been scarred and continue to suffer from the historical legacy of colonization—of dispossession, trauma, discrimination, and the devaluation of indigenous authority (25). However, Pearson sees Western education as the only long-term solution for Aboriginal people to sustain language and culture, and the sentiment expressed is that he has had enough of Aboriginal people positioning themselves and living according to a victim mentality (55). In *Radical Hope,* he proposes a "no excuses" response to poverty, violence, addiction, illiteracy, and truancy, based upon the way in which he believes he himself has taken personal responsibility to secure his own future as an Aboriginal man in Australia.

The no-excuses approach is based upon Obama's famous 2009 address on the 100th anniversary of the founding of the National Association for the Advancement of Colored People (NAACP) (Pearson 2009, 13). Pearson highlights Obama's concern for African American people in the United States to aim higher, to take personal responsibility for their own destiny, and for society as a whole to "get schooling right" so as to close the achievement gap between students of racial backgrounds (Pearson 2009, 16). Obama also addressed the broader structural disadvantages experienced by people of color in the United States and Pearson similarly asks, "Can educational disadvantage be overcome without overcoming broader socio-economic disadvantage?" (16). Heartened by the successes achieved in the United States in the reduction of educational disadvantage by adopting this approach, Pearson has subsequently embraced and implemented the no-excuses framework in Cape York. The Pearson version of no-excuses targets educators and explicitly states:

> The fact that some of our children come from disadvantaged backgrounds, and even dysfunctional, backgrounds, will no longer be an excuse for educational failure…It will not be an excuse for the children. It will not be an excuse for the parents or community. It will not be an excuse for the principal and the teachers. It will not be an excuse for the education system and all of us who say we are committed to Indigenous education reform. (Pearson 2009, 21)

The no-excuses approach as described by Pearson is in many ways paradoxical. There is a tension between wanting to "achieve," according to mainstream standards *and* wanting young Aboriginal people to "walk in two worlds and enjoy the best of both" (34). The no-excuses approach assumes that Aboriginal people are already assimilated and that participation in the dominant education system is the only way forward. The education system, as we are well aware, was built and is sustained by discourses of white-race dominance, power, and privilege and does not easily or willingly make space for the other world that Pearson wants for the next generation of Aboriginal people. The catch is that the no-excuses approach removes accountability from educators for ensuring that it is possible for indigenous students to sustain their strong sense of identity as Aboriginal and Torres Strait Islander peoples, and actually *gives* them an excuse for perpetuating the disempowerment of indigenous people through education by ignoring the cultures with which they identify.

Pearson expects educators to engage in "explicit instruction" (after Engelmann 1980; Engelmann and Carnine 1982; Engelmann 1983) with Aboriginal students, that is, "a means of communication that allows only one interpretation and which is capable of transmitting the relevant concept or skill to any learner" (49), which in practice, plays out as "explicit, phonics-based reading instruction" (53). Already this approach is at odds with the multiple ways of knowing, which exist in indigenous Australian communities and the diversity across those multiple ways of knowing according to location, landscape, and law. It is not possible—nor is it equitable or ethical—to assume that all indigenous communities are the same, yet the "explicit instruction" that he strongly advocates, seems to rest on the understanding that all indigenous children are a homogenous group.

In Pearson's model, the teacher and the school then become ultimately responsible for performing a "faultless" communication and transmission of information to indigenous students, an expectation that further muddies the very notion of personal responsibility that Pearson is promoting. The no-excuses tone adopted for the discussion provides a limited scope for effectively responding to the sociopolitical forces that have created inequities and discrimination in the past. The approach appears to accept that the nonindigenous (white) dominated teaching profession can continue to go about "business as usual" and avoid embarking on a meaningful and genuine reflexive self-critique. Indeed, the question of privilege becomes even more complex when it is considered that while Pearson is offering a vision of an empowering postcolonial and decolonizing education for indigenous students, his discussion fails to adequately respond to concerns that the approach draws on his own "success" within an "elite" secondary school setting, and is premised on instructional reform from the United States. Furthermore, while Pearson may draw his inspiration for hope from multiple sources, and while it may very well be radical, the colonial underpinnings do not bode well for delivering the promise of empowerment, self-determination, and freedom that Pearson holds onto.

Another Pedagogy of Hope: Chris Sarra's "Strong and Smart" Philosophy

Chris Sarra's widely known and acclaimed approach to Aboriginal education, the "Strong and Smart" philosophy (Sarra 2012a and 2012b), developed from his deep reflections on his experience as school principal at Cherbourg Aboriginal community school in Queensland from 1998 until 2005. His philosophy also emerged from his reflections on his own schooling as an Aboriginal male; here he wanted to challenge head-on what he refers to as the "downwards aspirations" of indigenous students constructed through their schooling. Indeed, in a way similar to postcolonial theorists Franz Fanon and Homi Bhaba's accounts of how colonization deeply affects the very psyche of both colonizers and colonized, Sarra ensured that the Aboriginal children in his school were able to see that daily-lived realities such as domestic violence, alcoholism, and so on were the legacy of colonization and a colonized Aboriginal identity. They were not the consequences of being Aboriginal, rather they were the consequences of colonization and the colonial present. In a broader sense, then, his approach could be seen as one of decolonization. Sarra reflected on this matter in relation to his time as principal at Cherbourg and to student identities and aspirations, "I was determined they would never be subjected to the stench of a school culture of low expectations" (2012a, 65). At the same time, he has noted how he did not ever denigrate white identities.

On the basis of his experience and intellectual reflections, Chris Sarra framed his philosophy within the school as one that focused on achieving two things—positive and enabling Aboriginal identities and school academic performance that matched that of other schools. As with Pearson, this was a no-excuses approach. Sarra reports how his approach resulted in many teachers leaving the school after he developed the philosophy at Cherbourg. He also reports subsequent great achievements of improved attendance and performance. Specifically, he documents (2012a, 66) the reduction of unexplained absenteeism, the huge improvement in attendance, the wonderful improvement in literacy performance from 1998 to 2004. In 1998, no students had achieved state-average performance, whereas in 2004, 81 percent were within the state-average band. On this point, he notes how it was actually easier to get Cherbourg students onside with the philosophy than it was with teachers. He has also documented how he worked with new teachers to ensure that they were onside with the strong and smart philosophy and how he developed the *A-Z Manual of Teaching at Cherbourg* to ensure teachers were inducted into the school change culture and knew what was expected of them.

Since leaving Cherbourg, Sarra has outlined the strong and smart philosophy as holistically consisting of the following elements:

- Acknowledging, embracing, and developing a positive sense of Aboriginal identity in schools
- Acknowledging and embracing Aboriginal leadership in schools and school communities
- High-expectations" leadership to ensure "high-expectations" classrooms, with "high-expectations" teacher/student relationships
- Innovative and dynamic school modelling in complex social and cultural contexts
- Innovative and dynamic school staffing models, especially for community schools (Sarra 2012a, 66)

The embracing of positive Aboriginal identity was enacted across all the school, but it was specifically addressed in the Aboriginal studies program of the school curricula. Here the students learned about ancient, traditional, and contemporary aspects of Aboriginal society and cultures and importantly, about the multifarious ways colonization and politics (both past and present) affected Aboriginal identities and expectations. One of us, Bob, had the privilege of sitting in on a couple of classes Chris taught on these topics and was deeply impressed by the awakening effects (politically and in terms of identity) that his pedagogies, philosophical approach, and curricula content had upon all the students in the classroom. In terms of whole school change, where his approach had similar politicizing effects, he has commented:

> On school assembly, I would say to the entire school things such as "Hands up if you're Aboriginal! Keep your hand up if you love being Aboriginal! When we leave this school what are we going to be?" The entire school would roar back to me from the pit of their gut, "*Strong and Smart!*." I would then say to children, "What does that mean?" They would reply enthusiastically, "Work hard," "be nice to the teachers," "keep our school clean and tidy," "*don't let anyone put us down*."
>
> This was a powerful time. I explained to the children that our school would be a place where you could get power, that historically our people had been denied power, but we were never going to miss

out. It really was an extraordinary time for all of us—staff, students, and parents—to bask in the magic of taking control, by rejecting absolutely the negative stereotype held out for us, and embracing a new and positive sense of identity on our terms. (Sarra 2012a, 68)

Sarra's philosophy about Aboriginal leadership and school-community relationships at Cherbourg was another very important aspect of the subsequently articulated strong and smart philosophy. He talks about how he instituted regular community elders assemblies, how he established a dedicated elders' room and space at the school, how he employed more Aboriginal people at the school, including men, and how he utilized local Aboriginal tradespeople to work in the school, thus encouraging community pride in the school itself. He has written specifically of the ways in which he teamed up with Mum Rae (Sarra 2012, 69), an important and powerful community leader, who, when he arrived in the community, appeared to be powerless inside the school. He worked assiduously to change this, and Mum Rae subsequently became a powerful ally in the effective educational changes he wrought at Cherbourg. He notes how this partnership ensured that he was "aligned with real authority in the community." Likewise, he changed the role of Aboriginal teacher aides, getting teachers to acknowledge and utilize their community contacts and knowledges, rather than simply using them to carry out menial and unmeaningful tasks. Here we can see how he worked to change the positioning of the school in the community and the community in the school around Aboriginal leadership and presence. He worked with the funds of knowledge in the community and in the school.

On leadership, Sarra articulated a high-expectations approach aligned with a focus on ensuring high teacher expectations generally and importantly in relation to teacher/student relationships. Here he explicitly recognized the very deep significance of classrooms and teacher pedagogies to achieving the best learning outcomes for all students. He has observed: "The classroom is undoubtedly the most sacred place" (Sarra 2012a, 70). Sarra outlines the mix of pressure, demand, and support he placed upon the teachers in his school. He was supportive, yet always challenging; he committed to large amounts of professional development to encourage ongoing teacher learning; he also monitored teachers' classroom practices and intervened where necessary. He honestly acknowledges that sometimes this was difficult, particularly in relation to a few teachers at the school, including an Aboriginal teacher and teacher's aide.

As with Noel Pearson, Chris Sarra adopted a no-excuses approach, one that assumed that schools and teachers could, should, and must make all the difference to indigenous schooling. This is a real pedagogy of hope. Perhaps, however, it downplays, at one level at least, as does Pearson, the negative impacts structurally and historically of colonization on Aboriginal students and schooling. Such a stance is seen by both as necessary to the rejection by Aboriginal students of a "victim mentality." Yet, the moral and ethical imperatives in both approaches are very obvious; to both Pearson and Sarra, it seems that any unreflective recognition within schools of these historical effects is akin to reproducing Aboriginal disadvantage and failing to close the gap in school performance and outcomes. Our position would be to recognize the power of both stances, but also the imperative need to address such structural disadvantages as complementary to school-based approaches, and not, of course, as a way of denying that schools can and must make a difference for the learning of Aboriginal students. We agree deeply with Chris Sarra's sage observation: "As a society, then, we are much poorer for failing to enable the capacity of Aboriginal students" (Sarra 2012a, 68). There are echoes here of John Dewey (1900), the American pragmatist philosopher of education, who noted at the turn of the twentieth century that what all good parents want for their children's schooling, we also should demand for the schooling of all children; this is very true of contemporary Aboriginal schooling. Anything else, Dewey (1900) added, would be "unlovely" and "undemocratic," and we would add, it would be socially unjust. The moral imperatives for schooling and teachers in regard to Aboriginal schooling articulated by both Noel Pearson and Chris Sarra are absolutely necessary and explicable, yet they need to be matched by other policy changes addressing disadvantage and what Gloria Ladson-Billings calls the "educational debt," that long neglect of indigenous schooling that accompanied colonization.

Noel Pearson (2009, 84–88) recognizes that Chris Sarra's approach is also of the no-excuses variety, but he refers to Sarra's pedagogical approach as an "identity pedagogy." He then goes on to challenge what he sees as Sarra's assumption in relation to education policy and practice, "that institutions of the state—public schools—are appropriate places for the cultivation of racial esteem" (85). In contrast to his representation of Sarra's "identity pedagogy" and strengthening of Aboriginal identity as the basis for improved school performance, Pearson observes, "The surest basis for esteem is effort and achievement" (86).

Sarra's strong and smart approach fits more with a progressive politics, with the additions of high expectations and a no-excuses disposition linked to a strong advocacy that schools and teachers must make a difference for indigenous students. It also aligns more closely with the school-reform literature that emphasizes the role of leadership in brokering school reform. It does not articulate a specific pedagogy, but rather stresses high expectations to frame all that schools do. Pearson's approach, in contrast, focuses more on the pedagogical relationships, emphasizing direct instruction, and politically, it is offered as a challenge to the liberal left establishment (as Pearson sees it) in Schools of Education in universities. Pearson's somewhat ambivalent view of Paulo Freire's work on the "pedagogy of the oppressed" is a good indication of his critique of left, progressive politics. In terms of Pearson's commitment to direct instruction, we would note that pedagogical research demonstrates that perhaps different pedagogies are required for achieving different types of educational goals. Interestingly, we note how Pearson (2011) also utilises John Hattie's (2009) research on what in-school factors have the biggest effects on student learning to provide an additional evidence base for his support of direct instruction. We would, though, point out that Hattie (2009, 243) also demonstrates from his synthesis of multiple research projects, that teacher pedagogical strategies around meta-cognition and challenging goals also have powerful effects when used by teachers. We would argue that they are essential for achieving higher order intellectual outcomes.

"Closing the Gap" on Educational Inequality

The election of the Rudd-led Labor federal government in 2007 and the promise of an "education revolution" has contributed to significantly altering the education landscape within Australia. Perhaps most significant here, was the shift in emphasis to increase transparency and accountability with a view to stimulating markets, increasing parental choice, and improving the quality and competitiveness of student outcomes within global comparative data (e.g., PISA). Underpinning these changes, then, was a renewed zeal that "data" and evidence were central to the solution; that "data" could help identify sections of the education sector (including indigenous students) that would benefit most from targeted and strategic responses.[2] One area within education that immediately, and one ponders unsurprisingly, emerged as a particular renewed concern were the disparities when indigenous and nonindigenous student outcomes and engagement were compared. Of particular alarm, according to the government, the data showed significant discrepancies in access to early childhood education (in remote settings); achievement in literacy and numeracy outcomes; and retention to year 12 (grade 12) and attainment of year 12 (or equivalent) qualifications (*Closing the Gap*, 2009). This concern gave rise to a political climate that Allan Luke (2009) described as an "unprecedented moment of...bipartisan support for a strong focus on reform and renewal in the education of Aborigines and Torres Strait Islanders." Within this shift, the federal government took a leading role with steering through the Council of Australian Governments (COAG)[3] toward a national agenda for schooling that is broadly framed by a human capital and productivity argument (Rizvi and Lingard 2010).

The growing emphasis on numbers orchestrating policy, or "policy as numbers" (see Rose 1999), is an approach that can be seen to permeate government activity within this current political climate, with numbers becoming a "technology of governance" (Lingard 2010). (See also Gillborn (2010) on the color of numbers in education policy.) In turning attention toward the government developing a policy approach in regard to indigenous people, the *Australia Summit 2020: The Future of Indigenous Australia* (2008) suggests that future indigenous policy needs to be evidence-based, to develop innovative evaluative strategies, and to assign specific roles to key representatives. Building on this approach, *Closing the Gap on Indigenous Disadvantage: The Challenge for Australia* (2009) established six clear and measurable targets to focus and evaluate "success." Three of the targets relate directly to education: all indigenous four year olds (in remote settings) will have access to early child care within five years; the reading, writing, and numeracy gap will be halved within a decade; and the gap for indigenous students in year-12 retention and attainment (or equivalent) rates will be halved by 2020. In establishing explicit targets such as this (and linking it with funding), the federal government is taking steps toward redefining the roles and responsibilities of the state-education providers. In part, this is one element in the broader move toward a more a national approach to schooling in Australia set in the context of globalization.

In the wake of these changes, Education Queensland, the state department of education in Queensland, developed their *Closing the Gap: Education Strategy* (2009). The general aims of the strategy are to: deliver clear, concise messages for regions and schools; specify a small number of targets; and contain a small number of evidence-based service lines, priority areas, and initiatives designed for sustainability. Hinting at the ongoing power struggle between federal and state structures, the Education Queensland policy establishes three specific targets that appear to be only loosely based on the broader COAG agenda—to halve the gap in year-three reading and numeracy by 2012; close the gap in student attendance by 2013; and close the gap in year-12 retention by 2013.

While it is not our intention to offer a detailed critique of these documents here, they do raise a number of concerns. Foremost is that the suite of policies mentioned here may ultimately contribute to further entrenching education inequities and discrimination. In focusing on narrow targets, and importantly, when connecting ongoing funding to these results, conditions are created that may lead to a narrowing of the curriculum and pedagogy made available to some indigenous students and perhaps deny difference. This was a concern identified by Giroux and Schmidt (2004) in their critique of similar strategies that were designed to close achievement "gaps" in the United States as part of the No Child Left Behind policy. The actual tools designed to measure the "gap" are a further worry. Klenowski (2009) draws attention to problems associated with the assessment instrument centrally implicated in measuring the gap, NAPLAN, as it can be critiqued on the grounds that it is not "culture fair" and that it discriminates against those without requisite cultural capital, including most indigenous Australians. Additionally, the logic underpinning the "gap" approach to indigenous education is itself unstable. Altman and Fogarty (2010) are critical of the targets as not being realistic; the approach continues to be limited in its capacity to effectively cater to the diversity of education contexts in Australia for indigenous students; and ultimately, it is a strategy that continues to be imbued with assimilationist ideas that are built upon racialized assumptions. Performance is measured only in relation to the one-size-fits-all NAPLAN exams on literacy and numeracy that all year 3, 5, 7, and 9 students in all Australian schools sit for each year.

Conclusion

In respect to the question, "Can education contribute to the cultural confidence of peoples and communities who have endured centuries of oppression and marginalisation?," we would answer in a hopeful affirmative, while acknowledging that schools alone cannot compensate for society, nor address the education debt, nor the colonial violence of the past and ongoing colonial present. Any school-level reforms must also be accompanied by broader, effective, and genuine policies of reconciliation with indigenous Australians and addressing of severe material and economic disadvantage. Postcolonial theory also makes us aware of a necessary discursive politics to confront elements of the colonial present. However, schools *can* and *must* make a difference. Here we are thus aligned with the educational goals articulated by Pearson and Sarra and recognize their decolonizing stances and acknowledge the significance within Sarra's philosophy of strong and smart of the need to work with Aboriginal funds of knowledge within schools and their communities. This demands broad policy changes, but also specific and localized responses. Pearson's approach offers one useful local response, but we are doubtful that direct instruction can achieve all of the goals we would want to see achieved in indigenous schooling in indigenous communities across the nation.

These are easy assertions, of course, from our comfortable chairs within academe, but we would make the point that indigenous voices must be encouraged and active listening on behalf of white educators and policy makers become the norm. Both voicing and listening are central to moving this "must" beyond mere aspiration. One of our major criticisms of the postcolonial stance in respect to indigenous schooling in Australia is that it is aspirational in tone, and as such, seems to lack suggestions for pragmatic ways forward, beyond a discursive politics. And while we have raised issues to do with the acceptance of indigenous ideas from leaders such as Pearson and Sarra, it must be kept in mind that their voices currently are and indeed should be heard as powerful contributions to these debates. Nonetheless, their voices need to be read and understood cautiously within broader debates that circulate in indigenous education. Following Bhabha (1994, 45), we would see their voices (as with our own, of course) from a postcolonial perspective, as hybrid forms, marked to varying degrees by the colonial present, and as such, they can be cautiously heard as representing neither "the noisy command of colonialist authority" nor "the silent repression of native traditions." Their approaches can be seen as attempts at decolonization through schooling; decolonization seems better placed to describe the political and educational activism of Pearson and Sarra than the aspirations of postcolonialism, which perhaps offers more to our theoretical understandings of the colonial present. Nonetheless, as Rizvi

(2007, 257) argues, "postcolonial theories can perform a valuable role, not least because they draw attention to the false universalism of globalization and show how contemporary social, political, economic and cultural practices continue to be located within the processes of cultural domination through the imposition of imperial structures of power."

At the forefront of our approach has been the implicit effort to move beyond deficit and compensatory strategies by working across the terrain of global north and global south epistemologies and ontologies. It is our strongly held belief that to effectively meet the educational needs of localized indigenous communities, it is essential that local epistemologies and ontologies are taken up robustly in the culture and practices of schooling relevant to that particular setting. Furthermore, it is our contention that offering theoretical strategies alone is inadequate for the task; approaches to decolonization, and indeed, indigenous knowledges, remind us that there must be meaningful and purposeful action in moving toward meeting the educational needs and aspirations of these people and communities. In Raymond Williams's (1983, 240) felicitous words, our strategies need to be about making hope practical rather than making despair convincing.

In investigating such working across knowledge terrains and bringing these terrains closer together, interesting creative and productive lines of flight for meeting the needs and aspirations of indigenous students in education might open up. Such lines of flight would offer policy, curricula, and pedagogical possibilities that not only would differ across the divergent and multifarious indigenous communities across the nation, but they would also lend confidence to indigenous peoples and communities within those educational settings. There is a multiplicity of indigenous local communities within Australia that demand specific and localized responses in schooling. These responses need to be positioned within a policy frame that might work as an assemblage, allowing for different localized re-articulations of the policy assemblage, rather than as a universal framework to be applied with fidelity in all contexts. The imperatives of current closing-the-gap policy in Australian schooling, while well intentioned, deny such difference. This policy works instead with a politics of the same, and it also inadvertently facilitates amnesia toward the continuing effects of colonization and their manifestation in structural inequalities in indigenous communities in the colonial present.

Notes

1. We would like to thank Dr. Sam Sellar, Postdoctoral Fellow in the School of Education at the University of Queensland, for his helpful comments on this chapter and for his assistance in finalizing the references.
2. The 2010 Prime Minister's Report asserts that: "Without a sound evidence base it was impossible to understand what was and what was not working well; and impossible to track our progress, in closing the gap on Indigenous disadvantage."
3. Consisting of the prime minister, state premiers and territory chief ministers, and a representative of local government.

References

Ah Sam, M., and C. Ackland. (2005). "The Curriculum: A Doorway to Learning." In *Introductory Indigenous Studies in Education: The Importance of Knowing*, edited by Jean Phillips and Jo Lampert. Sydney: Pearson Education Australia.

Altman, Jon, and William Fogarty. (2010). "Indigenous Australians as 'No Gaps' Subjects: Education and Development in Remote Australia." In *Closing the Gap in Education?: Improving Outcomes in Southern World Societies*, edited by Ilana Snyder and John Niewenhuysen, 109–128. Clayton, Victoria, Australia: Monash University Publishing.

Appadurai, Arjun. (2001). "Grassroots Globalization and the Research Imagination." In *Globalization*, edited by Arjun Appadurai. Durham, NC: Duke University Press.

Beresford, Quentin. (2003). "The Context of Aboriginal Education." In *(Reform and Resistance in Aboriginal Education: The Australian Experience*, edited by Quentin Beresford and Gary Partington. Perth: University of Western Australia Press., 10–68.

Bhabha, Homi. (1994). *The Location of Culture*. New York: Routledge.

Connell, R. W. (2008). *Southern Theory: The Global Dynamics of Knowledge in Social Science*. Cambridge: Polity Press.

Dewey, John. *The School and Society*. Chicago: Chicago University Press, 1990.

Engelmann, S. (1980). *Direct Instruction*. New Jersey: Educational Technology Publications.

Engelmann, S. (1983, 2007). "Theory of Instruction." *Performance and Instruction Journal* 22 (2): 13–16.

Engelmann, S., and D. Carnine. (1982). *Theory of Instruction: Principles and Applications*. Eugene: ADI Press.

Fraser, N. (1997). *Justice Interruptus*. New York: Routledge.

Gillborn, David. (2008). *Racism and Education: Coincidence or conspiracy?* London: Routledge.

Gillborn, David. (2010). "The Colour of Numbers: Surveys, Statistics and Deficit-Thinking about Race and Class." *Journal of Education Policy* 25 (2): 253–276.

Giroux, H., and M. Schmidt. (2004). "Closing the Achievement Gap: A Metaphor for Children Left Behind." *Journal of Educational Change* 5:213–228.
Gray, J., and Q. Beresford. (2008). "A 'Formidable Challenge': Australia's Quest for Equity in Indigenous Education." *Australian Journal of Education* 52 (2): 197–223.
Gregory, D. (2004). *The Colonial Present*. Oxford: Blackwell.
Hattie, J. (2009). *Visible Learning*. London: Routledge.
Klenowski, V. (2009). "Australian Indigenous Students: Addressing Equity Issues in Assessment." *Teaching Education* 20 (1): pp. 77–93.
Ladson-Billings, G. (2006). "From the Achievement Gap to the Education Debt: Understanding Achievement in U.S. Schools." *Education Researcher* 35 (7): 3–12.
Lingard, B. (2010). "Policy as Numbers: Ac/counting for Educational Research." Radford Memorial Lecture, Australian Association for Research in Education (AARE) Annual Conference, November, University of Melbourne.
Lingard, B., and P. Douglas. (1999). *Men Engaging Feminisms*. Buckingham: Open University Press.
Lingard, B., S. Creagh, and G. Vass. (2011). "Education Policy as Numbers: Data Categories and Two Australian Cases of Misrecognition." *Journal of Education Policy*, 24 (2): 149–162.
Luke, A. (2009) Introduction: on Indigenous Education. *Teaching and Learning*, 20, (1): 1–5.
Luke, A., M. Nakata, M. Garbutcheon Singh, and R. Smith. (1993). "Policy and the Politics of Representation: Torres Strait Islanders and Aborigines at the Margins." In *Schooling Reform in Hard Times*, edited by B. Lingard, J. Knight, and P. Porter. London: Falmer Press.
Malin, M., and D. Maidment. (2003). "Education, Indigenous Survival and Well-Being: Emerging Ideas and Programs." *Australian Journal of Indigenous Education* 23: 85–99.
Mellor, S., and M. Corrigan. (2004). *The Case for Change: A Review of Contemporary Research on Indigenous Education Outcomes*. Melbourne: Australian Council for Educational Research.
Pearson, N. (2011). "Education Guru Teaching to the Converted." *The Australian* (30, April): doi: http://www.theaustralian.com.au/national-affairs/opinion/education-guru-teaching-to-the-converted/story-e6frgd0x-1226047199220
Pearson, N. (2009). "Radical Hope Education and Equality in Australia." *Quarterly Essay* 35: 1–105.
Power, S., and Frandji, D. (2010). "Education Markets, the New Politics of Recognition, and the Increasing Fatalism Towards Inequality." *Journal of Education Policy* 25 (3): 385–396.
Rizvi, F. (2007). "Postcolonialism and Globalization in Education." *Cultural Studies <—> Critical Methodologies* 7 (3): 256–263.
Rizvi, F., and B. Lingard. (2010). *Globalizing Education Policy*. London, Routledge.
Rose, N. (1999). *Powers of Freedom*. Cambridge: Cambridge University Press.
Said, E. (2000). *Reflexions on Exile and Other Essays*. Cambridge, MA: Harvard University Press.

Sarra, C. (2012a). "Reflections of an Aboriginal School Principal on Leading Change in an Aboriginal School." In *Changing Schools: Alternative Ways to Make a World of Difference*, edited by T. Wrigley, P. Thomson, and B. Lingard. London: Routledge.

Sarra, C. (2012b). *Strong and Smart – Towards a Pedagogy for Emancipation: Education for First Peoples*. London: Routledge.

Spivak, G. (1990). "The Post-Modern Condition: The End of Politics?" In *The Postcolonial Critic: Interviews, Strategies, Dialogues*, edited by S. Harasym, 17–34. London, Routledge.

Spivak, G., D. Landry, and G. M. Maclean, ed. (1996). *The Spivak Reader*. New York: Routledge.

Swadener, B. and Mutua, K. (2008). "Decolonizing Performances: Deconstructing the Global Postcolonial." In *Handbook of Critical and Indigenous Methodologie*, edited by N. Denzin, Y. Lincoln, and L. Smith, 31–43. Thousand Oaks, CA: Sage.

Tuhiwai Smith, L. (1999). *Decolonizing Methodologies: Research and Indigenous Peoples*, London: Zed Books.

Williams, R. (1983). *Towards 2000*. Harmondsworth, UK: Penguin.

Young, R. (2003). *Postcolonialism: A Very Short Introduction*, Oxford, Oxford University Press.

7

Border Crossing: Conversations About Race, Identity, and Agency in South Africa[1]

Dennis Francis

Introduction

This chapter draws on the insights of research on nine Indian-white biracial youths to consider how they interpret their social reality. Life-history research was used to discover the complexities that make up the participants' everyday lives and to understand what they believe about themselves. The key findings reveal that the participants' struggles with identity indicate the complexity of identity, but those struggles are not always related to race. The participants' descriptions of their identity formation reveal an ongoing dialectical process that involved the making of choices among various social identities as they moved from one circumstance to another. Drawing on different postcolonial perspectives, my chapter contributes to the cultural confidence of biracial people living in South Africa who have endured years of apartheid legislation, racial oppression, and marginalization. Most importantly, my findings are likely to trouble theorists on marginality because I argue that labelling groups of individuals as marginal provides those groups with a coherent identity from which resistant counter-identities may be formulated.

It was my son Cameron's seventh birthday, and we had invited ten of his friends to enjoy his favorite pancake meal at home. Later, as parents of the seven-year-old guests arrived to fetch their children, one of them mentioned to Emma, my partner, and me that her son had asked her "what was Cameron?" When she saw that Emma and I seemed confused by the question, she framed it differently and continued that she did not know whether to answer "Indian-white," "mixed-race person," or "colored." All the descriptors she offered were linked to race and none made reference to other social identities, such as Christian, Hindu, boy, South African, or simply a seven-year-old, who loves pancakes. The racial references may have been triggered by the fact that Emma is white and I am Indian. When Emma asked the woman if it mattered what racial descriptor was used for Cameron, she gingerly alerted us to the possible identity confusion and pain that children of interracial unions experience. I do not believe that this woman is alone in making these assumptions, as these have informed much of the literature on biracial identity. Funderburg (Funderburg 1994, 10) writes "(F)or as long as blacks and whites have chosen to settle down and marry, they have been confronted with the question: But what about the children?"

The implication is that the racial divide between white and black is vast and unbridgeable and, therefore, that mixed children, because of their ambiguous social position, will automatically have identity problems (see Funderburg 1994; Kahn and Denmon 1997; Wilson 1987). There are at least two possible implied positions in this view—the one is that their biological status of "race mix" leads to problems, and the other is that society will make it problematic for the child, as the parent of the seven-year-old inadvertently implied. In various ways, many assumptions are made about biracial individuals without any reference to what they themselves think, feel, and experience, and one could rightfully interrogate the quality of research on which they were based. I believe that this is where my exploratory study adds to the small body of South African literature on this topic. At the heart of my study is an exploration of how a select group of nine Indian-white biracial young adults interpret their social reality, especially with regard to their understanding and experience of racial identity.

Talk About Race

Most South Africans describe their race in terms of the fixed racial categories that were legislatively assigned in the apartheid era, namely, African, Indian, white, and colored (see Posel 2001; Singh 1997; Zegeye 2001). These racialized identities are deeply embedded in the South African social structure and remain part of the nomenclature of the post-apartheid system (Posel 2001). I understand that to talk about race and racial categories, such as mixed race, interracial, biracial, and mixed descent, is to use terms and habits of thought inherited from the very race science that was used to justify oppression and marginalization (Erasmus 2001). It is always difficult to talk about what is essentially a flawed and problematic social construct without using language that is itself problematic (Tatum 1997). In this article, I view and use race as a social construct and not as an indicator of absolute, pure strains of genetic material or physical characteristics. Also, while I will make reference to racial categories such as Indian and white that should not lend legitimacy or credibility to the many popular cultural stereotypes and caricatures that accompany these descriptors. By using the categories, it allows me an opportunity to engage a select group of young adults to establish how they make sense of and communicate about the existence of the idea of race and racial identity, noting and reflecting on the possibility that my use of the terms, and the ways of thinking that accompany them, may influence my research methodology and analysis (see Francis 2006).

The term *biracial* is used in the United States to refer to people who have parents from two socially defined races. In South Africa, Blankenberg (2000), Morral (1994), Ledderboge (1996), and Maré (2005) have used *biracial* to refer to children of interracial unions. The term *biracial*, however, is perplexing because it implies that an individual has two halves, in this particular case, one Indian and one white. I am not suggesting that an individual can be divided into halves or can fall "in the middle" between two identities. Nor am I suggesting that there are black and white races and that there is a space between these called biracial. Biracial is a category of race, just as colored, African, Chinese, and Indian are constructed. Given the myriad possible combinations of different racial groups, the biracial category is indeed diverse and can comprise Indian African, white African, Chinese Indian, and so on, and thus differ significantly in terms of appearance, cultural practices, and life experiences (Wijeyesinghe 1992). South African research on interracial relationships (Morral 1994; Ratele 2002; Ratele 2002) and transracial adoptions (Ledderborge 1996; Miller 1999) have explored, albeit indirectly, the notion of biracialism. Morral (1994), Ledderboge (1996), Miller (1999) and Ratele (2002), based on participant responses in their research studies, reported that there is a perception that children of interracial unions will be born into a racial netherworld of marginal situation.

The Literature

The term *marginal* has become a convenient shorthand to describe any person "who does not fit into the mainstream mould and who, for whatever reason, straddles two or more confliction social identities"

(Wilson 1987, 37). Marginality theorists, Park (1950) and Stonequist (1937), suggest that individuals who were caught between two conflicting social groups were particularly prone to feelings of social unease, divided loyalty, and psychological distress. Park (1950, 370), for example, suggested that people of mixed-race origin could not claim full membership to either the black or white race and, thus, were "divided selves." This was said to intensify "self-consciousness, restlessness and [...] psychological malaise" which was internalized and experienced as an identity crisis. Thus says Park (1937, 881) charitably, while the marginal man (*sic*) lives a "fate, which condemns him to live, at the same time, in two worlds," his situation need not be entirely negative. He can have insight into the workings of two social groups, which he could use to his advantage if he can "look with a certain degree of critical detachment."

Unlike Park, Stonequist (1937, 8) described the marginal person as "poised in psychological uncertainty between two or more social worlds; reflecting in his soul the discords and harmonies, repulsions and attractions of the worlds." He writes of the "racial hybrid" as the "most obvious" type of marginal man, who "will be ambivalent in attitudes and sentiments, have divided loyalty, be irrational, moody, and temperamental" (Stonequist 1937, 201). Stonequist even suggests a three-part life cycle in marginality. In the first part, childhood, the person of mixed-race origin is unaware of his marginal situation. In the second part, proceeding to adolescence, the marginal man experiences a crisis of rejection as he becomes aware of his mixed race and marginal identity, because he does not belong to the white group. In the third part, adulthood, he attains some sense of "adjustment" by assimilating himself into the "dominant" society where he can pass as white. Alternatively, he will become absorbed into the black group, where he will have overcome negative feelings toward black people. Stonequist (1937, 138) concluded that mixed-race individuals who choose to remain marginal by resisting assimilation into either group would experience despair.

Dickie-Clark (1966), a South African sociologist, challenged Park and Stonequist's view of marginality by suggesting that they had confused the concept of marginality by failing to make a clear distinction between marginal situation, marginal person, and marginal personality. Dickie-Clark (1966, 10) argued that the mere fact of being in a marginal situation does not lead to a marginal personality. While Stonequist (1937) assumed that having the characteristics of more than one group meant that one was both in a marginal situation and had a marginal personality, Dickie-Clark (1966, 10) argued that it was possible to be in a marginal situation, and to negotiate the attitudes one encountered accordingly, without necessarily being deeply affected in one's personality.

In discussing the theories of Park (1937 and 1950), Stonequist (1937), and Dickie-Clark (1966), one could argue that their works are over 40 years in the past, and, therefore, their theories would be irrelevant to understanding how a group of biracial young adults experience identity in 2011. I can understand this trope. However, I have argued that a number of assumptions are still made about biracial individuals, many of which reflect the theories posited by Park and Stonequist. It is on this basis that I draw on the theories of Park (1928 and 1950), Stonequist (1937), and Dickie-Clark (1966), because I believe they still represent popular thinking, even if not informing such thinking, on whether it is the biological status of "race mix" that leads to problems, or whether it is society that makes it problematic for the individuals who describe themselves as being of mixed race.

More recent studies provide an alternative perspective that refutes Stonequist's (1937, 8–37) argument that mixed-race children have "identity problems" and "no sense of who they are or where they belong." For example, Wilson's (1987) study of a group of 51 Afro Caribbean white mixed-race children between the ages of six and nine in Britain reported that "mixed-race children do not necessarily conform to the stereotype of the social misfit, caught between the social worlds of Black and White." Wilson (1987, 199) concluded that it would be "outmoded" to suggest that the children would necessarily be "racked by malaise," "confused," or "psychologically maladjusted."

In another study designed to compare the social adjustment of biracial adolescents in the United States, Cauce et al. (1992) compared a group of black-white biracial adolescents with a monoracial control group. Cauce et al. (1992, 217–218) concluded that biracial adolescents did not differ from the comparison group on any qualitative aspects of family and peer relations (e.g., support trust, alienation) and that there were no significant differences between the groups in terms of life stress, behavior problems, psychological distress, or poorer competence, and sense of self-worth. Similarly, participants in Gibbs and Hines's (1992, 230–231) two-year study of twelve African American white adolescents and their families in California reported that they liked their "appearance, being different and unique and [...able] to fit in with all groups." They had difficulty, though, being "targets of racial slurs, being questioned about their appearance, their parents, and whether they were black or white [...but had] good relations with peers and classmates [...and had established] positive relationships with black, white and mixed race people" (Gibbs and Hines 1992, 232).

Tizard and Phoenix (1993, 65) explored the racial identities of 60 young people of mixed parentage. The participants regarded their mixed-race identity as an asset, to a degree that was not possible in the past. Tizard and Phoenix (1993) attribute this finding to changed societal attitudes to mixed marriages, the rise of black youth cultures, admiration from sectors of white youths, and the antiracist ethos in London schools. The researchers conclude that the "great majority of the sample did not experience the feelings of social isolation and rejection by both black and white groups" (Tizard and Phoenix 1993, 86).

Recent research takes the view that, on the whole, biracial children, adolescents, and young adults are not social misfits caught between the social worlds of black and white, nor are the obsessed or burdened with working out issues related to their racial identity. What such studies (see Wilson 1987; Cauce et al. 1992; Gibbs and Hines 1992; Tizard and Phoenix 1993) bring to the fore is that biracial individuals do not experience identity in terms of a progression of stages, nor do they report confusion or maladjustment as hypothesized by earlier theorists, such as Park (1950 and 1928) and Stonequist (1937). This does not mean that biracial individuals do not experience personal difficulties, rather that clinical studies (see J. T. Gibbs 1987; Kahn and Denmon 1997; Logan 1987) in this area generally report that individuals experiencing problems come for treatment not because they are biracial, but because of other related factors.

The Present Study

I used the life-history method of data collection in line with my view of social identity as a resource that people draw on in constructing personal narratives, which provide meaning and a sense of continuity to their lives. I chose to adopt the short life-story approach (Plummer 2001) as it requires less time than long life stories, tends to be more focused, and allows for a series of autobiographical presentations. I assumed that, by asking the participants to tell me stories of their lives, I would have gained access to how biracial young adults interpret their social world and what they believe about themselves. I began my article with a story from my life, to allow you, the reader, to gain access to my social world. From a quick glimpse, you would have read that I have self-identified as an Indian heterosexual father. From reading between the lines you may have also gathered that I am possibly Hindu or Christian, and a South African. It is against this background that I approached nine Indian-white young adults, ages 18 to 21, to tell me stories of how they interpret their social reality, especially with regard to their experience of identity. I asked the participants to tell me their life histories in three-in-depth interviews. Each interview lasted approximately 90 minutes. An interview guide was used to prompt respondents. The interviews were audio taped, and written transcripts were prepared of each interview. I conducted all the interviews. Other issues discussed during the interviews, not reported in this chapter, included what racial identities Indian-white biracial young adults chose to identify with, how their racial identities were constructed and experienced, and what the factors were that influenced their choice of racial identities (see Francis 2005).

I used the following criteria in selecting the participants. First, participants had to have biological membership in a family where one parent was identified as Indian and the other parent was identified as white. The South African Population Registration Act, Act 30 of 1950, imposed a specific racial grouping and, therefore, a formal identity on an individual, effectively shaping the individual's life story through this classification (Reddy 2001, 74). As the Population Registration Act was repealed only in 1991, parents of the 18- to 21-year-old biracial participants would have been racially classified, as this formed the basis of the National Party's policy of separate development. Secondly, participants were young adults. I have specifically chosen participants who were between 18 and 21 years of age because, as a researcher, I assumed that I would be able to gather sufficient life experiences from this age group as compared to using a younger adolescent sample. These ages (18 to 21) are also a critical period for the selected participants, as they would have just emerged from the norms of the school systems and now would be full of plans and choices for mapping out their futures. Interracial families and biracial young adults were identified through schools, universities, and religious, sporting, and social service organizations in the Ethekweni Metro area. In no way can the nine participants been seen as representative of Indian-white biracial young adults living in the region. Out of the 12 identified as Indian-white biracial young adults between the ages of 18 and 21, only nine were willing and able to participate. Table 7.1 reflects some characteristics of the final sample.

All nine participants received a clear explanation of the tasks in which they would be expected to participate, enabling them to make an informed choice for voluntary participation. They were also informed about the parameters of confidentiality of the information

Table 7.1 Summary of participants' identity

	Name	Gender	Age	Class*	Race# of Mother	Race# of Father
1	Kerry	female	18	working	white	white
2	Ishmael	male	21	upper middle	white	Indian
3	Natalie	female	21	upper middle	white	Indian
4	Dayallan	male	21	working	Indian	Indian
5	Mayuri	female	19	upper middle	Indian	white
6	Daniel	male	21	upper middle	Indian	white
7	Prashantha	female	20	middle	Indian	white
8	Marlon	male	20	working	Indian	white
9	Nicole	female	20	working	Indian	white

*Named by participant
#Named by Population Registration Act

they supplied and their anonymity. The names of all participants, and references to places and people, have been changed for the purpose of confidentiality. The study was approved by the ethics committee at the College of Humanities, University of KwaZulu-Natal. In analyzing the life histories, the purpose was to expand, refine, develop, and illuminate a theoretical understanding of how nine Indian-white biracial young adults interpret their social reality. The analysis involved a cross-case analysis for the purpose of theorizing from experiences drawn from the in-depth interviews, theoretical framework, and literature.

More Than Just a Race

Like Wijeyesinghe's (1992) study on race, for the nine Indian-white biracial young adults in my study, was not the sole or even the most important consideration in the construction of their identities, even though they had to confront such demands all the time as a contextual given. Race was simply an aspect of a much more complex and multidimensional whole that was made up of gender, class, religious, age, and sexual-orientation identities. For example, when the participants talk about religion as an important identity marker, what they are saying is that religion is different from the role played by race and, therefore, largely independent of it. Ishmael, Natalie, Prashantha, and Mayuri spoke of religion and faith as being important, if not more important, in their lives than other aspects of their identity. For example, Ishmael stated explicitly:

> On reflection I felt that [my identity as] being a Muslim has been more prominent than any other aspect of my identity. You see I define myself as a Muslim.

For Ishmael, *"Islam is a way of life,"* and he shared a number of experiences, which were centred on his Muslim identity. In similar ways, Mayuri mentioned how religion, and not race, was often a cause of tension between her boyfriend and herself, and claimed, *"I never realized that Catholicism would be so important to me but it is."* For Natalie, religion takes on a different meaning as it is seen as a source of conflict within her home. She argues that it was not her *"parents' race that has bothered [her] as much as it's their religious differences."* In her life history, she clarifies the distinction between race and religion by stating that her parents' arguments were centred on the latter. For Natalie, religion is not viewed as an essentialist version of what race is, in that it often (in the local context) encompasses religion. Of course, this is not true for all the participants. Nicole and Mayuri, who were socialized as Christians, shared their experiences of how they interpreted and participated in the Hindu prayers and rituals when they visited their *"Indian relatives."* Mayuri tells:

> I did not know what to do, but my Indian cousins used to show me how to hold the lamp and what the different prayers were for. Sometimes I would hold the lamp with my cousins and turn it around. I remember that while I would do the [Hindu] rituals, I would pray to Jesus, the Christian God.

While the participants do racialize identity in a particular way, it is not crudely done, by linking religion to race in an essentialised way. The participants' stories reveal a grappling with different aspects of their identity, such as religion, age, class, and gender that would contribute to a sense of complexity and are not directly linked to race. Their stories indicate clearly that the participant see themselves as more than just racial beings.

Life Cycle in Marginality

Earlier in this article, I included Stonequist's (1937, 137) discussion on marginality where he argues that the most difficult time for the biracial individual occurs between adolescence and adulthood when they would endure a "crisis stage." All nine participants in my study are between the ages of 18 and 21 and, according to Stonequist (1937, 137–8), should be experiencing the "feeling of confusion," "guilt and alienation," and "self-hatred as a result of being of mixed race." However, there is a disparity between the life histories of the nine participants and the time-specific stage theories posited by Stonequist. All nine participants spoke about their current experiences and challenges but did not describe "feelings of confusion," "guilt and alienation," and "self-hatred" as a consequence of being of mixed race. The participants in my study described their identity formation as an ongoing dialectical process that involved the making of choices among various social identities as they moved from one circumstance to another. All nine participants spoke about current challenges and issues that were far more significant in their lives than grappling with "having to choose one racial identity that is not fully expressive of one's background" (Stonequist 1937, 138). Marlon, for example, spoke about his newly acquired identity as a husband and father and narrated his current dilemmas:

> *I feel like I have failed as a man, you know; I mean the man has to look after his family and to be the breadwinner and all.*

For him, class identity is part of his interaction with the world around him and is something he is always aware of wherever he goes. In the same way, the other eight participants spoke about current challenges:

> Natalie: *According to my father, that's the ideal of what a woman should be: " learn how to cook, go do the dancing… You remain submissive." That's his belief. He says to me, "Natalie, it's a man's world"*'
>
> Nicole: *She [mother] would argue that "A boy can do this and that because he can protect himself," and I'm thinking, to myself, "Girls can do the same." She and I always argue until we are blue in the face.*
>
> Daniel: *I mean, I'm heterosexual, and I also happen to be a man. But being heterosexual doesn't make me more "manly" than a man who is homosexual.*
>
> Natalie: *He was a suitable date only because my parents saw him as a Gujarati boy from a similar wealthy class to us. When boys had these two characteristics they were considered good prospects, but if they were different, my parents had a whole lot of problems.*

> Mayuri: *I wanted to be a chef. They [parents] said, "You are not allowed to do that. It's not a proper job. There's no degree."*

The diverse, complex, and inconsistent ways in which the nine participants made sense of their identity, challenges the usefulness of models, such as those proposed by Stonequist (1937), that view the racial-identity development of biracial individuals as taking place through a progression of stages. In attempting to squash rich and diverse experiences into stage-development models, such as the one proposed by Stonequist, much of the meaning that an individual makes of his or her life and sense of identity is diminished. Such approaches to identity overlook other social identities and experiences that may have played a more prominent role in identity construction.

"Marginal Man" and Racism

Park (1928) and Stonequist's (1937, 138) argument that the marginal man will experience "feelings of isolation or of not quite belonging" did hold in some instance for the nine participants. It holds in the sense that all nine participants did experience racism similar to the findings reported by Wilson (1987), Cauce et al. (1992), Gibbs and Hines (1992), and Tizard and Phoenix (1993). What emerges in the nine participants' life histories is that they have learned positive ways of understanding racial difference and developed creative ways of dealing with racism (Francis 2007). For example, Dayalan recalls coming home from school upset because the other children told him he was not Indian and his grandfather making him feel better:

> *He said that we are all one race. And that God made all people in this world and whether you were white or brown or black it did not matter. All that mattered was what color your heart was.*

This helped Dayallan see the good in people, beyond the color of their skin, and not to allow racist remarks to deter him. This helped him through high school to deal with other racist name-calling. Another participant, Ishmael, used his unique family situation to get his classmates to talk about race. He chose "What it is like to be part of a multicultural family" as the topic for his class oral presentation. The discussions after Ishmael had finished helped him dispel the myths that some of his classmates harbored about biracial children and interracial families.

Most of the participants mentioned their irritation at continuously having to answer the question, "What are you?" Mayuri found that by challenging people about the question and asking them to clarify it, it became more obvious that fitting into a racial category was not the only defining point to a person. A certain amount of humor was also present when the participants described people's frustrations and efforts to classify them. Perhaps the following examples make explicit that marginality was less of an issue for the participants than it was for those who were attempting to classify them. For example, Prashantha mentioned how much amusement she found in confusing people by answering, *"I'm half Scottish and half Tamil."* Nicole also found humor a good way of dealing with her classmates' continuous need to know her race:

> *At school everyone's asking us, "What are you?" It's like every time you say, "No my mother's Indian and my father's white." And they say, "You can't be white." And I would say, "No really, we are tanned whites...the sun tanned me. I am a really tanned white person." I think most were convinced. I even remember some of them saying, "I wish I was as tanned as you...it's so unfair that you tan so easily." And I would say, "Oh, it's just natural."*

The participants do not see their social world as "problematic" or "disorganized" but see their situation as a creative challenge and positive resource.

Beyond Marginal

All of the nine participants in my study have constructed their personal narratives as being stories of minor success and saw advantages in their situation (Francis 2007). Kerry's situation was one that could be envied by others. She felt that being half-Indian, half-white gave her a kind of unique attractiveness that other girls did not have:

> *I remember once in Standard 7, when we had an "Eastern extravaganza," I wore a punjabi and everything and ended up being the first princess. The Indian girls looked at me and talked to each other, because I looked so good in the outfit I was wearing. I think they were jealous.*

Natalie also stated that she thought she was beautiful and that this put her at an advantage over both boys, because they wanted to go out with her, and girls, because they wanted to look like her. She also sees her looks as positive because no one can define her or put her in a box. She recalled a situation in which she was sitting in a café with her friends and a woman came up to her and told her that she *"looked like the UN."* She saw this as a compliment and as giving her freedom from having to fit into a racial category.

Park (1928) argued that the biracial individual had the advantage of allowing the individual an insight into the workings of two social groups, which provided a "wider horizon" for them (Park 1928, 881). When looking at the following comments made by the participants, the latter seems to be true. Daniel, Prashantha, Kerry, and Natalie found that being part of two different groups helped them understand both points of view. This was often used as a mediating point or in bridging the gap between the racial groups at school and freed them in a way that the other children could not experience. Mayuri remembers an incident in which her white friends did not want to attend an Indian girl's party because she lived in an Indian township, which they perceived as *"dangerous."* She managed to challenge these stereotypes and could make them see the situation from a different angle, which resulted in their attending the party together.

For Daniel, being half-Indian, half-white proved advantageous, especially when it came to finding a date for his school dance. He told his classmates, "I've *got a passport to do whatever I want—I could go white, I could go Indian—it's a privilege"*. Being biracial also allowed him access to two worlds, something that he described as *"like a pendulum, you can swing between the two extremes."* This placed the participants in a position where they had access to not just the Indian and the white groups, but a number of different racial groups. For example, Daniel and Prashantha both described how at breaks they could move between the different groups. The point here is that such wider social acceptance is important to teenagers, with the general insecurities that often accompany this age. Daniel explains:

> I remember how at break times, we used to have almost like a "group areas act" happening, because there would be an area where all the Indians would sit, an area for the African group, and then there would be an area where the white group would sit. I could mix between them.

This he also saw as having a positive effect on his fellow students, as he says, *"Maybe it was good that people could see me moving around and realize that you didn't have to stick to any particular race group."* David and Prashantha's narratives highlight how they have been able to use their unique situation as change agents in their desegregated schools in a post-apartheid South Africa.

It could be argued that to compare the participants' positive responses to the negative theories regarding "the marginal man" may be unhelpful. It is true that some of the participants did speak of a certain amount of confusion (Francis 2007, 267). However, these in no way overshadowed their generally positive outlook about their identities. The confusion the participants spoke of only operated at a superficial level when their identity was problematized by external sources, such as when classmates and officials attempted to lock them into rigid racial identities, such as by asking *"What are you?"* It should be noted, however, that the issue of the participants' grappling with their identity negotiation is not uncommon for any individual of their age, and not just in relation to "race." As Steyn (2001, xxi–xxii) argues, all population groups in South Africa, whether willingly or unwillingly, successfully or unsuccessfully, are engaged in the renegotiation of their identities.

What the participants' stories bring into focus is that the participants see their biracial identity as something positive and not as something that burdens them (Francis 2007, 267). Perhaps a connection can here be made to McNay's (1994, 25) point that the labeling of certain groups of individuals as marginal provides those groups with a coherent identity from which resistant counter-identities may be formulated, for instance, the idea of "queer" politics. As Nicole shows:

> I have half of each race in me. I am happy with that mix: I am blessed with the better of two beautiful worlds. I am not cursed, I am blessed…I would not have had my situation any different.

Conclusion

In giving an account of their identities, the nine biracial young adults in my study described their life worlds as the sum of many parts, a sum that included but was not limited to their racial identity. Their descriptions of their identity formation suggest an ongoing dialectical process that involved the making of choices among various social identities as they moved from one context to another. All nine participants spoke about current challenges and issues that were far more significant in their lives than grappling with having to choose one racial identity that is not fully expressive of one's background. Despite all the assumptions that biracial individuals will be born into a racial netherworld, destined to be confused, unstable, maladjusted, and perpetual victims of a racially polarized society, the participants' stories in my study reveal that they see their biracial identity as something positive and not as something that burdens them.

Note

1. An earlier version of this chapter appeared in *Acta Academica* (2008), 40(3), 33–51.

References

Blankenberg, N. (2000). "That Rare and Random Tribe: Albino Identity in South Africa." *Critical Arts* 14 (2): 6–48.
Cauce, A. M., Y. Hiraga, C. Mason, T. Aguilar, N. Ordonez, N., and N. Gonzales. (1992). *Between a Rock and a Hard Place: Social Adjustment of Biracial Youth*. Thousands Oaks: Sage Publications.
Dickie-Clark, H. F. (1966). *The Marginal Situation: A Sociological Study of a Coloured Group*. London: Routledge.
Dickie-Clark, H. F. (1966). *The Marginal Situation: A Sociological Study of a Coloured Group*. Atlantic Highlands, NJ: Humanitites Press. (University of Kwa-Natal, Durban.)
Erasmus, Z. (2001). *Coloured by History Shaped by Place: New Perspectives on Coloured Identities in Cape Town*. Cape Town: Kwela Books.
Francis, D. (2005). *Between Race; Beyond Race: The Experience of Self-Identification of Indian White Biracial Young Adults and the Factors Affecting Their Choices of Identity*. University of KwaZulu-Natal, Durban.
Francis, D. (2006). "Between Race; Beyond Race: the Experience of Self-Identification of Indian-White Biracial Young Adults and the Factors Affecting Their Choice of Identity." *Psychology in Society* 34: 1–16.
Francis, D. (2007). "Researching Children of Mixed Race; Exploring Implications for Transracial Adoptions." *Journal of Social Work* 43 (3): 261–271.
Funderburg, L. (1994). *Black, White, Other: Biracial Americans Talk about Race and Identity*. New York: William Morrow.
Gibbs, J. T. (1987). "Identity and Marginality: Issues in the Treatment of Biracial Adoloescents." *American Journal of Orthopsychiatry* 57 (2): 265–278.
Gibbs, J. T., and A. M. Hines. (1992). *Negotiating Ethnic Identity: Issues for Black-White Biracial Adolescents, in Root M P P*. Thousand Oaks: Sage Publications.
Kahn, S., and J. Denmon. (1997). "An Examination of Social Science Literature Pertaining to Multiracial Identity: A Historical Perspective." *Journal of Multicultural Social Work*, 6 (1/2), 117–138.
Ledderborge, U. (1996). *Transracial Placements of Children in the Durban Metropolitan Area*. Durban: The Department of Social Work, University

of Kwa-Natal, South Africa. Logan, S., E. Freeman, and R. McRoy. (1987). "Racial Identity Problems of Biracial Clients: Implications for Social Workers Practice." *Journal of Intergroup Relations*, 15 (11–24).

Mare, G. (2005). "Mixing Blood: What Does 'Biracialism' Do to the Notion of 'Race'?" *Psychology in Society* 31: 99–105.

McNay, L. (1994). *Foucault—A Critical Introduction*. Cambridge: Polity Press.

Miller, E. (1999). *What Perceptions of Cross-Racial Adoption Reveal of Race, Culture and Identity: A Qualitative Study of Young White South Africans*. Durban: University of Kwa-Natal, South Africa.

Morral, L. (1994). *Interracial Families in South Africa: An Exploratory Study*. Rand Afrikaans University, Johannesburg.

Park, R. E. (1937). Introductionto *The Marginal Man: A Study in Personality and Culture Conflict*, edited by E. V. Stonequist. New York: Russell and Russell.

Park, R. E. (1950). *Race and Culture*. London: Collier-Macmillan.

Plummer, K. (2001). *Documents of Life 2*. London: Sage Publications.

Posel, D. (2001). "What's in a Name?: Racial Categorisation Under Apartheid and Their Afterlife." *Transformation* 47: 50–74.

Ratele, K. (Ed.). (2002). "Interpersonal Relations Around Race". In *Discourses on Differences, Discourses on Oppression*, edited by N. Duncan, P. Gqola, M. Hofmeyer, T. Shefer, F. Mulunga, and F. Mashige, 371–406. Cape Town: Centre for Advanced Studies of African Studies, South Africa.

Reddy, T. (2001). "The Politics of Naming: The Constitution of Coloured Subjects in South Africa." In *Coloured by History Shaped by Place: New Perspectives on Coloured Identities in Cape Town*, edited by Z. Erasmus. Cape Town: Kwela Books.

Singh, M. (1997). "Identity in the Making." *South African Journal of Philosophy*. 16 (3): 120–123.

Steyn, M. (2001). *Whiteness Just Isn't What It Used to Be: White Identity in a Changing South Africa*. Albany: State University of New York Press.

Stonequist, E. V. (1937). *The Marginal Man*. New York: Russel and Russel.

Tatum, B. D. (1997). *Why Are All the Black Kids Sitting in The Cafeteria?* New York: Basic Books.

Tizard, B., and Phoenix, A. (1993). *Black White or Mixed Race?* London: Routeledge.

Wijeyesinghe, C. (1992). *Towards an Understanding of The Racial Identity of Bi-Racial People*. Amherst: University of Massachusetts.

Wilson, A. (1987). *Mixed Race Children: A Study of Identity*. London: Allen and Unwin.

Zegeye, A. (Ed.). (2001). *After Apartheid: Social Identities in the New South Africa Volume One*. Cape Town: Kwela Books and South African History Online.

8
Constructing a Nation: The Role of Arts Education in South Africa

Lorraine Singh

Introduction

Can education contribute to the cultural confidence of peoples and communities who have endured centuries of oppression and marginalization? In this chapter, I argue that education in the arts can make a significant contribution to cultural confidence because it provides a potent platform for interrogating cultural difference. In doing so, it contributes to identity formation both on a personal and a national level. I quote from the relevant arts curricula and arts policy in South Africa to elucidate my argument.

If we accept the view of Fanon (1959, 1), who maintained that colonial domination disrupts the cultural life of a conquered people and that the colonized person is made to admit the inferiority of his/her culture, then South Africa, which suffered doubly under centuries of colonialism and apartheid, is in dire need of reconstruction and cultural reimaginings. In traditional African society, education and culture are linked in conception, theory and practice with learning and culturalization, which are seen as lifelong continuing practices and core to the formation of the individual and the collective (Mugo 1999, 213). Today, in all societies, it is accepted that no educational process can avoid imparting some culture, whether in language, customs, or morality (Scruton 1991). In a culturally diverse country, questions arise about the binding and acceptable aspects of culture that give rise to the sense of belonging, to the sense of national identity and pride that promote the cultural confidence introduced in this chapter's opening question.

Nation and Culture

What unity and coherence can we call on to provide for ourselves the conditions of existence to create a nation called South Africa? We have established within our borders a concept of "rainbow nationalism," which we already see as a patched-together, convenient compromise for work-a-day politics. Professor Njabulo Ndebele articulates why we are in this situation today:

> We have never had social cohesion in South Africa...what we definitely have had over the decades is a mobilising vision. Could it be that the mobilising vision, mistaken for social cohesion, is cracking under the weight of the reality and extent of social reconstruction, and that the legitimate framework for debating these frameworks is collapsing? (Ndebele 2006)

While Ndebele goes on to propose a political solution, the problem of social cohesion remains. Unless we feel truly comfortable in our South Africanness, every issue facing the country, whether party political, economic, or moral, threatens to split the country along racial, ethnic, and class lines. Cultural theorizing in South Africa, because of its history of segregation, has tended to focus on "the over-determination of the political, the inflation of resistance, and the fixation on race, or more particularly on racial supremacy and racial victimhood as a determinant of identity" (Nuttall and Michael 2000, 1). With democracy came the emphasis on reconciliation, on affirmation and inclusion; it seemed that preservation of what was familiar to people, what had been denigrated during apartheid, and what offered safety in the face of the unknown, became part of the prevailing discourse. Equality, redress, and access in cultural practices and the arts meant first assessing what was and what is, before stepping out into what could be. So the idea of the rainbow nation was enthusiastically adopted by the emerging nation.

The rainbow nation is supposed to encourage a single nonracial identity, made up at the same time of many different strands. Despite this nonracial description, the nonracial aspects of rainbow nationalism are difficult to see. The rainbow nation version of nation-building cannot be said to be transformative, because it leaves little room for regroupings (Fraser 1998). Identities can never be fixed; so our focus should be on identity formation and how we shape this, not on fixing identities, for ultimately, only color is fixed. This is why the concept of the rainbow nation, for all its convenience, is seen by many as so stultifying. A new identity that has more in keeping with a vision of a nonracialized society is not being re-imagined. Neither the rhetoric of the African renaissance nor the amelioration of the rainbow nation has really worked for us in the way we expected.

Fanon (1959) makes a strong case for the reestablishment of the nation in order to give life to national culture. He clarifies that national consciousness is not nationalism, and it is from the former that culture emerges. National liberation and the renaissance of the state are for him prerequisites for the creation of culture. Having achieved its liberation, South Africa faces the task of arriving at a national identity, a core of common values, interests, and practices. The African National Congress (ANC) government in South Africa has adopted a nation-building approach in nonethnic and nonracial terms (Zegeye 2001, 337), with the Bill of Rights protecting the cultural and other rights of groups of people. The policy is to encourage the development of national identity based on unity-in-diversity (Zegeye 2001, 340).

The Present Context

As Ntuli points out, even now in the "post colony we do not encounter singular pristine identities determined by a single organizing principle," but rather a number of contesting identities (Ntuli 1999, 186). Nuttall and Michael refer to the "complex configurations" of identity that the new nation has tried to mask by foregrounding an "oversimplified discourse of rainbow nationalism" (Nuttall and Michael 2000, 1). Recent events in South Africa suggest that the mask is slipping. In 2007, xenophobia exploded into ugly incidents of violence that shocked the nation. This violence was significant because it was directed not at white but specifically at African and Asian foreigners. This showed a strong biocultural bias and an ingrained acceptance of white authority. It would seem that many South Africans define themselves by what they are not—not Zimbabwean, not Somali, not Pakistani. Other daily incidents of racial, ethnic, and religious intolerance occur that indicate the birth pangs of the nation. The work of liberation is not yet done; there is still a culture of victimhood in South Africa, and we still have race as the primary signifier of identity. In 2010, the murder of a notorious right-wing Afrikaner

Eugène Terre'Blanche by black farmworkers and the singing of a freedom song "Kill the Boer," by Julius Malema, leader of the African National Congress Youth league, has inflamed the tensions and allowed extremists on both sides of the political divide to come to the fore, prompting President Zuma to call for calm. Moderates are calling for a return to the middle ground. But perhaps these openly racist events and people help us confront more honestly our own hidden racism. Is this, then, how the vision of the new South Africa, proudly inaugurated by Nelson Mandela in 1994, plays out?

Education and the Nation

In 1994, at the dawn of democracy in South Africa, leaders faced the mammoth task of bringing together a country fragmented, polarized, and unsettled. Questions of culture and identity were fraught with the tensions of the past, of racial domination and cultural hegemony. Homi Bhabha could have been describing South Africa when he wrote:

> We are confronted with a nation split within itself, articulating the heterogeneity of its population...internally marked by the discourses of minorities, the heterogeneous histories of contending peoples, antagonistic authorities and tense locations of cultural differences. (Bhabha 1994, 148)

What the democratic process had to do was try to deal with this nation "split within itself." In South Africa, the laws of apartheid enacted the minority culture as the dominant one and while the majority of the people were relegated to the periphery, their culture was regarded as the "other," an object of derision or exoticism. The opening question in this chapter is echoed by Peter Abbs (2003), who in his defense of ethical judgment and aesthetic discrimination in arts education, asked, "What should education serve, what should art serve, and what is culture for?" I would like to use these questions to argue for arts education in South Africa as a site for postcolonial cultural imaginings and negotiation. I maintain that education can and must contribute to cultural confidence and identity formation. Furthermore, I am convinced that education in the arts is particularly suited to this project. Theatre director, Richard Schechner, wrote, "Theatre is the art of actualising alternatives, if only temporarily, for fun" (Schechner and Schuman 1976, 4). This "what if" facility of being able to imagine and "perform" another ideal reality is one of the reasons that I believe that the arts lead the way in bringing about social change. My argument rests on the notion that education in the arts for the youth of South Africa provides the fulcrum for the transformation needed for national consciousness and identity formation—the cultural confidence that forms the central focus of this book.

Dolby's (2001) work on identity construction in a South African school suggests that global flows of popular culture have become critical in the discursive formation of identity among the youth. She argues that these appropriations and reinterpretations of global commodities provide a site for the constructions of post-apartheid identity (Dolby 2001) and can be viewed as constructions of the new ethnicities described by Hall (1989). These reinterpretations and reconstructions allow students to create a "third space" that opens up possibilities for challenging local issues of power and race. It is a space much larger than that of the rainbow nation. The notion of a third space as posited by Homi Bhabha (1991, 1994) refers to the construction of a cultural hybridity, which, at the moment of challenging a dominant culture, constitutes a third space that displaces the histories that set it up. This third space straddles two or more cultures and constructs a new hybrid identity within the conditions of oppression and inequity. When young people appropriate costume, language, and other cultural markers of a dominant group and mix and match these to suit their own style, sometimes in an ironic way, they are giving expression to a new identity formation.

The changes in the educational scenario in South Africa were prompted by a large-scale political upheaval in the dismantling of the apartheid state and the move to a constitutional democracy. Studies of curriculum change show that it is usually prompted by social and economic changes within political systems (Milburn, Goodson, and Clark 1993). One of the significant ways in which the new leadership, after the first democratic election, attempted to deal with the "split" nation was through a new approach to education and the institution of a system of values in education emanating from the aims of the constitution of the country. The principles underlying the new curriculum included social transformation and democracy. These principles were embedded into a national curriculum that was driven by a human-rights pedagogy that sought to promote social justice, equity, and redress (DOE 2001). Consequently, curriculum as a means to realize a vision, with the vision being social transformation, provides a clue to the questions posed by Abbs.

To illustrate my argument, I interrogate and analyze the nature of the Arts and Culture curriculum for schools (grades R to 9), which came into being in 1997, was revised in 2001, and had again come under review in 2010. Arts and culture had a particular symbolism for South Africa because it was through the cultural processes and the arts of the resistance movement during the liberation struggle that popular attention worldwide could be focussed on the atrocities of apartheid. The new-learning area (school subject) was called significantly, Arts *and* Culture, an emphasis that grew out of the period of political and cultural struggle. Perhaps it was prompted by a view similar to that of Fanon's that "a nation which is born of the people's concerted action which embodies the real aspirations of the people while changing the state cannot exist save in the expression of exceptionally rich forms of culture" (Fanon 1959, 7). The naming of the learning area then is particularly significant because it signals an intention to engage with cultural issues and, more importantly, to do this with young people. While I focus on arts education at school level, my assertions about the power of the arts in education applies equally to all levels.

In the apartheid era, the arts associated with the liberation struggle served many purposes: they gave hope and pleasure in a life that often had neither; they became the means around which to mobilize people; and they became the means of recording the histories of the struggle. The arts, considered by some to be mere entertainment, were seen to have a power to move people and challenge ideology. It was not surprising that resistance experiences became the driving force for arts in the new dispensation. The new learning area allowed for those art forms and cultural expressions that had long been suppressed to be revealed and celebrated. The colonized person was free to revel in and bring his or her culture to the foreground. Not only was this being done in a social and political arena, but now there was legitimation through inclusion in a formal school curriculum. The first version of the Arts and Culture curriculum stated:

> Despite these adverse conditions, indigenous arts and cultural practices have proved irrepressible. They must now be actively preserved, developed and promoted within the educational system and the broader society. (DOE 1997, AC–3)

This is an edifying example of how curricula originate, are reproduced, and respond to new prescriptions; socially constructed, passing from the domain of everyday life and societal knowledge into the more codified knowledge of the academic domain. What I intend to do here is highlight aspects of the Arts and Culture curriculum to show how it consciously sought to contribute to building cultural confidence and affirming difference. I quote in detail from the curricula to provide evidence to support my contention. I use narrative theory as a tool for analysis as I uncover the discourse of the arts curricula and education policies. The "voice" and focalization of each policy emerges in the direct quotations given and the theorizing around these.

An Arts and Culture Approach

Version I

The first Arts and Culture curriculum framework stated:

> The Learning Area seeks to mediate the acculturative process and affirm, honour, respect, acknowledge and salvage elements of indigenous culture which are constitutionally aligned and therefore worthy of preservation for posterity. Considering that cultural change is a worldwide process affecting all societies, comparisons between reconstructed indigenous and acculturated settings become centrally important and invite learners to ask basic questions about the future of humankind. (DOE 1997, AC6)

Culture is thus conceptualized as inclusive, giving voice to the dispossessed and marginalized, and narrating an imagined national identity. In seeking to "mediate the acculturative process," the curriculum acknowledges the dynamics of culture formation and raises questions of why and how cultures are shaped. The curriculum points out that South African society, up to this point, had been accustomed to the historical domination of Western art and culture forms. Although indigenous arts proved irrepressible, this was often represented through a Western view of the "other." The learning area seeks to explore how "institutional bias" acknowledged and promoted some arts and culture forms and relegated others to a "lesser status" (DOE 1997). It hopes, then, to nurture a common cultural identity and at the same time to undo the effects of the "entrenched social divisions" caused by "unequal resourcing and provision of Arts and Culture Education and Training" (DOE 1997, AC–3).

This first version of an Arts and Culture curriculum for the new nation was influenced in some measure by the government's "White

Paper on Arts, Culture, and Heritage," (1996) the seminal arts policy of the time. Chapter 1 of the white paper states:

> This White paper deals with one of the most emotive matters to face the new government. Cultural expression and identity stand alongside language rights and access to land as some of the most pressing issues of our time. (RSA 1996, 1–7)

A summary of the education section (chapter 4 of the white paper) sees the role of arts education as serving the social and political needs of South African society and the democratic project. Educators and educational institutions are identified as part of the mechanism of reconceptualizing the arts. Since education was used to deny the values of "other cultures" during the apartheid era, it is now to be used to redress that injustice. Education is expected to create a new means for shaping, challenging, affirming, and exploring personal and social relationships and community identity. It is expected to build a sense of pride in our diverse cultural heritage (RSA 1996, 4: 32). This is the official arts policy of the government and remains in place to date. Given this background, it is not surprising to find the following injunction in the curriculum which was developed a year after the white paper:

> Using culture and arts processes to advance principles of equity, redress, nation-building, transformation and development at various levels including culturally, structurally, gender-wise, race-wise and class-wise. (DOE 1997, AC7)

This quotation captures the epistemology of this Arts and Culture curriculum. The arts were included in Curriculum 2005 (what the new government named its education policy) as a formal learning area because they could be *used* so effectively to achieve the political ends that needed to be met at that time. In my analysis of arts education policies and in my interviews with policy makers, I frequently encountered the phrase "bringing people together." Other similar concepts were: "the need to understand each other," "learn about particular cultures," and ensuring a "cross-pollination of cultural enrichment" or "intercultural exchange." So showing "pride in our diverse cultural heritage" may not then be intended as a move to reverse and, thereby reify, those heritages; it may also imply "appreciation" as a means of bringing those diverse cultures together.

Some may say that this curriculum and those who developed it were idealistic, but their vision for the future is clear. This curriculum is committed to the support of a newly developing democracy concerned with creating an imagined nation and culture. It continuously frames education in the arts as a means of achieving sociopolitical aspirations, and, therefore, the arts become valuable because of this factor. What should education serve, and what arts should serve, asked Abbs. This curriculum has given a clear answer.

Version 2

In 2001, all the existing curricula in South African schools were revised. The revised arts and culture curriculum, outlined in the Revised National Curriculum Statement (RNCS), moved from a broad experience, involving several art forms within diverse cultural contexts, toward increasing depth of knowledge and skills in and about the arts themselves. This second curriculum stressed the need to provide learners with exposure and access to all art forms and a variety of cultural practices. The approach toward culture is to encourage learners to be active participants rather than passive inheritors of culture. They are encouraged to reflect critically and creatively on cultural practices and to understand and affirm the diversity of South African cultures. An interesting approach to culture in the curriculum is that learners are expected to identify the links between cultural practice, power, and cultural dominance (DOE 2002). This more critical stance builds on the position adopted by the first version. A stated intention of the curriculum is "to develop awareness of national culture and promote nation-building" (DOE 2002, 4). While the focus in this curriculum may be on high knowledge and skills, the political needs of the country have not been abandoned. The curriculum states that the intention in this learning area is to:

- develop creative and innovative individuals as responsible citizens, in line with the values of democracy according to the Constitution of South Africa;
- provide access to Arts and Culture education for all learners as part of redressing historical imbalances;
- develop an awareness of national culture to promote nation-building. (DOE 2002, 4)

It is assumed in this curriculum, as in all the related policies, that everyone has a common understanding of what is meant by nation-building and, indeed, by "nation."

In the first version, there were two specific outcomes about culture. In this version, there are none. Issues about culture are, nevertheless, addressed within the actual assessment standards. Cultural processes and activities also provide a context for arts learning through the use of the organizing principles, particularly in the senior phase. Examples of these official organizing principles, from the South African Department of Education for grades 7 to 9, are given in italics in the pages that follow.

Grade 7

Organizing Principle

> *The learner will be able to engage collaboratively in Arts and Culture activities to develop good social relations and explore ways of promoting nation-building.* (DOE 2002, 86)

And...

> *The learner will be able to explore, express and communicate the role of heritage in South African arts, past and present.* (DOE 2002, 92)

These principles are then exemplified in the official Assessment Standards in the different art forms, for example:

> *Researches and presents an example of indigenous performance, such as praise poetry or folk tales.* (DOE 2002, 92)

> *Investigates and explains the purpose, function and role of different instruments used in indigenous, traditional or Western forms of music in South Africa.* (DOE 2002, 92)

Grade 8

Organizing Principle

> *The learner will be able to think critically and reflect on Arts and Culture processes and products in relation to human rights issues in Africa.* (DOE 2002, 79)

And...

> *The learner will be able to explore, express and communicate issues of stereotyping, discrimination and prejudice in contemporary culture.* (DOE 2002, 93)

Examples of official Assessment Standards are:

Debates the roles traditionally assigned to different genders in dance by recognising and expressing different points of view.
Identifies age, gender, class and cultural stereotyping in stories, theatre, film, television or radio over time and in the present.
Develops a short skit to highlight problems of stereotyping, discrimination and prejudice in school or local community.

Grade 9

Organizing Principle

The learner will be able to offer a critical interpretation of the relationship between global and local cultures. (DOE 2002, 81)

And...

The learner will be able to use group activities to explore and share experiences of power relations. (DOE 2002, 87)

Examples of official Assessment Standards are:

Shows willingness to explore new cultural ideas and an ability to reconsider stereotypes. (DOE 2002, 87)

Discusses and interprets concepts of power, control and dominance in mass media and popular culture. (DOE 2002, 79)

These formal Assessment Standards illustrate a wonderful potential for cultural engagement and negotiation. This curriculum becomes a site for debate and discussion through songs, dance, drama, and artifacts. There are also composite Assessment Standards that address issues of culture more directly, for example:

Analyses the interplay between global and local culture...
Analyses how cultures affect one another and undergo change...
Identifies sources of cultural information such as elders, scholars and artists from the communities, libraries...(DOE 2002, 79)

These Assessment Standards offer an opportunity for engagement with traditional cultural practices as well as contemporary and popular culture. As far as the latter is concerned, young people are generally willing to engage with film, fashion, music, and new media. Bringing these into the classroom creates a space for challenging and examining cultural issues. Human rights, nation-building, power relations, and cultural practices become the context for arts education. For example, if we work on play-making, the play could be about xenophobia or HIV/AIDS. Power relations within cultural practices can safely be explored in a drama role play. Then, if we examine the lyrics of some popular songs, a whole debate can be opened up on gender issues and how women are portrayed in the media and, more importantly, how students themselves talk and think about these issues. Many traditional African cultural practices are based on paternalistic notions of gender roles that are at odds with contemporary society. Family prejudices of race and ethnicity are carried into the classroom where they can be challenged in a nonthreatening way. Many young people feel trapped within the conflicting demands of family and tradition, on the one hand, and peer pressure and popular role models, on the other. Performance pieces and artworks allow them to give expression to these inner struggles and through discussion and debate to find alternative ways of addressing their concerns. This is why I maintain that the Arts and Culture curriculum can play a strategic role in shaping how culture and identity are fashioned in the coming decades. The "voice" in this curriculum is at once idealistic and pragmatic as it attempts to balance the tensions of educational demands against transformation. What should arts serve? What is culture for? The arts can serve themselves, when learning is *in* the arts, and the arts can serve cultural understandings when the arts are used to challenge and extend these.

And Version 3

Perhaps the most significant change in 2010 has been in the name of the learning area. The schools arts curriculum will now be known as Creative Arts (DOE 2009). In fact, the proposal in the early years of schooling (grades 1 to 3) is to call it "Arts and Crafts," a name reminiscent of nineteenth-century schooling and apartheid differentiation. What change in ideology and focus does the dropping of "culture" as part of the title signify? Unlike the original naming, which was highly contested and widely debated (Singh 2007, 4), this name change has gone by barely noticed. The new curriculum focuses specifically on content because this is the mandate given to the curriculum developers. The grades 4 to 7 Creative Arts curriculum, which is located within a subject called Life Skills, says that the main purpose of creative arts is to develop learners as creative, imaginative individuals, with an appreciation of the arts. It maintains that a safe and supportive environment is created for learners to explore experience and express thoughts, ideas, and concepts within an atmosphere of openness and acceptance. Creative arts, the curriculum says, assists learners to give expression to their feelings and understandings, alone and in collaboration with others, and it creates a foundation for balanced creative, cognitive, emotional, artistic, and social development. No mention is made of cultural difference or diversity; one assumes that teachers will address these issues, if they wish to.

The insistence on the inclusion of culture in the first version can be understood in the light of the role played by "struggle artists" in helping tell the world the stories of South Africans under oppression. Ntuli confirms, "culture became the first instrument used to resist," and notes that this was a strategic and tactical move in the struggle since overt political engagement was proscribed (Ntuli 1999, 194). The discourse of resistance arts, the Black Consciousness Movement's theater pieces, the liberation songs, and the toyi-toyi[1] dances became a weapon of the mass-liberation movement. The story of the struggle for liberation through the arts is well-documented (see Coplan 1985: Cross 1992: Orkin 1991: and Sitas 1990). Culture was used as ideology, which, in turn, demonstrated an enormous power for mobilization, conscientization, and resistance (Ntuli 1999, 194). Resistance art did not exist only in the arena of leisure activity, but formed an integral part of the life of the working person as well. It was no wonder that those who came from the struggle ranks and the returned exiles, who had been sustained by those same cultural products, wanted to include culture and the arts in the curriculum to build this new nation. They had experienced the unifying effects of a common cultural ethos and hoped to recreate these experiences for all. It was their voices that were heard in the corridors of power, their voices that carried the most weight at the time of political transformation.

Now the question arises, since we have achieved our liberation, is it no longer necessary to forge cultural bonds through the medium of arts education? In the 1997 version of the curriculum, mention is made of the "healing" power of the arts and the white paper states: "Arts and culture may play a *healing* role through promoting reconciliation" (RSA 1996, 1:13). The arts are seen as having the power to heal and reconcile; hence their place in the new curriculum. The healing and reconciliation so assiduously pursued by our arts education policies must surely mean getting beyond the idea that the first defining characteristic of anyone is their race or ethnic group. The question we have to ask is whether we can remove race and racism from our thinking and our visualizing of identity. Are we whole and secure enough to confront this challenge? Who are "we"?

Artists Speak

Writer and director Ashraf Jamal (2000) suggests that the notion of a "new" South Africa is a misnomer: there is no "wholeness" yet; we lack the dimensions of a new country and a new people, coming as we do from a painful past of fragmented identities. This past experience, which has left permanent scars on our collective psyche, must affect our emerging future. But Jamal says:

> ...within this wreckage, the fallout of decades of repression and inequality there remains a hope that we will heal and will be unchained from a past that remains ever present. (Jamal 2000, 198)

The hope that Jamal referred to ten years ago can be aligned to the development of what the white paper (RSA 1996) calls the fertile and unique South African culture that is inclusive and eclectic. Perhaps it includes the hope that in the future the first defining characteristic of any South African will not be race. The nation-building so glibly referred to in the arts curricula needs to be a concerted effort that allows for public debate and growth more rapidly and among more people. Where is the locus for debate and negotiation in a democracy in which dissent or disagreement is today seen as disloyalty and disrespect to the ruling liberation party? In April 2010, there were two glaring examples of this inability to debate. One instance was of right-wing leader Andries Visagie who stormed out of a television interview, hurling abuse and threatening revenge at the interviewer, and the other was where a BBC journalist was sent out of a press conference and verbally abused by Julius Malema for asking a question. (Both interviews are on YouTube.) Again, while these people may represent extremist views, they bring to light deeply held prejudices and resentments.

South African author and columnist Fred Khumalo, reporting in 2009 on the conference held in Johannesburg to commemorate the fall of the Berlin Wall, writes of the "palpable sense of the search for reconciliation in both countries" (Khumalo 2009, 2). At this same conference, Malcolm Purkey, a radical theater practitioner and innovator in liberation theater in the 1980s and 1990s, stated:

> I am all for nation-building, I am all for reconciliation, but I do not believe the artist should be imposed upon to think in a certain way, or create works that necessarily respond to calls for nation-building or reconciliation through the arts. (Khumalo 2009, 2)

This statement does more than call to question the role and purpose of the arts in society; it indicates a move away from the attitude of resistance artists, whose works were a weapon for the struggle. Other presenters at the conference spoke of the hopelessness of reconciliation, which is one-sided, as it is seen to be coming from black people only. Khumalo however asserts that artists are involved in a new struggle, "against corruption, avarice, greed, disease, illiteracy, political opportunism and intolerance" (Khumalo 2009, 3). So, there is a need for artists to respond to the needs of these times. And, indeed, this is happening, for example, in dramas that deal with subjects like child rape (*Tshepang*), traditional culture (*iMumbo Jumbo*); exhibitions that portray images of African homosexuality (formally a taboo subject), and many other challenging and hard-hitting works. The emerging South African film industry is also contributing to the exploration of social and identity issues—movies like *Tsotsi* and *District 9* make hard-hitting statements. The good that we have achieved is also celebrated in the arts through fusion dance and music and in youth subculture, which blends and borrows language, clothes, and style without self-consciousness. Unfortunately, the debates triggered by artists' efforts affect only a minority; youth subcultures are out of the mainstream debates. Such debates do not have a large-scale impact. Spaces are needed where we can all interrogate our cultural difference, examine our shared histories, and negotiate a sense of what it means to be a South African. "There are multiple ways in which the world can be known," says Eisner, "Artists, writers, and dancers, as well as scientists, have important things to tell about the world" (Eisner 1998, 7). Schools and the arts curriculum offer a space and a way of knowing about our world and how we act in it to thousands of young people.

Nation and Arts Education

Given the present-day scenario discussed above, have the arts curricula any real solution to offer? Can the building blocks of nationhood that emerged from my study of the various arts policies—access, redress, equity, reconciliation, transformation, inclusivity, democracy, social justice, human rights, social reconstruction, economic development, and cultural diversity—actually be made to mean more than trite politically correct platitudes? I believe that if the arts are taught with passion and power, then issues of race, class, and gender, can be brought into the classroom, where they can be teased out to have the kind of long-lasting impact we are looking for. If we cannot deal with the fallout of apartheid ourselves, at least we can help the generation to come to forge a new cultural identity. Cultural diversity as it exists now has to be interrogated more vigorously. On the one hand, we have a call for a return to traditional African culture with tribal values and practices, while on the other hand, we see South Africans striving to be part of a Western global society How do we negotiate these polarities?

If we go back to the "White Paper for Arts, Culture, and Heritage" (WPACH) and to the Arts and Culture curriculum documents, we find constant references to acknowledgement of our cultural diversity. The principle of celebrating cultural diversity and heritage is not in itself a problem. It becomes a problem if that is *all* we do. Cultural diversity, says Bhabha, is an epistemological object—an object of empirical knowledge that remains "unsullied," whereas cultural difference is the process of the enunciation of culture as "knowledgeable," authoritative, adequate to the construction of systems of cultural identification (Bhabha 1994, 34). What he is suggesting is that cultural difference could draw attention to common ground and focus on the problem of the ambivalence of cultural authority, the attempt to dominate in the name of cultural supremacy (Bhabha 1994, 34). When we think of difference, we tend to think of separation and apartness. Again, Bhabha's articulation exemplifies the South African situation:

> Once the "liminality" of the nation space is established, and its signifying difference is turned from the boundary "outside" to its finitude "within," the threat of cultural difference is no longer a problem of "other" people. It becomes a question of otherness of the people-as-one. (Bhabha 1994, 150)

So there is also difference that is positional, conditional, and conjectural, and that recognizes that we all speak from a particular place, history, and experience (Hall 1989). What we need to explore are the intertextualities of our positions, the liminal spaces in which we can forge a yet unseen, unknown identity. In this regard, the Revised National Curriculum Statement for Arts and Culture speaks of *"showing adaptability to new ideas or situations, affirming and acknowledging diversity."* Cultural diversity must be seen as inclusive, employing social justice and democratic principles. Together they provide a vision of how the new nation was conceived.

Imagining the Future

If the policies for transformation are to be achieved, if the social, economic, and political goals of democracy are to be realized, education must become key to the discourse of transformation. Only in this way can the large-scale transformation of people be achieved. The Arts and Culture curriculum policy can play a strategic role in shaping how culture and identity are fashioned in the coming decades. By being mainstreamed, the arts have been thrust into a more powerful position than ever before in our history. Nation-building is, after all, an educational enterprise. It develops through mass schooling and public-school institutions. In this regard, education in the arts assumes a significant role. In both the modernist and postmodernist society, schools are seen as producers and reproducers of culture. Micere Mugo notes that education "acts as a communicator as well as a reservoir of culture" (Mugo 1999, 218). Shain, reviewing the work of Dolby (2001) and Tsolidis (2001), makes the following assertion about the mediation of schools with cultural identity:

> Schools, through both formal and informal relationships, represent powerful interpretations of what it means to be "British," "Australian" or "South African" that is, of belonging and non-belonging, inclusion and exclusion. The institutional practices and discourses of schooling frame understandings about who can legitimately make claims to such labels and who cannot. (Shain 2003, 120)

The Arts and Culture curriculum of 2002 raised questions and posed challenges about issues of race, power, and traditional cultural practices. It examined notions of diversity and difference, and in so doing, it became a vital cultural text, a vehicle offering a transformatory pedagogy for shaping the reinvention of our identities as South Africans and challenging fixed multicultural notions. Arts and culture can play a vital role in fashioning the ethos of post-apartheid South Africa through its effects on school-going youths. Our development as a political and economic entity depends on, and is affected by, our sense of national identity and cultural coherence. The influence and impact of arts and culture education comes as part of the transformation process in identity formation and nation-building.

Conclusion

How we see ourselves as a nation depends on our sense of identity, which, as has been suggested, is never a static thing. This identity formation depends on how successful the transformation process has been. Given the present day uncertainty and polarization within South Africa, we are more than ever before in need of every aid to promote transformation. For me, this need brings into sharp focus the importance of the Arts and Culture curriculum as a cultural tool to raise and address issues of cultural difference and promote cultural confidence. The removal of the term *culture* in arts education, then, denotes a lack of imagining and a failure to engage with the exciting and affirming possibilities of hybridization (Bhabha 1994) and creolization offered by our cultural difference. While the new Creative Arts curriculum, which is to be implemented in 2012, may prove to be effective in equipping young people with art skills, it can contribute little to building cultural confidence and creating a nation at peace with its own identity, unless these notions are built into the curriculum. The developers of the previous Arts and Culture curricula may have been idealistic, but they had at least a vision of how the arts could serve the nation. My thesis maintains that arts and culture education lies at the intersection of nation-building, identity formation, and transformation. If education and the arts cannot serve the nation, then like Abbs, we also have to ask: What is education for?

Note

1. The toyi-toyi dance, or toyi toyi, is a military dance style that had been used in training camps and that is now used primarily in protest marches, often accompanied by chants and protest songs.

References

Abbs, P. (2003). *Against the Flow Education, the Arts and Postmodern Culture.* London: Routledge Falmer.

Bhabha, H. K. (1991). "Third Space: Interview with Homi K. Bhabha." In *Identity: Community, Culture, Difference*, edited by Jonathan Rutherford, 207–221. London: Lawrence and Wishart.
Bhabha, H. K. (1994). *The Location of Culture*. London: Routledge.
Coplan, D. (1985). *In Township Tonight South Africa's Black City Music and Theatre*. Johannesburg: Raven Press.
Cross, M. (1992). *Resistance and Transformation Education, Culture and Reconstruction in South Africa*. Johannesburg: Skotaville.
Department of Education. (1997). *Senior Phase (Grades 7–9) Policy Document*, October 1997, Pretoria, South Africa.
Department of Education. (2002). *Revised National Curriculum Statement Grades R–9 (Schools) Policy Arts and Culture*. Pretoria, South Africa.
Department of Education. (2009). *Report of the Task Team for the Review of the Implementation of the National Curriculum Statement*. Pretoria, South Africa.
Dolby, N. (2001). *Constructing Race: Youth, Identity, and Popular Culture in South Africa*. Albany: State University of New York Press.
Eisner, E. W. (1998). *The Enlightened Eye Qualitative Inquiry and the Enhancement of Educational Practice*. New Jersey: Prentice-Hall.
Fanon, F. (1959). "Wretched of the Earth." Speech by Franz Fanon at the Congress of Black African Writers. Accessed on March 28, 2007. doi:http://www.marxists.org/reference/subject/philosophy/works/ot/fanon.htm
Fraser, N. (1998). "From Redistribution to Recognition? Dilemmas of Justice in a 'Post- Socialist' Age." In *Theorising Multiculturalism A Guide to the Current Debate*, edited by Cynthia Willet, 19–49. Oxford: Blackwell.
Hall, S. (1989). "New Ethnicities." In *Black Film, British Cinema*, ICA Documents 7. London: Institute of Contemporary Arts.
Jamal, A. (2000). "Stagings." In *Senses of Culture. South African Culture Studies*, edited by S. Nuttall and C. A. Michael, 197–211. Oxford: Oxford University Press.
Khumalo, F. (2009). "Art Should Still Be Wielded as a Weapon of Social Change." Accessed April 1, 2010. doi:http://www.timeslive.co.za/opinion/columnists/article183981.ece/We-need-break-out-the-laager
Milburn, G., I. F. Goodson, and R. J. Clark, ed. (1989). *Re-Interpreting Curriculum Research: Images and Arguments*. London: Falmer Press.
Mugo, M. G. (1999). "African Culture in Education for Sustainable Development." In *African Renaissance The New Struggle*, Makgoba, M. W. 210–221. Cape Town: Mafube Tafelberg.
Ndebele, N. (2006). "True Leadership May Mean Admitting Disunity." Edited extract from the inaugural King Moshoeshoe Memorial Lecture, University of the Free State. *Sunday Times,* June 4, 2006, p. 21.
Ntuli, P. P. (1999). "The Missing Link between Culture and Education: Are We Still Chasing Gods That Are Not Our Own?" In *African Renaissance The New Struggle,* edited by M.W. Makgoba. Cape Town: Mafube and Tafelberg.
Nuttall, S., and C. Michael, ed. (2000). *Senses of Culture South African Cultural Studies*. Oxford: Oxford University Press.

Orkin, M. (1991). *Drama and the South African State*. Johannesburg: Witwatersrand University Press.
Republic of South Africa. (1996). "White Paper for Arts, Culture, and Heritage." Pretoria, South Africa.
Schechner, R., and M. Schuman, ed. (1976). *Ritual, Play and Performance Readings in the Social Sciences /Theatre*. New York: Continuum Books.
Scruton, R. (1987). "The Myth of Cultural Relativism." In *Anti-Racism: An Assault on Education and Value*, edited by F. Palmer. Nottingham, UK: Sherwood Press.
Shain, F. (2003). "Creating Third Spaces: Youth, Schooling, and Difference." *Discourse: Studies In The Cultural Politics of Education*. 24 (1): 119–126.
Singh, L. P. (2007). "Birth and Regeneration: The Arts and Culture Curriculum in South Africa (1997–2006)." Doctoral thesis, University of KwaZulu-Natal, Durban.
Sitas, A. (1990). "The Voice and Gesture in South Africa's Revolution: A Study of Worker Gatherings and Performance Genres in Natal." In *International Annual of Oral History*, edited by R. J. Grele, 93–105. Johannesburg: Raven Press.
Zegeye, A., ed. (2001). *After Apartheid: Social Identities in the New South Africa*, vol. 1. Cape Town: Kwela Books and South African History Online.

YouTube Interviews

Julius Malema. (April 2010). Interview. doi:http://www.youtube.com/watch?v=-Wlh_HF2Y8E
Andries Visagie. (April 2010). Interview. doi :http://www.youtube.com/watch?v=0IVdrJ1zKXk&feature=related

9

Calypso, Education, and Community in Trinidad and Tobago: From the 1940s to 2011

Gordon Rohlehr

Introduction

This chapter has grown out of an address delivered on January 28, 2009, at a seminar on the theme "Education through Community Issues and Possibilities for Development." It seeks to explore the foundational ideas of Eric Williams,[1] an international scholar and former Trinidad and Tobago prime minister, about education as a vehicle for decolonization through nation-building, most of which he outlined in *Education in the British West Indies* (1950), a report that, having been prepared under the auspices of the Caribbean Research Council of the Caribbean Commission between 1945 and 1947, he then published in 1950 in partnership with the Teachers' Economic and Cultural Association (TECA) of Trinidad and Tobago. Drawing heavily upon De Wilton Rogers's *The Rise of the People's National Movement* (1981), this chapter will detail Williams's association with the TECA and its education arm, the People's Education Movement [PEM], between 1950 and 1955, when Williams made the transition from research to politics via lectures. It will also explore the issues of education, community, and nation-building during the early years of the People's National Movement (PNM), and when in his first term in office, Williams struggled to sell his ideas about educational reform and development to a skeptical, and sometimes hostile, hierarchy of entrenched interests.

The bulk of the chapter reads Williams's mission and performance through the lenses of 100 calypsos (in the original lecture), which serve as the people's voice, which at times echoes and at others qualifies and critiques, official rhetoric about education, social transformation, and community-building. If both the PEM and the nascent PNM engaged in education as a one-way process, in which a committed intelligentsia voluntarily undertakes the tasks of uplifting and illuminating their less fortunate brethren in the rural and peri-urban borderlands, the calypsonians, fierce guardians of independent grassrooted opinion, assume the right to dialogue, to talking back to their certificated intellectual supervisors, weekend schoolmasters and schoolmarms.

The calypsos used in this critical, historical analysis revealed that the world of the streets, the urban yards, the ever-burgeoning ghetto, the world, indeed, of Williams's southeast Port-of-Spain constituency in Trinidad, has its own curriculum of constant crises and survivalism—its alternative economy of cutting and contriving and its own hierarchy of muscle and blood. Calypso texts uncover the distressing distance between Williams's efforts to create through education an enlightened and articulate modern national community, and the impermeable indifference to Williams's curriculum of the unmanageable rebels, outcasts, knife-and-razor technicians, gunslingers, and blood-and-sand gladiators in his constituency who have created their own cinematic lifestyles, counter-cultural mores, values, and modes of earning, granting respect, and self-recognition. Although these people constituted only a minuscule percentage of the citizens of locations such as John John, Laventille, Shanty Town, Sea Lots, Morvant, or Gonzales, peri-urban Port-of-Spain "Behind the Bridge," and beyond, became negatively profiled in their name and through the reality and fable of their deeds.

This critical, historical, and cultural analysis is presented in three thematic accounts, expressed as a textual collage to highlight the relationship between education, community, and culture. Indeed, there is a conversation presented in this chapter between the texts of the intellectual and those of the grassroots commentary about community nation-building. The texts traverse the contested terrain of the historical by using Williams's work *Education in the British West Indies* and the indigenous music of the calypso, which provides contrapuntal reading as "the classroom of the road" to intellectual discourse.

Background: Education in the British West Indies

To examine Williams's education platform is to begin by establishing his relationship with the Teachers' Economic and Cultural Association (TECA). After succeeding in the campaign for equality in wages for female teachers, TECA decided in 1950 to establish an "Education Movement with a further reach than merely cultural" (Rogers 1981, 10). This was the People's Education Movement, which did not limit itself to teachers' issues, but sought to recruit "the housewife, the teacher, the proprietor, the shop-keeper, the chauffeur, the peasant, the clerk, the labourer, the domestic and the Civil Servant" (Rogers 1981, 10). Its war cry was "All must join. None must be out. We are at war against ignorance and poverty" (Rogers 1981, 13). The PEM's program ran on the principle of voluntary self-help, and there were in Tobago 60 volunteers who accepted the PEM's mission "to share knowledge with others" in the "war against poverty and Ignorance" (Rogers 1981, 20). The PEM set up units in 18 areas throughout the length and breadth of Trinidad and Tobago.

Soon after its inauguration, the PEM, through its founders De Wilton Rogers and John S. Donaldson, invited the deputy chairman of the Caribbean Research Council, Eric Williams, to become their consultant. At the same time, TECA, the parent organization of the PEM, published Williams's canonical *Education in the British West Indies* in 1950 and requested via Williams, access to the library of the Caribbean Commission with its data on vocational and adult education. TECA also wanted to prepare "a handbook on Caribbean facts and figures such as population, employment, and unemployment," statistics, they said, that would aid them in their efforts "to improve the education and cultural standards of the people in these parts." Evidently, Williams's growing involvement in the affairs of TECA and the PEM was the result of the need he shared with these bodies for visibility and acclamation in the context of the nascent nation of Trinidad and Tobago. Williams needed the activism and the enthusiasm of the PEM to give life to his ideas and as the springboard for his leap into politics. The PEM needed Williams for ideas and data that could validate their program of educational outreach and for his power in structuring their wayward agenda into a coherent mission. Their need was mutual, though Williams, engrossed in engineering his own charismatic emergence as a leader of a brand new nation, seldom acknowledges either the process or the people involved in his propulsion toward leadership.

Beginning in 1945, when, under the auspices of the Caribbean Commission, Williams commenced work on *Education in the British West Indies*, the draft manuscript that he completed in 1946. There was a gulf between Williams's notion about the trajectory of research and what the Caribbean Commission required: a survey that would be a compendium of facts about the subject researched, in which the researcher, a neuter and objective gatherer of data, should have no say as to the use to which such data, would be put. Williams, the academic as activist, believed that his research should be the beginning of a mission to fill the gaping void in colonial education, which had left the colonized subject/object disconnected from his/her past, and hence, incapacitated as a potential citizen of the yet nonexistent new nation. Williams believed that relevant education would instill in the colonized the sense of confidence they needed in order to build a nation.

Education, he argued, "is designed to serve" particular interests and purposes, implying that the interests and purposes of the colonized are of necessity different from those of the colonizers. In his preface to the 1945 draft of *Education in the British West Indies* (1950), he wrote:

> Education in the modern world is, more than anything else, education of the people themselves as to the necessity of viewing their own education as part of their democratic privileges and their democratic responsibilities. (1945, 17)

One war had just ended, another was just about to start: the struggle toward an independent nation at whose center Williams located the engagement of the people in, and the responsibility of the people for, the content, design, trajectory, and quality of the education they received.

Williams shared his ideas with educators, politicians, trade unionists, and other interested persons in Trinidad, Barbados, the Virgin Islands, and St. Thomas. In preparing the document, he had consulted a number of his Howard University colleagues, themselves important avant-garde intellectuals, along with educators from India, South Africa, New Zealand, Australia, and the United Kingdom. He wanted to make his ideas available:

> For the consideration not only of the ordinary citizen in the British West Indies, but also of those people who were interested in the very

important problem of education in colonial and semi-colonial countries. (Williams 1950, xi)

It must have been Williams's openness in declaring his interest in making an impact on both the Caribbean and the wider anticolonial world that made his bosses at the imperialistic Caribbean Commission delay publication of his report for four years after its completion. Williams shared his report with the Teachers' Economic and Cultural Association (TECA) who found in its logically argued and systematically structured pages justification for their own program of educational reform. The possibilities suggested by Williams's as yet unpublished blueprint, inspired the leaders of the TECA to create the People's Education Movement (PEM), its energetic and militant arm, for whom educating teachers about pedagogy soon became providing lecture series on politics, economics, and sociology for the edification of the general public.

In *Education in the British West Indies,* which TECA published in 1950, Williams accorded education a major role in the engineering of radical change in societies, shaped by colonialism. To perform this function, however, the education system itself needed to be radically transformed from being an agency for the reinforcement of the status quo to becoming "a midwife to the emerging social order" (Williams 1950, x). Caribbean societies were in the main, dominated by large plantations controlled by foreign capital and producing for export, and landless labouers and small peasant farmers who had little control over their circumstances. Williams observed that "the system of land tenure . . . is an effective obstacle in the way of giving agricultural education the place in the curriculum that it demands" (Williams 1950, 10).

The question of land tenure has remained one of the bitterest issues two generations after Williams's death. The concomitant issue of agricultural education, pertinent to peasant farming communities, has only been partially addressed, despite the efforts of successive governments over nearly five decades of independence. *Education in the British West Indies* identified most of the traditional problems and suggested possible solutions. Yet efforts to implement plans for solving problems have proven inadequate, and in some cases, the problems have increased, outstripping the state's capacity to solve or contain them.

In considering the social structure of Caribbean societies, Williams focused especially on the ambivalence of "mulatto" intellectuals confronted with the necessity of inventing or discovering a national identity. While, traditionally, this class had found itself ground "between the upper millstone, which was white. and the nether, which was black" (Williams 1950, 5), some of its more enlightened members had in recent times discarded old colonial attitudes of despising blackness, aspiring to whiteness, and measuring people in terms of color and lightness of skin. Williams disclosed that:

> In Jamaica mulattoes are consciously seeking back into their own history, are reviving and resurrecting West Indian songs, local artists of talent are coming to the fore and receiving recognition in poetry, art and dramatics. A West Indian culture is slowly but surely emerging. (Williams 1950, 7–8)

Williams, at this early stage, seemed to place great hope in this sector of Caribbean society, which by the forties had begun to find common ground with the broader Creole intelligentsia that had for decades been involved in associations, such as debating societies, welfare societies, lodges, literary clubs, and musical groups. TECA was one such association that had begun to make a transition from a preoccupation with cultural matters to the beginnings of a kind of politics. Williams observed this happening all over the Caribbean during the 1940s.

> With the development of political consciousness, the more alert West Indians, in their clubs, organizations and journals, are discussing federation, nationalization of the means of production, tenancy reforms, industrialization, slavery, race relations, and other questions that constitute the warp and woof of British West Indian—and international—society. (Williams 1950, 8)

Perceiving this new spirit, Williams, in the decade between 1946 and 1956, held dialogues with distinctly different groups of committed intellectuals, notably with TECA/ PEM and the (southern) San Fernando–based group "Bachacs," described by Winston Mahabir as constituting himself, Ibbit Mosaheb, Norman Girwar, Telford Georges, Claire Sloane-Seales, George Wattley, Edward Lee, Gerard Montano, Donald Granado, and Dennis Mahabir (Mahabir 1978, 17). Bachacs and TECA/PEM were, it seems, quite separate from each other; yet both were connected to Williams's dream of fathering a rational and articulate national movement, and both were dedicated to the greater plan of mass political education, while each group felt flattered by its closeness and feeling of being special to the leader. Winston Mahabir, for example, claimed that:

> San Fernando was, even then, the intellectual centre of Trinidad, the clumsy but honest progenitor of almost every relevant idea or movement that stirred the people to a belief in their own potential. (Mahabir 1978, 17)

Mahabir doesn't even mention the People's Education Movement, which, according to one of its founders, De Wilton Rogers, facilitated Williams's triumphal entry into the northern districts of southeast Port-of-Spain and the University of Woodford Square.[2] Rogers, in turn, has nothing to say about Bachacs.

The irony of this rivalry between Bachacs and PEM is that both represented different segments of an emerging middle class that Williams, in his *History of the People of Trinidad and Tobago,* would condemn for its mediocrity, emptiness, materialism, and individualism. Williams, much as he recognized and constructed his charismatic image on his own academic superiority, placed on the educated middle class the special burden of having to subvert the very education system that had created them. Colonial education, he declared, was a "distortion" that had created a middle class of civil servants, minor administrative functionaries, "parasites" who scorned manual labor and had separated themselves from the workers and peasants in what were essentially agricultural communities. The colonial curriculum, designed to serve only the purposes of the colonizer, ignored the history and culture of the colonized. *Education in the British West Indies* painted a dismal picture of inadequate enrollment in schools, high dropout rates—nearly 80 percent in some cases—and consequently, high illiteracy rates (Williams 1962, 281–282). To change the educational systems in the colonies, one would have to change political representation. Educational change would come only with vigorous nationalism, and such nationalism could not flourish under an educational system that Williams termed "aristocratic" (Williams 1950, 19).

The transformation that had taken place in post-revolutionary Mexico became the template from which Williams dreamed to construct both Caribbean education systems and Caribbean societies. Mexico had instituted a program of "land and schools" (Williams 1950, 19) through which her leaders hoped to undermine "the old Latin American convention of 'enlightened classes exploiting ignorant masses.'" Mexico had sought to educate the peasant to acquire skills relevant to an agrarian existence. Education was practical, geared to preparing the student for work and life. It emphasized knowledge and love of country and taught civics and the revolution's reconstruction of history (the way that Cuba would three decades later). The curriculum included theater (mainly of a propagandist nature), portraying national customs and manners; music, physical education, social education via "festivals, concerts and friendly gatherings" (Williams 1950, 83). It also emphasized adult education and perceived education as a means of building community.

> The rural school is openly envisaged as a community agency to lead in community life, help spend leisure and guide all community activities. (Williams 1950, 24)

Education in the colonial Caribbean was, by contrast, divorced from the needs of the community. Teacher training and supervision at the primary level ignored "the vital and organic connection between the school and the community" (Williams 1950, 25). Secondary education was ideally geared toward the production of scholarship winners, who were destined for "affluence and prestige" or dysfunctional General Certificate of Education (GCE) Ordinary Level (O-level) candidates who filled the lower level of the public service. Those educated in commerce, typewriting, and bookkeeping, ran the risk of having to face race and color discrimination from the banks, airlines, shipping companies, import/export firms, and even department stores, when they sought employment in these institutions. Private-sector business imported their staff at the higher levels and recruited only the highly colored (that is, those with a lighter shade of skin color) at the middle and lower levels (Williams 1950, 36). Williams exposed the undemocratic nature of the society and the historic roots of race and class discrimination, and wanted to create a more equitable society based on a reformed education system. He was aware of the large numbers of church-owned and church-managed schools, and of the likelihood of protest coming from religious denominations if any attempt were made to replace their schools with state-owned institutions. Williams, however, asserted that: "The educational system...must safeguard the superior right of the community as a whole to control the general trend of education" (Williams 1950, 33). The questions posed here were: Who or what constituted "the community as a whole" and "whose and which rights" were "superior," and which and whose rights were "inferior" or of lesser importance? Williams felt that the right of the community as a whole was superior to that of any of its component elements. The religious denominations were, arguably, the most important component of the educational system, insofar as the ownership and administration of the schools were concerned. Williams foresaw that educational reform, legislated by the state on behalf of the undefined "community as a whole," would lead to headlong confrontation with the religious denominations.

This confrontation did indeed take place early in Williams's long tour of duty (1956–1981). The issue was never satisfactorily resolved, though the main antagonists, the State, the Church, Mandir, and Masjid, did arrive at a compromise in the famous Concordat of 1960 and the Education Act of 1965, which enabled the religious bodies to retain power and authority over the administration of their schools and choice of a percentage (20 percent) of the annual intake of suitably qualified students. Critics of the Concordat have portrayed it as a concession by the state to the old status quo of class and perhaps ethnic elitism, the maintenance of a small élite of rulers. The very elite had, in fact, created Williams and the intellectual class of his generation. This was ironic when one considers that Williams had vowed to transform society by expanding educational opportunity and by making the curriculum more relevant to the national community. Williams was recommending nothing short of an educational revolution that would lead to either the abolition or the transformation of the very system that had produced Williams and his contemporaries. But he would never seriously enact a policy that he had so acerbically and clearly articulated one decade before he came to power. This may be because he anticipated that:

> The establishment of special schools for vocational education incurs the danger that these schools will be regarded by the community as inferior to the traditional, academic schools. (Williams 1950, 35)

He recognized since 1946, that the idea of "prestige" schools, that is, traditional and "superior" grammar schools, was deeply inscribed in the public mind, and that his suggested emphasis on the rural school might actually serve to widen the divide between rural and urban that he was seeking to close. So he recommended an alternative plan, which was the creation of the "the multilateral school, which will include classical, modern and technical curricula" (Williams 1950, 41). Efforts to create such schools did not destroy deeply engrained notions of so-called prestige schools that remained most people's first choice at the secondary level of education. The issue of government schools versus denominational ones; of the junior secondary/senior comprehensive and multilateral schools versus prestige schools, has survived the Williams era to become the cyclic subject of intense and futile national debate whenever one dares open that Pandora's box of suppressed subterranean controversy. Education, Williams well knew, was a "dual process" (Williams 1950, 89) involving exchange between the teaching intelligentsia and the learning communities. But political necessity and ideological urgency prompted a much more schoolmasterish encounter between the (PNM) party's intellectuals and the masses. As our examination of calypsos will soon indicate, the masses have constantly "talked back" to their would-be schoolmasters, as the curricula of the college and the communities have continuously clashed in the classrooms of the road.

Calypso: The Classroom of the Road

Calypso evidence spanning the 25 years (1956–1981) of Williams's political leadership of Trinidad and Tobago and the three decades since his death, suggests that a gap in sensibility has persisted between intellectuals and ordinary folk, who have clung to the ancient belief that "common-sense make before book-sense," and who have at times dismissed the entire class of intellectuals as being "too bright" (Allen 2010) or have considered them more contemptuously as "educated donkeys" (DeFosto 2008). Calypsonian[3] Chalkdust is a teacher, University of the West Indies (UWI) graduate, University of Michigan doctorate, and has been a seven-time calypso monarch as well as an author of several books and essays on Trinidad's social history. Chalkdust advised the George Chambers government in Trinidad and Tobago in *Ram the Magician* (1984):

> If you can't run the country
> Then call in Kirpalani. (Liverpool 1984)

Important aspects of the nation's administration had been put in the hands of certificated technocrats by the last Eric Williams regime (1976–1981). Chalkdust's calypso was a signal of the dissatisfaction felt by sections of the public at the performance of these technocrats. Ram Kirpalani was the country's most successful businessman whose family, originally from India, had over eight decades of residence in Trinidad and built a considerable conglomerate of businesses in Trinidad and Tobago and other parts of the West Indies. Chalkdust points out that:

> Ram never went to university
> But he got a PhD in money. (Liverpool 1984)

Academic knowledge, then, was being measured against an acumen developed through long and practical experience of the marketplace.

There has been an ongoing concern in calypsos with the quality, scope, and content of education, and a scathing scrutiny of syllabi, teachers, schools, textbooks, and methods of discipline. Calypsos, such as Sparrow's *Dan Is the Man in the Van* (1963), Chalkdust's *Teach the Right History* (1969), Pretender's *History in We Own Backyard* (1972), Composer's *Proper Teaching* (1971), Prowler's *Build More Trade Schools* (1969), or more recent ones, such as Delamo's *Looters* (1991) or Chalkdust's *Rescue QRC* (2002) and *No More Licks in School* (2002), are a fair sample of the larger body of songs that have reflected the nation's preoccupation with what is being taught, what is being produced, the quality of both teachers and students, the relationship between education and employment, and Eric Williams's original concern with transforming the national community through education.

There are as many calypsos that ask whether Williams and the seven governments that have succeeded his unbroken relay of five, have failed, wholly or partially, to correct deficiencies in the system that were identified and denounced since *Education in the British West Indies*. By the early 1980s, the dedicated cadre of intellectuals and persons of culture on whose zeal and selfless effort Williams built the PNM, have become the "headhunters" of Black Stalin's *More Times* (1980), and by the end of the century, they have morphed into David Rudder's "mindbenders," "various smart-men and politicians," with hidden agendas in *The Ganges and the Nile* (1999). Black Stalin's grassroots citizen, faced with the almost universal duplicity of people who "come out so for your mind," humbles himself and "takes aside": that is, detaches himself from the festering social and political scenario, practicing what the Mighty Gibraltar grew to call, "avoidism."

Something has snapped—some line of trust that seemed briefly to have existed in those early Williams years, a line that, however tenuously, connected the intelligentsia with the masses. Delamo in calypsos like *Apocalypse* (1981), *Sodom and Gommorah* (1982), and *Armageddon* (1984)—the years of recession and George Chambers's cost-cutting measures—chronicles disintegration as he paints a dismal portrait of the professional class of doctors, lawyers, and big and small merchants and concludes: "So you see, the system is like unto an abscess" (Delamo 1984). Worst of all, he thinks that the solution is beyond human ability, that "There'll be no solution / Until the last days of Armageddon."

David Rudder observes not so much the breach in the line that once bound intellectual to community, but a strange and unhealthy levelling off of classes, races: "convent girl" and "rude bwoy," product of prestige (traditional grammar) school and graduate from the academy of the streets, strangely united in the delirium of the nightclub (Rudder, *Madness*, 1986). Rudder shows in *Another Day in Paradise* (1995) that certain of "the new Greeks"—that is, the current generation of intellectuals—and the new "gorgons"—that is, the region's stony-hearted young men of crime—have come together in a coalition that is the diametric opposite of what Williams had at the Republic of Trinidad and Tobago's independence hoped for that generation of children who, he said, held the country's future in their book bags. In the mid-1990s, the national community faces new and horrible alignments and configurations of class: "For when a gorgon shoot another gorgon," it is up to the doctor and the lawyers to save these youths: and "Now he back on the streets/ terror in your tail" (Rudder 1995).

Calypsonians, products of the classroom and curriculum of the streets, have both shared in and preserved a detachment from the euphoria of the Woodford Square magical moment. The Mighty Sparrow, who was 21 in 1956 when Williams and the PNM first rode to power, sang *Dan Is the Man in the Van* in 1963, in which he caricatured Captain Cutteridge's colonial reading primer as absurd, designed to produce comedians. He ends the calypso with the unforgettable couplet:

> They beat me like a dog to learn that in school
> If my head was bright, ah woulda been a damn fool. (Sparrow 1963)

It was 1963, the year after independence, and *Dan Is the Man in the Van* was signaling a necessity to break from the old brutality and absurdity of the inherited system of education; that is, it was in its bizarre way proclaiming a oneness with the Williams mission to reform education, from nursery to tertiary levels.

Sparrow's *Education* (1967) was first sung 12 years after the University of Woodford Square lectures and five years after Independence. It captures the fervor of the PEM/PNM years and articulates the creed of self-improvement through education, by which most citizens have lived and still do live. *Education,* sometimes called *Education a Must,* is an excellent example of the exhortatory, nation-building calypso in which the calypsonian as solid rational spokesperson for the population at large affirms the mission of his government to create a new world of the Caribbean. The lyrics of *Education* are a restatement of cherished Eric Williams and PNM policy. Its tone is that of the prophet as part warner and part divine messenger, imparting to the new nation the message of the gods. The calypsonian temporarily abandons his guise of social critic, protestor, or satirist, trying to keep a government or its leader in check, and dons the mask of medium or mediator between the masses and the maximum leader who, overburdened by work and the nightmarish vision of enemies—imperialists, capitalists, and worse, communists—hiding behind every fig leaf, has begun a retreat from the dais of the University of Woodford Square into the twilight of a fortress of solitude.

But Williams had, as we have seen, inscribed his ideas about the urgency of the nation's need for education at all levels. Education was, he had preached, the main article of faith, the major foundation block upon which the new nation and transformed community of the Caribbean and the post-colonial New World were to be built. It was the only way that a coherent and well-balanced nation could be constructed out of the darkness and shambles of colonialism. Sparrow in *Education,* then, assumes the crusading spirit and voice of the Williams of 1955, or of one of his lieutenants, exhorting the masses, delivering the message: "Education, education, this is the foundation...To enjoy any kind of happiness/ Knowledge is the key to success" (Sparrow 1967).

The chorus is directed at the nation's children. Williams had said at its independence that the nation's future lay in the book bags of its children. This declaration stuck in the nation's mind, and thirty years later, would be invoked by Luta, the schoolteacher calypsonian in *Think Again* (1991) and David Rudder in *Another Day in Paradise* (1995), in ironic reflection on the sad state into which the nation and its youth had fallen, now that the children's book bags were "packed up with gun, knife and chain" (Luta 1991).

In 1967, however, the nation was still young and full of hope, amid early signs of the disintegration of certain peri-urban communities.

Sparrow restates the text of Williams's sermon, though one detects in Sparrow's insistent and repetitive exhortations, the beginnings of a certain desperation, signs perhaps that the government's programs of Special Works, Better and Best Villages, Education and Community Development were not running as successfully as citizens might have expected. Illiteracy remained a major social problem and would, well into the twenty-first century, be cited as a major cause of youths turning to crime. Sparrow in 1967 warned that the future of the nation was in the hands of the youth.

Why did Sparrow see the need to reinforce Williams's and the PNM's foundational mission statement with such repetitive insistence? On the face of things, Williams's two administrations, 1956–1961 and 1961–1966 had performed well in implementing fundamental reforms and improvements in education. Williams himself outlined the changes that had taken place in his November 3, 1967, preface to the American edition of *Education in the British West Indies*.

1. Free Secondary Education (1960)
2. Advances in Vocational Education and teacher training
3. Creation of the Ministry of Education and Culture whose mission is the rationalization of the Education System
4. The Education Act of 1965, making the Denominational Schools part of the system "as they never were before" (i.e. the Concordat mentioned earlier)
5. Prioritizing the issue of a Caribbean Examinations system (NB. Such a system, the CXC, took another decade to materialize)
6. Independence of UWI in 1962
7. Plans to establish faculties of Law and Dentistry
8. Decentralization of UWI, leading to the location of Agriculture and Engineering in Trinidad and Medicine in Jamaica
9. The establishment of the Institute of Social and Economic Research in Jamaica
10. The establishment of Extra-Mural centres of the UWI in smaller territories
11. The establishment of Liberal Arts Colleges in Jamaica, Trinidad and Barbados
12. Compulsory University courses in the Development of Civilization and in West Indian History and Society (Williams 1967, x)

From this list, it can be seen how closely Williams and his colleagues in the federated, then unfederated West Indies, now either fully independent or on the road to that blissful state, had followed the template for educational development in the region that Williams had set out since 1946 in *Education in the British West Indies*. Yet the transformation of community, a major objective of Williams's, the PEM's, and after 1955 the PNM's lectures in the University of Woodford Square and throughout Trinidad and Tobago, had not visibly occurred. Indeed, community development had become something of an orphan child in the scheme of things. Conceived of as social welfare, community development had been attached to the Ministry of Education until 1956, when the PNM first assumed office. Successive governments headed by Eric Williams seemed to have little idea of how to nurture the dream of a relationship between education and community, or how to stimulate the transformation of community. Social and educational voluntarism, however, noble and sincere their beginning years before Williams, gave way to hard pragmatic party politicizing, in which it became dangerous to "invade territory" controlled by the PNM's border guards. University of the West Indies lecturers, who voluntarily lectured to young men in Renegades panyard[4] in 1969 on West Indian history, government, and popular music, all received threats of death and dire injury in 1970 from unknown sources, who termed themselves, "Desperadoes Will Protect," "The Death Squad," and "Simbutu Warriors." They had trespassed on holy ground—the electoral constituency of Dr. Williams (Rohlehr 1995). A small act of voluntary service, linking intellectuals to community—a cherished PNM ideal—had led to this manic, this delirious reaction.

From the late 1950s, calypsonians had been recording the grim paradox of educational improvement and community disintegration. First, there were all those "badjohn" and "bravado" calypsos (Sparrow's own terms) that Sparrow sang between the late 1950s and mid-1960s: *Gunslingers* (1959), *Renegades* (1961), *Hangman's Cemetery* (1961), *Don't Touch Me* (1960/ 1961), *Royal Jail* (1961), *Bull Pistle Gang* (1964), *Ten to One Is Murder* (1960), and *The Rebel* (1966). Periurban communities, such as Williams's Port-of-Spain southeast constituency were sites of constant and violent male-versus-male encounters, as they had been since emancipation. Protagonists in Sparrow's badjohn calypsos are usually isolated males under attack from other males, and either defending themselves or threatening to retaliate with extreme violence. In *Shanty-Town People* (1966), the Laventille citizen portrays himself as a decent and respectable man who has been driven to his wit's end by the "fire and brimstone" he has had to endure from a gang of "rats" who hail from Shanty-Town, a nether circle of hell where the narrow plain at the bottom of Laventille Hill trails into the La Basse and swamp. These former swamp-dwellers fight, curse, gamble, steal whatever they can, defy the police, reduce the protagonist's life to misery, and block his passage when he tries to escape to the remote but then comparatively peaceful countryside of Claxton Bay, miles away from this urban theater of stress and torment. Their final act of anarchism is truly grim:

> They thief all meh furniture and carry it to pawn
> Set fire to meh house and gone. (Sparrow 1966)

In *Royal Jail* (1961) the violence, significantly, extends toward even the deputy prime minister, himself an island scholar, a past participant in the party's program of consciousness-raising lectures and the party's first minister of education.

> Just imagine the Minister of Home Affairs
> He and all have to walk with care. (Sparrow 1961)

Threatened, the minister, like a gunslinger who has been "called-out," adopts the falsely heroic, violent rhetoric and register of the street. This signals not his oneness with the street, but on the contrary, a breakdown, a failure, the fatuity even of those earlier efforts to illuminate a community comfortable with its own darkness, and capable of reducing educated national island scholars and dedicated PNM missionaries to its own level of histrionic encounter and rhetoric.

The Rebel (1966) is unique because Sparrow creates in this calypso the persona of a young badjohn-in-formation, who portrays himself as having been the innocent victim of his social environment. The streets, where he receives his informal education, have their own curriculum and professors. Foremost among these are:

1. Bullying older males, "all o'dem badjohns" who handle the protagonist violently, commit crimes or sometimes pranks for which the protagonist is blamed and punished
2. Teachers in school, particularly the headmaster, who doesn't sympathize with his situation and eventually expels him
3. Parents who put him out from home when he is expelled from school

His self-portrait is that of an innocent, misunderstood scapegoat and victim of the perverse masculinity of his world: that of the city. This perverse masculinity demands a constant violent testing and initiation—a putting-down and a putting-in-place of the young neophyte, who, socialized into a *sans humanité* environment, absorbs its values of confrontation of the "other" perceived as enemy, and of harboring thoughts of future revenge. There are borders in this world of the city street, raised to separate small man (i.e., little boy) from youth man (i.e., teenager) and both of them from big man (i.e., adult male). There are also harsh rites of passage from one stage to the next. *The Rebel* describes the street education and testing of one of these young males as he progresses from small man to youth man about to graduate into full (or empty) manhood; i.e., the status of badjohn and rebel grown strong enough to challenge his former persecutors.

Grown up, the protagonist now welcomes the aging badjohns of his youth, who, it seems, have grown weak and vulnerable. Now that they need compassion, he will not be the one to provide it. This is his time to play, not badjohn—(he never admits to having grown into and become the mask he most deeply hates)—but rebel. He seems to regard the role of rebel as a worthier one, one that exonerates him from any responsibility for what he has become. It is the theme and ethic of scores of Western movies: the emergence of the rebel out of a history of suffering, oppression, and trauma. More often than not, he has witnessed the annihilation of his entire family and, having grown up, has returned to a town or territory to exact vengeance from his parents' killers. The stanza about school excludes details about the narrator's far from happy school days. Sparrow would six years later sing *Happy Schooldays* (1972) where school days are portrayed as a time of joyful enactment of the poetry, songs, verbal, and physical games of a childhood steeped in play and folklore. Bill Trotman, too, sang of wanting to go back to school, a world and time of pure delight. Sparrow's rebel, however, has experienced no such delight in child's play, and seems to have grown up in, and in constant fear of, a world of men; the world of the street where the big men provide only falsely heroic role models for the small men (i.e., boys), who grow up simultaneously to rebel against and adopt the mask of the badjohn to conceal the remembered wounds of boyhood.

In school, the headmaster is the badjohn in authority, different from the badjohn on the street only in the sense that he is spokesperson for the positive strategies of straight society, and guards the doorway toward lower and middle-class respectability. We are note told anything about him, except that, exasperated by his failure to control or change this youth man, he tells him that he wishes the police would "hold"—that is, arrest, "take down," incarcerate, and straighten him out. The police constitute a hierarchical brotherhood of uniformed badjohns, precariously oscillating between their roots in impoverishment and the well-to-do class of proprietors they serve. To the bruised youth man, they would be worse than the badjohns on the street. Expelled from school, the young rebel becomes a problem of the street, because expulsion has led to a further expulsion from home where, it is implied, the system of parental discipline has also failed to contain rebellion or point the rebel toward a more positive pathway. *The Rebel*, this calypso of silences and spaces, does not describe either the confrontation at school with the headmaster or the one at home with parents. However, one may surmise that both confrontations involve the youth caught at the point of transition between "youth man" and "adult," or boyhood and young manhood, and being repelled or expelled into a sort of no man's land or wilderness of the street "out there," by the gods or gatekeepers of the crossroads of transition, the schoolmaster, in one case, his parents, in the other.

The urban wilderness that the PNM's peripatetic lectures sought to enlighten and tame with their lessons on history, civics, politics, and sociology, had its own codes, values, its certificate of bruises and modes of survival in which the methods of the street transcended those of the school, even though there could be considerable areas of overlap between them. "They beat me like a dog to learn that in school," declares the narrator of *Dan Is the Man in the Van*. He could easily have been describing life on the street. Preemptive and retributive violence is widely accepted by both street and school as a means of straightening the young sapling that displays a tendency to bend. While one of Williams's repeatedly stated objectives was to educate a nation of people so that the country could confidently locate itself in the modern world, there must have been many features of contemporary Western civilization from which he would have liked to shield the nation, but could not.

Williams also had profound doubts about the viability of fragile local cultures. His assumption was that the ancestral origins of the various ethnic groups in his country were too remote to be retrieved, revived, or understood. In "Politics and Culture," he stated the case for people of the diaspora accepting their disconnection from ancestral roots. He questioned: What do we have as our own in the West Indies? And he replies:

> ...Something, but not too much. A few relics of the aborigines, a few survivals of the African transplantation somewhat stronger influence

among the older generations of Indians which reactionaries strive to use for their personal ends. The rest is Europe – language, games, economy, externals of culture, values, way of life. Add to this at present a few local dances (far more authentic in the French islands than in Trinidad) our calypso whose value is not sufficiently appreciated, our Carnival and street bands, a more pronounced tendency nowadays in the local environment, some first rate literature from Roumains (sic) Cesaire, Zobel, Selvon, Naipaul and Lamming, and, most important of all, the elevation of CREOLE in Haiti to the status of national language – and what you have is a West Indian version of Europe, Europe with a difference indeed, but Europe. It is for the future to decide how far, with national independence and the assimilation of the various groups which constitute our society, we will develop something so distinctive, so removed from the original, that it becomes indigenous. (Williams 1958)

Williams then defined the role of the political leader as being not only "to govern" and "improve the material way of life," but to protect, encourage, and foster "the infant indigenous culture." Politics must help nurture culture, while culture, "through the nationalist movement in the arts and in literature," will in its turn support "the political movement and help...to give it a wider international audience" (Williams 1957). The plurality of culture was challenge and opportunity, not impediment. Williams recognized that:

> The existence of various racial groups and different cultural strands is an opportunity for the political leader as a man of culture to weave a native, indigenous cloth—not the patchwork of coexistence but the integrated harmonious pattern of assimilation. (Williams 1957)

Williams, at this point (September 1958), stood more for "interculturation" (Brathwaite 1974), which emphasizes what is shared between transgressive ethnic cultures, a commonality in the process and product of their becoming, than for multiculturalism, which seeks to distinguish between and keep distinct the differences in their origins and evolution. What he did not here anticipate was what Leveller in 1966, Naipaul in *The Middle Passage* (1962), and a chorus of voices after the neo-Garveyite Black Power awakening of 1970 loudly declared: that the ancestral void, within which the imagined patriarchal leader begins, might become filled with the worst elements of European civilization; that the fragile, indigenous culture of "relics" that the new postcolonial nation brings to the void or vortex, might simply crumble and give in to the culture of a new imperialism even more insidious and corrosive than the old one had been. The "modern world" within which Trinidad and Tobago was rapidly learning, both on their own and via the insights and policies of their maximum leader, to locate themselves, had its considerable deficiencies, the absorption of which was catalyzing into existence a nation that was quite different from anything Williams or anyone else could have imagined or controlled.

Yet, in 1966, Leveller had an apprehension of what was soon to come. His fears about the kinds of young men and women who were emerging out of the complex blend of historical, social, racial, and cultural sources would be enunciated several times over by concerned citizens in the decades that were to follow. He did not think that the government fully understood the complexity and severity of the situation, and his third stanza is a direct critique of the state's effort to curb what had begun to seem like an uncontrollable situation. In 1965, the government, far more sensitive than Leveller gave them credit for being, had recognized the imminent collapse of communities throughout the country and had initiated an intense program of community development via the construction of 57 community centers and several youth camps. Such development in fact paralleled and was based on the same principle as confronting the problem of education in the post-independence years by the construction of schools.

Such construction of buildings, as Leveller observed, was merely the beginning of the mission to transform both education and community. More schools did not mean improvement in what took place inside them, just as more community centers did not mean a more coherent or harmonious community life throughout the nation. Indeed, because of the widening racial divisions, community centers soon became sites for interethnic contestation as to which group had the right to determine how they were to be utilized.

Leveller is saying in his 1966 calypso that all the palliatives tried by the state have either failed or proven inadequate to contain the exploding problems. Apart from slum clearance, expansion of the army, the building of schools, there is the habit of appointing committees to investigate problems (then ignoring the recommendations and shelving the reports of these committees). Youth rallies are a weak placebo for the enormous headache of expanding unemployment among even the certificated youth.

Neither "our *intellectual* government"—note the implied derogation of academic intelligence—nor grassroots Gramscian "organic" intelligence, such as Leveller abundantly demonstrates in *How to Curb*

Delinquency, has any real idea of how to solve the ever-expanding problem of delinquency. Has education failed or has the government failed to create a relevant curriculum, and if so, what should such a curriculum include? Ironically, this is precisely the question that Eric Williams had been asking since *Education in the British West Indies*.

Conclusion: The Final Decade

Calypso discourse on education and community during Williams's final decade reformulates ideas that Williams had articulated several years before: more vocational schools, revised and locally oriented syllabi. Chalkdust, for example, in his calypso *The Answer to Black Power* (1971), could be repeating Williams's public address on "National Reconstruction," when he advises:

> Doctor, the answer to stop Black Power [protests]
> ...Teach the young ones before it's too late. (Chalkdust 1971)

It is Prowler's message in *Build More Trade Schools* that we see more of Williams's themes in *Education in the British West Indies*. Sparrow's *Children Must Learn* (1972) is, like his *Education* (1967), an exhortation to parents and children to support the agenda of the state:

> ...to take proper care of their child
> ...So teach them the correct way, don't let them run wild. (Sparrow 1972)

The parents' responsibility is to teach the children "the difference between right and wrong," "the light of true love," thrift, self-reliance, independence, kindness, fair play, generosity, and the virtue of hard work. All of these qualities, taught and inscribed in the home, will "make our land a much better place to be." Education in the home will become the foundation for a better nation. This sermon has all the moral earnestness that one might expect from a "peripatetic lecturer" of the late 1950s, or an acolyte, inspired by Williams's call in 1970 for a renewal of voluntary service.

The final stanza enjoins the parents to "teach them that drugs, rum and crime ain't no friend," and signals the growing concern of citizens with these three enemies of a healthy nation. Drugs, alcohol, and crime were to become the major agencies of community destruction in this post-independence Caribbean. They steadily designed the curriculum of the street, competing with, and in many places displacing, the curricula of the home and school. Sparrow in 1974 sings *No Future*, a calypso that warns young people that drug addition will destroy their chance of success in life, while Bomber laments *The Crime Wave in Trinidad*. Sparrow in 1974 also exhorts the nation to abandon all forms of uncivil behavior and to remember *We Pass That Stage*, wearing an academic gown and mortarboard to deliver his sermon at what had become the "university" of Queen's Park Savannah, at the culmination of the Carnival competitions in Trinidad at the Dimanche Gras concert in 1974. So mesmerized were the calypso judges by this back-in-times mimicry of the professorial pose, that they failed utterly to recognize the compelling originality of the calypsonian Shadow's rendition called *Bass Man*, with its image of a man pressured and driven by a demon of rhythm, "a man in his head" (an ear worm!), that he needed to kill.

Sparrow, on the other hand, wore a different mask in *Drunk and Disorderly* (1972) and *Rope* (1972). In *Drunk and Disorderly*, the protagonist celebrates his patently self-destructive, antisocial behaviour. He's always under police arrest, spends his weekends in jail, has exhausted the patience of friends and family, and is always short of money. Neither his anarchic behavior nor his self-lionization could make sense to the narrator of *Children Must Learn*. Did Sparrow's celebration of such contradictory roles—moralizing professor or preacher, rabid self-glorifying alcoholic—suggest a contradiction in the actor, his audience who relished both supreme moralist and supreme amoralist, or the bewildering society that has produced both masks?

In *"Rope,"* the protagonist is a peacekeeper and peacemaker who takes it on himself to make the streets safe for masqueraders on Carnival day, by taming a band of ruffians whose aim is simply to cause trouble by violently disrupting the performance of other players. The narrator, something of an old-time badjohn, one of whose responsibilities was to keep peace on his block, threatens to meet violence with superior violence ("rope") in putting down a younger generation of ruffians, bred now on the amoral and bloody spaghetti Westerns. There is a clash of generations and styles on the streets, a collision of types of anarchic behavior.

Clearly, the peacekeeping badjohn of three years earlier, the community leader of an older generation, has failed in his attempt to control the turbulence of the age. The entire nation is manifesting the same anomie in which civic existence has been reduced to "a free-for-all." Williams had in his independence addresses and in *History of the People of Trinidad and Tobago* (1962) identified savage individualism and an absence of commitment to any greater concept of community or any larger entity than self, to have been the worst obstacles in the pathway toward the intelligent, aware, self-confident, rational, balanced, and altruistic nation that he envisaged and to whose construction he had dedicated his life. *Ah Digging Horrors* is a calypso that describes a nation in which such individualism as Williams deplored has intensified and broken through all restraining barriers. Such anomie is recognized by Sparrow to be an illness of mind and spirit; maybe even madness.

In the midst of such mental confusion, Williams's role of teacher, professor, father, guide, and guardian of the prematurely aging nation, began to seem irrelevant, his vision and mission quaint old-time things. His subjects openly referred to him as "Deafy." Calypsos on education such as Brother Mudada's *Papers No Use* (1976), Explainer's *Strings* (1980), and Terror's *Madness* (1978) provide reasons why Williams's project in education seems to have failed. Mudada asserts that one's certificates are "no use," if one does not have a patron to promote one's cause. This is true, he affirms, whether one is applying for a job with the government or private sector:

> The papers [certificates] no use, darling, no use, no use. (Mudada 1976)

Finding employment in the real world requires not only abundant qualifications, but "connections." The narrator cites the cliché: "It's not what you know, but who you know," and describes how this process is causing frustration, destroying such unity as already exists throughout the country and forcing many qualified persons to migrate, join the "brain-drain," about which Williams used to complain, and contribute their labor toward the building of another country's economy. It may well be that Williams had by the mid-1970s reconciled himself to the brain drain. In the third address of 1970, "National Reconstruction," he spoke about his government's plan to improve and expand vocational education to provide high-school graduates, "with additional skills needed in this technological age to secure, *at home and abroad*, the job opportunities which are readily available" [my emphasis] (Williams 1981, 172).

Brother Mudada, however, is saying that after two decades of political leadership, Williams had neither reformed nor significantly modified the pernicious colonial system of patronage and clientelism. Williams had noted in *Education in the British West Indies* that the colonial system was characterized by restricted educational opportunities reinforced by race, class, color, and caste discrimination in the narrow job market. If one by miracle or natural intelligence excelled in the quest for certificates, one would still need a patron to gain employment congruent with one's qualifications. Mudada's *Papers No Use* indicates that far from having disappeared, the system of patronage and clientelism has become entrenched in the practice of the neocolonial state itself, leaving Trinidad and Tobago in the contradictory situation of its prime minister, on the one hand, haranguing citizens to be idealistic, patriotic, and zealous in their efforts to create a united national community, and on the other, retaining systems-based, not on merit, but on the relationship between patron and client, thus undermining such trust and unity as already exist in the nation between individuals and ethnic groups.

Of particular importance is the connection Mudada sees between such systemic discrimination and the alienation unto madness of the victim of discrimination. Two years later, the Mighty Terror in *Madness* (1978) argued that, more than narcotics, it is frustration at not being able to acquire "suitable" jobs that is driving young men mad. Youths are going mad, not because of illiteracy, but because of dysfunctional education. "Youths with O Level/ on the projects pushing shovel" suffer a crushing sense of thwarted expectations. They have followed Sparrow's advice in *Education* (1967) and gone to school and learned well, yet they can find no suitable work. They have believed Williams's great message of independence (1962), about the future of the nation residing in their school bags; and though these youths are too young to have read *Education in the British West Indies*, citizens of their parents' and of Terror's generation would have ingested Williams's most fervently preached message since 1946, about the necessity of educating to suit the needs of the community, and about the urgent need to either replace or blend academic with vocational education.

Yet, Terror, and perhaps the great majority of his generation, had in their heart of hearts never accepted Williams's radical recommendations about destroying the "aristocratic" and prestigious grammar-school curriculum, which had, as they could clearly recognize, produced the entire coterie of scholarship winners both on the government and opposition benches, who were now their neocolonial rulers. Thus, unlike Prowler, who in 1969 argued the need for more trade schools, Terror despairs of a solution to the burgeoning lunacy that he claims has overtaken the nation's youth. He reiterates and holds up to gloomy scrutiny the mantra of his generation.

Educated youths
Lots are going mad. (Terror 1978)

In this chapter, I have used the calypso as commentary and critique to exemplify how a community comes to understand itself, and more so, how it interprets how it learns about itself. By using Eric Williams's agenda for education in the region, I have been able to examine the development and impact of colonial education on Caribbean societies, illustrating how the legacies of such a system have been contested, persist, and resist change. To imagine as postcolonial subjects requires us to "make projections," not merely to predict the future, as I have articulated elsewhere (see Rohlehr 2000), but to "document how a popular art-form such as the calypso has behaved in the face of both the localised or microcosmic and the global or macrocosmic aspects of change" (542).

Notes

1. Dr. Eric Eustace Williams, the first prime minister of Trinidad and Tobago, is widely known as an international scholar and leader having written extensively, from an anticolonial stance, on the experience of colonialism and the requirements for national, regional, and international development.
2. The name given to a public park opposite to the parliament by Dr. Williams. This is the site where he delivered his famous public political lecturers, which were attended by huge crowds.
3. It was and is the practice for artists who sing calypsos to voluntarily take on a sobriquet that would depict the genre of calypso that they would want to project. Here is an example of a calypsonian who is also a teacher by profession, assuming a performance name of Chalkdust. Calypsonians are referred to by their sobriquet or performing title throughout this chapter.
4. This term is used to describe the headquarters of steel-pan orchestras. It is also seen as pivotal to community life.

References

Brathwaite, Edward Kamau. *Contradictory Omens: Cultural Diversity and Integration in the Caribbean*, Mona, Jamaica: Savacou Publications, 1974.

Craig, Susan. *Community Development in Trinidad and Tobago, 1943–1973: From Welfare to Patronage*. Institute of Social and Economic Research, University of the West Indies, Mona, Jamaica, 1974.

Lewis, Gordon K. "The Social Sources in the West Indies." *PNM Weekly*, January 13, 1958.

Mahabir, Winston. *In and Out of Politics*. Port-of-Spain: Imprint Caribbean, 1978.

Roach, Eric. "I Am the Archipelago." In *The Flowering Rock Collected Poems 1938–1974*. Leeds: Peepal Tree Books, 1992, 128. (Poem first published in 1957.)

Rogers, De Wilton. *The Rise of the PNM People's National Movement*, vol. 1 In *In the Beginning: An Excursus and Biography*. San Juan, Trinidad: Ideal Press, 1981.

Rohlehr, Gordon. "Apocalypso and the Soca Fires of 1990." In *The Shape of That Hurt and Other Essays*. Port-of-Spain: Lexicon, 1992.

Rohlehr, Gordon. "The Dilemma of the West Indian Academic in 1970." In *The Black Power Revolution 1970: a Retrospective*, edited by Ryan, Selwyn, and Stewart Taimoon. St. Augustine, Trinidad: University of the West Indies, Institute of Social and Economic Research, 1995, 381–402.

Rohlehr, Gordon. "Change and Prophecy in the Trinidad and Tobago Calypso Towards the 21st Century." In *Contending with Destiny: The Caribbean in the 21st Century*, edited by Kenneth Hall and Denis Benn. Kingston: Ian Randle Publishers, 2000, 542–574.

Ryan, Selwyn. *Eric Williams: The Myth and the Man*. Mona, Jamaica: University of the West Indies Press, 2009.

Williams, Eric. "Party Group Recommends Establishment of Pool of Peripathetic Lectures." *PNM Weekly* 2, no. 51 (August 25, 1958): N.P.

Williams, Eric. "Politics and Culture." *PNM Weekly* 2, no. 52 (September 1, 1958): N.P.

Williams, Eric. "MP Attends PNM's First Week-end School." *PNM Weekly* 3, no. 4 (September 29, 1958): N.P.

Williams, Eric. "National Reconstruction." In *Forged from the Love of Liberty, Selected Speeches of Eric Williams*. Port-of-Spain: Longman Caribbean, 1981, 172. (Address of June 30, 1970.)

Williams, Eric. "Revolution and Dignity." In *Forged from the Love of Liberty, Selected Speeches of Eric Williams*. Port-of-Spain, Longman Caribbean, 1981.

Williams, Eric. "The Dangers Facing Trinidad, Tobago, and the West Indian Nation." *PNM Weekly* 2, no. 34 (April 21, 1958): N.P.

Williams, Eric. "The Dangers Facing Trinidad, Tobago and the West Indian Nation." *PNM Weekly* vol. 2, no. 34 (April 21, 1958): 1, 3, 4.

Williams, Eric. *Education in the British West Indies*. Brooklyn, NY: A and B Publishers, 1994. First Published in Port of Spain, Trinidad, by TECA, 1950.

Williams, Eric. *Federation: Two Public Lectures, Port-of-Spain*, New York: College Press, 1956.

Williams, Eric. *History of the People of Trinidad and Tobago*. Port-of-Spain: PNM Publishers, 1962, 281–282.

Williams, Eric. *My Relations with the Caribbean Commission, 1943–1955*. (Port-of-Spain: Ben Durham Printing Works, 1955.
Williams, Eric. Preface to American edition of *Education in the British West Indies*. New York: A and B Publishers, November 3, 1967.

Discography

Allen, Kurt. "Too Bright." From the album *The Last Badjohn in Calypso*, Fuluma, 2010.
Black Stalin (Leroy Calliste). "More Times." From the album, *Roots, Rock Soca*, Rounder, 1992. (Song composed and first recorded in 1980.)
Black Stalin (Leroy Calliste). *National Reconstruction*, 1971.
Chalkdust, The Mighty (Hollis Liverpool). "Ram the Magician." From the album *Kaiso with Dignity*, Hot Vinyl, 1984.
Chalkdust, The Mighty (Hollis Liverpool). *The Answer to Black Power*. Tropico, 1970.
Chalkdust, The Mighty (Hollis Liverpool). "No More Licks in School." From the CD *A Thread of Hope*, Juba Productions, 2002.
Chalkdust, The Mighty (Hollis Liverpool). "Rescue QRC." From the CD *Drums of the Millennium*, Strakers, 2000.
Chalkdust, The Mighty (Hollis Liverpool). *Teach the Right History*. Tropico, 1968.
Composer, The Mighty (Fred Mitchell). *Child Training*. Telco Record Label, Port of Spain Trinidad, 1969.
Composer, The Mighty. (Fred Mitchell) *Proper Teaching*. (No details) 1971.
Delamo (Franz Lambkin). *Armageddon*. (No details) 1984.
Delamo (Franz Lambkin). *Apocalypse*. (No details) 1981.
Delamo (Franz Lambkin). *Sodom and Gommorah*. (No details) 1982.
Delamo (Franz Lambkin). *Looters*. (No details) 1991.
Gibraltar, The Mighty (Sydney Benjamin). *Avoidism*. (Not dated).
Leveller (No name recorded). *How to Curb Delinquency*. (No details) 1966.
Luta (Morel Peters). *Think Again*. (No details) 1991.
Mitchelle, Boyie (Boyie Mitchelle). "Real Ole'l Time Ting." From the CD compilation *Kitchener's Calypso Revue: Kaiso Gems Live*, vol. 2. 1999.
Mudada, Brother (Allan Fortune). *Papers No Use*. (No details) 1976.
Pretender (Aldrick Farell). *History in We Own Backyard*. (No details) 1972.
Prowler, The Mighty (Roy Lewis; later The Mystic Prowler). *Build More Trade Schools*. 1969.
Rudder, David. "Madness." From the CD *No Restriction* (box set: disc 2), Musicrama/ Koch, 1999.
Rudder, David. "The Ganges and the Nile." From the CD *International Chantuelle*. J. W. Productions, 1999.
Rudder, David. "Another Day in Paradise" From the CD. *No Restriction* (Box Set: Disc 1). Musicrama/Koch, 1999. (Originally performed in 1995.)
Sparrow, The Mighty (Slinger Francisco). "Bull Pistle Gang." From the 7" Vinyl, *Bull Pistle Gang/The Village Ram*, Jump Up Label JU-523. 1964.

Sparrow, The Mighty (Slinger Francisco). "Don't Touch Me." From the Album *Carnival Bacchanal*, RCA, 1960/ 1961.
Sparrow, The Mighty (Slinger Francisco). "Hangman's Cemetery." From the CD *Early Years: Millennium Series*. Mighty Sparrow Label, 2001. (Originally recorded in 1961.)
Sparrow, The Mighty (Slinger Francisco). *Renegades*. From the CD *Early Years: Millennium Series*. Mighty Sparrow Label, 2001. (Originally recorded in 1961.)
Sparrow, The Mighty (Slinger Francisco). "Royal Jail." From the album *The Calypso King of Trinidad* (no details) 1961.
Sparrow, The Mighty. (Slinger Francisco). "Ten to One Is Murder" From the CD *Party Classics*, vol 1 and 2. Musicrama/Koch, 1994. (Originally released in. 1960.)
Sparrow, The Mighty (Slinger Francisco). "William the Conqueror." From the CD *Living Legend: Millennium Series*. The Mighty Sparrow label, 2001. (Originally recorded in 1957.)
Sparrow, The Mighty (Slinger Francisco). "Gunslingers." From the CD *King Sparrow in High-Fidelity* (Audio CD 2011), Smithsonian Folkways Archival. (Originally performed in 1959. Originally released as *Sparrow in Hi-Fi*, Cook, 1963.)
Sparrow, The Mighty (Slinger Francisco). "Children Must Learn." From the album *Many Moods of Sparrow*. Bestway, BW 1001, 1972.
Sparrow, The Mighty (Slinger Francisco). "Ah Digging Horrors" From the CD *True Awakening: Millennium Series* The Mighty Sparrow Label, 2001. (Originally recorded in 1975.)
Sparrow, The Mighty (Slinger Francisco). "Dan is the Man in the Van" From the CD *Quintessential Cd! Mighty Sparrow*, RIAA Label. 2006. (Originally released in 1963.)
Sparrow, The Mighty (Slinger Francisco). "Education.is Essential" From the CD *Quintessential, Cd! Mighty Sparrow*. RIAA Label. 2006. (Originally released in 1967.)
Sparrow, The Mighty (Slinger Francisco). *Shanty Town People*. 45 rpm National Record Company, Port of Spain Trinidad, 1966.
Sparrow, The Mighty (Slinger Francisco). "The Rebel." From the CD *Early Years: Millennium Series*. Mighty Sparrow Label, 2001. (Originally recorded as a 45 rpm National Record Company, Port of Spain Trinidad, 1966).
Terror, The Mighty (Fitzgerald Henry). *Madness*. (No details) 1978.
The Original De Fosto Himself (Winston Scarbrough). "Educated Donkey." From the album *From Beyond—Now and Then*. Fuluma, 2008.
Young Creole (Wilfred Barker). *Behind the Bridge*. (No details) 1970.

10

More in de Mortar dan de Pestle*: Recruitment into Secondary Teaching in Trinidad and Tobago

Joyanne De Four-Babb

"More to it than meets the eye. More to the story than was said."

—John Mendes, *Cote ci Cote la: Trinidad and Tobago Dictionary*[1]

Postcolonialism draws our theoretical attention to the ways in which language works in the colonial formation of discursive and cultural practices. It shows how discourse and power are inextricably linked. Politically, it enables us to provide an account of the ways in which global inequalities are perpetuated not only through the distribution of resources, but also through colonial modes of representation, and in doing this it suggests ways of resisting colonial power in order to forge a more socially just world order. (Rizvi, Lingard, and Lavia 2006, 250)

The excerpt above highlights that one concern of researchers who theorize about using concepts of postcolonialism is to unravel the complexity of construction of identity in the contested site of the, cultural-discursive, social-political, and material-economic (Kemmis and Grootenboer, 2008) postcolonial space. This chapter provides room for the postcolonial and post-independence voices of college-graduate,[2] secondary-school teachers from Trinidad and Tobago, who may have been "marginalised, silenced, ignored or denied" the opportunity to speak and gives them the opportunity to be "valued, heard and responded to" in this reinterpretation of identity formation through a recruitment process. It provides a critical look at a centralized practice of teacher recruitment in Trinidad and Tobago that occurred between 1966 (four years after Trinidad and Tobago gained independence from Great Britain) and 2000. This practice is in contrast to the neoliberalist, contractual employment arrangements that have crept into the public service after 2000 (Marchack n.d.). Nonetheless, today the practice of recruitment still looks very much like it did in the period under review.

Very little work has been done on analyzing public service recruitment practice in Trinidad and Tobago (see Marchack n.d.). Even fewer studies examine the influence of recruitment practices on secondary-school teacher identity in Trinidad and Tobago. Very few, if any, take into account teachers' voices in this process. This essay is an attempt to address all of these gaps.

Background

In Trinidad and Tobago, a highly centralized and bureaucratic practice for the recruitment of teachers was established in 1966. Today in 2011, the Teaching Service Commission (TSC), a civil-service bureau established by the Education Act of 1966, is still the only body with the authority to "hire, dismiss, promote, and transfer all teachers who work in public schools" (Stewart 1981, 192). The TSC, along with other constitutionally appointed service commissions (public, civil, fire, and prison) also exercise disciplinary control over persons employed within the various arms of the public services (government of Trinidad and Tobago 2011; Marchack n.d.). Until 2000, the TSC was part of the Public Service Commission, and teachers were regarded as "civil servants." They were subject to the laws governing the TSC, including the Education Act of 1966 and the Education (Teaching Service) Regulations, Chapter 39.01 of the Laws of the Republic of Trinidad and Tobago (Cabinet Appointed Committee, Republic of Trinidad and Tobago, 1999).

Prior to the establishment of the TSC in 1966, the director of education handled all recruitment of teachers and principals in government schools. The director delegated these responsibilities to the boards of management of each of the government-assisted schools (Campbell 1997; Stewart 1981). Consequently, some principals had discretion over who was recruited to teach at their schools, because they could make personal recommendations to their respective boards (De Four-Babb 2004). However, when the TSC was established, it served to "standardize the criteria" (Stewart 1981, 192) by which a teacher or principal could be hired. In so doing, the government was able to control those who were employed in the education system. Such an arrangement allowed for "stricter methods of surveillance [of teachers], a tighter partitioning of the population [and] more efficient techniques of locating and obtaining information" (Foucault 1977, 77) about who wanted to and who would be allowed to teach.

But in the post-independence era, especially between 1966 and 2000, little has been documented about who was "called forth" or "hailed" or "interpelated" (Althusser 1971) as secondary-school teachers by the Teaching Service Commission and Ministry of Education in Trinidad and Tobago. Who did the Ministry of Education think the college-graduate, secondary-school teacher was (Ellsworth 1997)? What dominant cultural-discursive, material-economic and social-political arrangements (Kemmis and Grootenboer 2008) enabled or constrained the recruitment process for these secondary-school teachers in Trinidad and Tobago? How did a person come to think about himself or herself as a teacher after having been through the practice of recruitment in this post-independence era?

I use poststructuralist, Foucauldian discourse analysis to "loosen the embrace...of words and things" (Foucault 1972, 49) said about and done in the process of recruitment of college-graduate, secondary-school teachers into teaching high school in Trinidad and Tobago. I analyze how disciplinary technologies (Foucault 1977; Gore 1998), such as surveillance, normalization of judgement, exclusion, classification, regulation, and examination operate in the social regulation of the college-graduate secondary-school teacher.

In *Discipline and Punish* (Foucault 1977), Foucault distinguished between sovereign power, which he viewed as something external and enforced on the body, and disciplinary power. He argued that disciplinary power is the dominant mode of social regulation of people in the modern world. It is invisible and does not rely on physical force, but relies on infinitesimal practices. Foucault argued that disciplinary power is internalized in people through disciplinary technologies and results in self-control (Foucault 1977; Llamas 2006; Marshall 1989). These disciplinary technologies are practices that result in subtle forms of social and self-regulation. They help to classify particular behaviors, actions, and attitudes as "normal" or "abnormal."

Gore (1998), in her analysis of Foucault's (1977) work, identified eight disciplinary technologies characteristic of modern societal institutions. These included: *surveillance*, which she explained as "supervising, closely observing, watching, threatening to watch, or expecting to be watched" (235); *normalization of judgement* through comparison by "invoking, requiring, setting or conforming to a standard defined as normal" (237); *exclusion*, setting apart from the normal—"the defining of the pathological" (238); *classification*, which is the differentiation and ranking of groups and individuals; the *distribution* of bodies in space, through separation or isolation; *individualization*—giving individual character to oneself; *totalization* defined as "giving collective character" (242) to individuals, by naming oneself as part of a group; and *regulation*, defined as "controlling by rule, subject to restrictions, invoking a rule, including sanction, reward and punishment" (243).

The data and analysis described in this essay is drawn from a qualitative study that formed the basis of my doctoral work (De Four-Babb 2004[3]). In that study, I drew upon transcribed interview data from 14 male and 15 female college-graduate secondary-school teachers recruited into teaching between 1965 and 2000. During that period, college-graduate secondary-school teachers in Trinidad and Tobago, were not required to have engaged in any preservice teacher-education programs before they were recruited. It was only in 2010 that graduates of a pre-service preparation program for secondary-school teachers entered the education system (Bristol, Brown, and De Four-Babb 2010). It is the experiences of recruitment given by these 29 teachers, my own experience of being recruited as a college-graduate secondary-school teacher in 1986, my analysis of documents, policies, and practices associated with the practices of recruitment that I present here.[4] I argue that the recruitment process in that period sought to normalize and categorize college-graduate secondary-school teachers as school-subject specialists rather than as educational professionals.

The Recruitment Process

In the *International Dictionary of Education,* the word *recruitment* is defined as "the process and methods of finding and attracting new personnel, members, etc." (Page and Thomas 1977, 286). And recruitment is critical for the continued existence of any profession (Hale and Starratt 1989; Lortie 1975). As Dan Lortie argued:

> From the perspective of the occupations, these processes are the means of its endurance: no occupation which fails to attract new members, inculcate its subculture, or sustain commitment through time can survive or maintain its identity. (Lortie 1975, 24)

Recruitment can be seen as a practice: a nexus of sayings, doings, and relatings (Kemmis and Grootenboer 2008; Schatzki, in press) involved in the process of selecting and moving individuals into teaching. It is during this process that potential teachers begin to construct new understandings of how they should act and be as teachers. They also begin to understand what is required of them as they seek to become members of the teaching profession. It is also an important time during which they begin to construct their identity as a teacher (Britzman 1991).

In Trinidad and Tobago, recruitment of teachers is a highly centralized process, controlled by the Ministry of Education and the TSC. Jesse, a female college graduate and teacher who began to teach in 1985, described her experience of the phases of the recruitment process in the following way:

> I filled out the forms with the Ministry. The Ministry asked for my degree certificate and my O'Level and A'Level certificates. There was an interview, I think a few months after I applied. And then I just had to wait to be called to a school. (Jesse 1985)

Jesse's description is quite similar to that of most of the other 28 interviewees' stories about the various stages of the recruitment; this is in spite of the historical period in which they began to teach. Yet, based on my personal experience of being recruited as a college-graduate secondary-school teacher in Trinidad and Tobago in 1986, and my analysis of the policies, procedures, and documents, the practice of recruitment is not as simple as Jesse described. Indeed, there was more to it than meets the eye.

The recruitment practice includes various activities: *registration, application, classification, interview,* and *placement*. Each of these activities is enabled and constrained by various cultural-discursive, material-economic, and social-political arrangements (Kemmis and Grootenboer 2008) at any given time. These arrangements, in turn, also create possibilities and constraints for how persons may come to think of themselves as college-graduate secondary-school teachers. I will now explore how engagement in these activities resulted in subtle forms of social and self-regulation of 29 college-graduate secondary-school teachers.

Registration

The Teachers' Register was established under the Education Act of 1966, Section 47 (1). It signaled the Ministry of Education's attempt to monitor all persons who wished to be appointed to teach in the public school system. The Act stated, "Subject to this Act, no person is eligible to be appointed to be, or to continue to be a teacher, unless his name is registered and kept in the Register of teachers herein required to be kept" (Laws of Trinidad and Tobago, Education Act, 1966, 26). The Minister of Education was put in charge of keeping this public record, which was first published in 1966 in the *Gazette*, the government newspaper. Since then, supplementary lists have been used to update the Teachers' Register. A person's name is removed from the register upon death or if found "guilty of gross misbehaviour, or gross inefficiency or other conduct unfitting him for employment as a teacher" (Laws of Trinidad and Tobago, Education Act, 1966, 27). This person would be informed in writing, and when his/her name is removed, he or she will no longer be permitted to teach in Trinidad and Tobago. He or she could appeal this decision within 42 days.

In order to be entered into the Teacher's Register, a person must have a minimum academic qualification of at least a pass in five Ordinary Level subjects (O-levels). As one of the interviewees, Sid Chase, explained:

> You registered, meaning that you simply go down—I cannot remember—I think it was the Treasury. You paid five dollars and you showed your certificates, your O'Level certificates and once you had a minimum of five O'Levels you could register as a teacher. (Sid Chase 1979)

Each person is then given a certificate bearing a teacher's registration number. This registration number is a requirement for the next phase of the recruitment process.

While this register is a bureaucratic and legal requirement for all persons wanting to teach, it is also a form of surveillance (Foucault, 1977) of prospective teachers by the government and members of the general public. There is the public naming and listing of those who will be allowed to teach. When the names of those who wish to teach are published, they become targets of the public gaze, and their private lives are up for public scrutiny for "gross misbehaviour" or "gross inefficiency." For example, Bumper recalled:

> I remember something happened in my private life, though, and my mother said to me that she did not very well like something that I was doing and she said, "You know you can be reported to the Ministry for that." And I said, "What? My personal life is my personal life. I don't want anybody meddling. And in fact after I persisted along that line, she told me that in fact somebody had told her that they would report me to the Ministry. And I was very, very upset. But I sat down to think about it again and I said "Listen, this probably is not very right and if you are to be some kind of role model and set some kind of example, maybe you should listen. (Bumper 1980)

Although Bumper did not disclose the "something" that happened in her private life, the threat of being reported served to make her modify her behavior. In her case, she was under surveillance by her own mother and other members of the public. In the same way, the registration process could induce self-control in prospective teachers who have made a public declaration to teach and have, therefore, opened their lives up for public scrutiny. Since there is no definition of "gross inefficiency" and "gross misbehavior," many practicing and prospective teachers will want to appear "well-behaved" and "efficient." From these subject positions, they would tend to try to display exemplary or conservative behavior, as they do not wish to be "struck off the list."

The registration process excludes from teaching those persons who do not possess the minimum academic qualifications to teach. Although a person may be extremely talented, if he or she does not possess the minimum qualifications, he or she cannot legally teach. At the same time, the registration process identifies a group of people who can perform the function of teaching. This normalization, or setting of a norm (Gore 1998), for those who *can* enter the teaching profession is based on an academic standard rather than the expressed ability to do the job. This leads to the public perception that anybody who has five O-levels can teach. As Cynthia explained:

> I think it all stems from the whole idea that anybody could go in a classroom and teach. Anybody! And that is a view held by society I

mean if anybody could go in a classroom and teach you are obviously not a professional, and the fact that we are not trained in advance emphasises that view. Just get five subjects and make sure you get Maths and a Science and you will teach and if you can't find anything better to do, teach. (Cynthia 1978)

Therefore, at the initial registration process for teaching, the Ministry of Education calls forth persons with minimum academic qualifications to be listed as part of a body of potential teachers. The underlying discourse is that any certifiably knowledgeable person could be considered as a prospective teacher.

Application

Prospective secondary-school teachers may find out about teaching vacancies from other teachers, principals, or advertisements for teachers put out by the Ministry of Education or denominational boards. For example, I found out about two teaching vacancies from my father, who sent me a letter a few months before I graduated from the University of the West Indies, Mona Jamaica. In the letter dated May 5, 1985, he commented:

> About job opportunities, I have no exciting news. Why? I have not investigated the ministry as yet. However, I must inform you, two vacancies (Geog.) will be created this month, at [name of school]. Are you interested? State your wish with dispatch. If interested send application. Tell me the earliest date you can be available, so I can talk it over with the principal. (E. De Four, personal communication, May 9, 1985)

My father was a college-graduate teacher at a government secondary school when he wrote this letter, and he had insider information on the vacancies at the other school. He knew the principal of the school and was willing to suggest me as a possible person for the job. I did not accept his offer at the time, but was able to secure my first job when another teacher told me about another vacant position several months after I returned home.

The Ministry of Education advertises for graduate secondary-school teachers when vacancies become available. For example, in 2000, the Ministry of Education in its attempt to find "suitably qualified persons to fill teaching vacancies" in specified subject areas for named secondary schools in Trinidad and Tobago, invited applications to be considered from:

1. Persons who hold degrees or diplomas from recognised Universities/Institutions
2. Non-graduates who have fulfilled partial requirements for the award of a degree from the University of the West Indies and are available for immediate employment
3. Persons who hold five (5) O level passes including English and Mathematics together with (2) Advanced Level passes, one of which must be in the relevant subject area.
4. Persons who are over the age of 45 years who possess the above qualifications would also be considered for employment **on contract only**. (bold in original; Ministry of Education, *Vacancies*, 2000)

For the Ministry of Education, "suitably qualified" refers to an academic standard—a graduate of a "recognized" university, an incomplete degree or A-level qualifications—rather than a professional or technical indication that one can teach. The prospective teacher is positioned first and foremost as a school-subject specialist. There is no requirement for previous experience of working with groups of young people. There is no requirement that one be familiar with how students learn. There is no requirement for the prospective teacher to have some ability to work with students of varying abilities, with students who have learning disabilities, or with students from various economic and social backgrounds. The absence of these requirements in an advertisement for teachers continues to feed into the idea that anybody with academic qualifications can teach.

The advertisement also calls forth persons to fill different categories of secondary teacher—the graduate, nongraduate, and A-level college-graduate teacher. Each of these categories represents different levels of experience in the education system and suggests that there can be no level playing field in terms of preparation and ongoing professional development for all secondary-school teachers. The policy of employment of persons over the age of 45 "under contract" discriminates against more mature persons who may want to change careers and enter teaching. This person still has 15 years to make a career in teaching before his/her compulsory retirement at age 60. Therefore, one questions the fairness of this policy. Applications are made in duplicate on prescribed forms. The application forms request verifiable data such as a person's name, age, educational history, nationality, weight, height, language, and nationality. Original academic, birth, and marriage certificates must be presented when a person submits the application forms to the Ministry of Education. In addition to these original documents, two recent photographs are required to confirm these aspects of biographical data. The Teacher Registration Certificate and number must also be submitted with the application forms. Other general information, such as available date for employment; father's biographical details and occupation; and the applicant's other jobs held, disabilities, and convictions are also required.

The focus on "father's occupation" is a slap in the face for the thousands of children of single or married working mothers, because mother's occupation is not requested. This policy hints at a patriarchal discourse that harks back to the "old boy's network" that flourished in colonial days when the sons of the religious and economic elite filled the spaces of the civil service. The application process can be viewed as a form of "administrative documentation" (Foucault 1977, 189) and represents a "whole mass of documents that capture and fix" (Foucault 1977, 189) prospective teachers. It puts them under surveillance by the Ministry and its representatives. However, while this biographical information is easy to collect (Reilly and Chao 1982) and gives some idea of the physical characteristics of the person being recruited to teach, the information gathered is not necessarily a good indicator of how well a person will be able to teach. A more detailed application process is needed for potential teachers to draw out whether or not they are able to engage students in the teaching-learning process.

Classification

College-graduate secondary-school teachers are classified in two ways: (1) as a class of teacher based on the level of academic qualifications and (2) as a specialist school-subject teacher. In its attempt to administer the large number and types of teachers recruited to teach at secondary schools, the Ministry of Education devised a hierarchical system of classifying secondary-school teachers based on academic qualifications. Up until 1999, the categories of secondary-school teachers included: (1) persons with degrees (Teacher II); (2) persons with incomplete degree qualifications (Special Teacher III); (3) persons with primary Teacher's Diplomas (Teacher I); (4) persons with A-level qualifications (Assistant Teacher III); (5) persons with technical vocational training (Technical Vocational Teacher, I–IV). In 2000, this system was replaced by a newer system of classification. However, the old classification scheme is used in this study because it was the system that was in place when the interviewees first began teaching.

In the pre-2000 classification scheme, the title of the secondary-school teacher at each level is constituted by a minimum academic qualification. According to Mackinnon (1960, 83), "Each teacher is put in a category and appropriately labelled." Academic performance may be an indication of how well someone has "learned" formal subject knowledge. It is not a direct measure of how well a person can teach. Every category was tied to remuneration. The post of college-graduate secondary-school teacher was the highest ranked and highest paid. However, academic qualifications beyond a first degree or professional qualifications, such as a Primary-(school) Teacher's Diploma or the in-service Diploma in Education, did not result in any change in rank or added remuneration. Foucault (1977) argued that "the distribution according to ranks and grades has a double role: it marks the gaps, hierarchizes qualities, skills and aptitudes; but it also punishes and rewards" (Foucault 1977, 181). Teachers who do not possess a degree have an incentive or reward of increased pay if they choose to improve their academic qualifications and move up the ranks to college-graduate secondary-school teacher status. However, those who do not hold degrees are "punished" because of their lack of tertiary qualifications. Those who hold degrees and teach in primary schools are punished because their degrees are not recognized. This bureaucratic standard subsidizes the weak and holds back the able (Mackinnon 1960). In other words, it punishes those who move on to higher education or professional development, because those teachers who pursue academic or professional qualifications are not rewarded for their efforts. The result is that those with added academic qualifications tend to move out of the classroom and into administrative posts or other jobs. Darling-Hammond and Sclan (1996) argued:

> For talented candidates to decide to teach and to remain in teaching, they must perceive opportunities for professional growth, advancement and financial rewards. (Darling-Hammond and Sclan 1996, 69)

This practice of no rewards for professional advancement continues to reinforce the discourse that those with degrees do not need professional training. If there were some recognition of the professional qualifications above the level of college-graduate secondary-school teacher, then this would probably signal that there is need for a professional requirement for teaching. There is need for a greater range of career options and rewards for those college-graduate secondary-school teachers who want to stay in the classroom and improve their academic qualifications.

The classification as a specialist school-subject teacher is based on a complex interaction of one's university specialization, the secondary school's school-subjects, and the vacancy available. For example, although I completed a double major in geography and geology, I was only classified as a geography teacher because geology was not part of the secondary curriculum. Two interviewees, whose names I have withheld because they have identified their subject areas, gave an example of how they were classified as geography teachers when they began to teach.

> Joyanne: *You said that you did Economics [at university], and yet you were sent to teach Geography and History. How did that come about?*
>
> Interviewee A: *When you are interviewed they look at the subjects you read for your degree and you're A'Level qualifications and they would assess your competence in specific subject areas. The vacancy at [name of school] was for History/Geography teacher and based on my assessment, I was deemed qualified to fill the vacancy.*

Interviewee A was assigned to teach geography and history as determined by his or her A-level qualification, rather than his or her specialization at university. He or she was needed to teach geography, because of a vacancy existed for a geography teacher, and since he or she had done it at A-levels he or she was classified as a geography teacher. Similarly, Interviewee B explained how he or she had to choose between his or her university specializations based on the vacancy at the school:

> I thought that when you went to the Teaching Service Commission for an interview, you were being interviewed for the job of a teacher. I was told point blank, "What subject would you like to be tested on?" I said, "I have a double degree..." "But no you have to choose a subject." So I chose Geography. So that is how I am classified as a Geography teacher. So right away you have said to me you can be a Geography teacher, but you cannot be a History teacher, when I did not mind teaching the History. I've never taught History.
>
> J: *You've never taught History?*
>
> Interviewee A: No. But I've been teaching Social Studies and I have not a clue.

As new teachers, both of these interviewees got jobs as geography teachers based on vacancies for particular types of teachers in the secondary-school system. The thinking behind this practice may be that an ability to understand the formal content knowledge of a discipline, can be an indication that one could teach a certain school subject, especially if one had already passed that level of qualification at O-level or A-level.

The college-graduate secondary-school teacher is classified and normalized first and foremost as a specialist school-subject teacher based on the individual's academic qualifications, and not based on the ability to teach that subject, that is, demonstrating practical understanding of what they should do as teachers.

Interviews

The interview was recommended in the 1960 Trinidad and Tobago Cabinet proposals as "an essential part of the procedure in making appointment" for teachers (Trinidad and Tobago Government 1960, 5). The interviews were supposed to be conducted by the five members of the Teaching Service Commission (TSC). Membership in the TSC [is] held by:

> Persons (male or female) with experience in teaching and educational administration, who could be relied upon to assess the technical requirements of a vacancy and the professional qualification of applicants. (Trinidad and Tobago Government 1960, 8)

Sid Chase described her meeting with these officials in the following way:

> I was called by the Teaching Service Commission to be interviewed for a post. When I entered the room I came with all my documents...my original documents that is. Of course nobody asked me for any original documents. There was a panel. I can't remember the number but it was certainly more than about four persons on the panel. I do remember a particular lady being on the panel...So this awesome panel...I have to say awesome because everybody looked very bureaucratic I must say...elderly people. (Sid Chase 1979)

The assumption is that these experienced educators are qualified to judge the prospective teachers. However, one wonders what is their concept of a "good teacher"? Will they be upholding the Ministry of

Education's view of a good teacher? Or will their concepts be based upon their own experiences as teachers and with teachers?

An interview provides an opportunity for face-to-face interaction between the interviewer and the interviewee. It is also useful for the assessment of the interviewee's personal characteristics, such as elements of physical character, such as height, build, race, voice, dress, well as communication skills of prospective teachers. Interviewers could convey information about the job and provide an opportunity for applicants to clarify questions (Reilly and Chao 1982). But one could also regard the interview as a disciplinary technology: an examination. As an examination, "it is a normalizing gaze, a surveillance that makes it possible to qualify, to classify, and to punish. It establishes over individuals a visibility which one differentiates and judges them" (Foucault 1977, 184). The interview uses surveillance.

While the main purpose of an interview may be to eliminate unsuitable candidates, in the face of teacher shortages in certain school-subject areas, especially mathematics and geography, or at periods of increased demand for teachers, many people will not be eliminated as classrooms and schools need to be staffed. Additionally, some applicants may try to make a good impression on the interviewers. As Salohcin explained:

> You know when it comes to people doing interview, they do fantastic because people could talk their way out of something and get in there [the classroom] and then muck it up. (Salohcin 1973)

As Salohcin suggested, a successful interview is not necessarily an indicator of what one *can* or will be able to do when one begins to teach.

The interviewees described these Teaching Service Commission interviews as usually under a half-hour. The questions asked in the interviews tended to be general rather than technical questions. For example, Kowen stated: "I guess knowing that I was just a university graduate they couldn't ask too many technical questions because I had no formal training" (Kowen 1990). The questions in the interviews were related to reasons for entering teaching and how to teach a particular topic or lesson. Poui described the interview as follows:

> I remember being asked questions like, some very general questions like how would you approach the teaching of a particular topic? That kind of thing. How would you deal with difficult students? General

questions like that. I mean other than the normal questions like why you would like to be there and that sort of thing. To me as I remember it was not a very in-depth kind of interview. They asked you these things and I suppose once you give a reasonable kind of answer, that was it. Once you did not obviously, I suppose, appear to be—I don't know-a total delinquent or something, that was the thing. (Poui 1979)

One wonders what kind of judgment about a person's ability to teach could be made during a 20- to 30-minute interview. Although the interviews were scored, no feedback was given to the interviewees about their performance in the interviews. The results of the TSC interviews are ranked, and names of prospective teachers are put on an availability list that principals can consult when they need new teachers.

Taylor and Driscoll (1995) warned about the "halo effects" of the interview, that is, the external factors that may influence interviewers to introduce an element of leniency in the interview. These "halo effects" are particularly significant in small communities, such as the education fraternity in Trinidad, where there is possibility of interviewers and interviewees knowing each other, directly or indirectly. Several interviewees mentioned examples of these halo effects. For example, Sid Chase recalled:

> I remember this particular panellist smiling and then the lady, the elderly lady who was a school supervisor at the time looked at me and she said "Who," and she called my last name, "Who is your family?" And she said "Is so and so your grandmother? "Are you related to so and so?" So I said yes. She said, "So your are so and so's granddaughter?" So I said yes. So the other panellist now who had asked me the first question said, "Oh! Your mother would have told you to make a statement like that then. No wonder you responded so eloquently." And the next thing I heard was "Thank you very much for coming. You have done very well in the interview." And the next thing I knew I was appointed. (Sid Chase 1979)

Many of the interviewees believed that the interview process was not rigorous enough. For example, Miss T&T explained:

> Now looking at it I felt that maybe it was too simple an interview. And I feel that...and in interacting with other people in the teaching profession sometimes I feel that maybe, people are ending up in teaching who do not want to be here and maybe the interview should interrogate

people a little more, because when you are in a job that you don't really want to be in, you don't perform to your maximum. (Miss T&T 1990)

Salohcin made recommendations on how more rigor could be imposed in the interview process. He explained:

> I believe you must have some kind of evaluation process other than the university qualifications. In much the same way you have jury selection. So much work has gone into education over the last 25 years, I am sure that some instrument could be designed so that close to 60% staying in the system could be determined. Really! People are coming into the system and the attitude they have towards people's children is frightening. They do more harm than good sometimes. That's the minority, but still it happens. So you have an instrument where you have them evaluated, psychologically, emotionally, so you "know" how they are likely to respond in a given set of circumstances. You must have some kind of orientation and some kind of pre-service training. I would say a minimum of six months in the first instance before people are placed in a secondary school. The approach today is a rush job, a quick fix which virtually unleashes some unfit candidates on the school children. (Salohcin 1973)

The interview was useful to make face-to-face contact between a prospective teacher and people who are well experienced in the education system. But the process as described by the interviewees was quite brief and not rigorous enough. It did not discriminate between one's ability to learn and one's ability to teach.

Placement and Support in the Beginning Years

The appointment of a new college-graduate secondary-school teacher depends upon the existence of a temporary or permanent vacancy in the teaching service. Permanent vacancies may be created when a teacher resigns or is promoted to a new post or when a new post is created with the expansion of the delivery system. Temporary vacancies may be created when teachers go on maternity leave for three months or on full-pay or no-pay study leave.

All first appointments of college-graduate secondary-school teachers are made on a temporary basis, and teachers are "on probation." The letters of appointment from the Ministry of Education state: "This appointment is purely temporary and may be terminated at any time by either party at short notice." However, this bureaucratic requirement is disconcerting to those persons who wish to make a career in teaching. As one interviewee stated:

> V: Even that was kind of strange because after a while when you started teaching, you know you are temporary and they keep sending these letters from the Teaching Service Commission telling you this does not allow you in any way to go and further your studies or do any other thing. [*Name of a person*] told me don't take that letter on, you go and do your DipEd because I was kind of scared to do it.
>
> J: *How often did you receive those temporary letters?*
>
> V: Once a term or twice a term. I think I have some of them home somewhere. I found that it was strange, getting into teaching, you are temporary. They don't want to allow you to go and study to do your Dip Ed, your Masters or whatever it is, but yet they send these letters for you. They tell you are a teacher. I mean that can't be. The system is messed up a bit. (Mr. Vogue 1991)

Before being confirmed in a permanent post by the Teaching Service Commission, college-graduate secondary-school teachers must complete a two-year probationary period and a medical examination to determine whether or not they are fit to teach. However, there is no professional requirement or additional certification required to move from probation to confirmation. These levels of appointment are bureaucratic requirements, since there is no professional standard to be achieved during the two years of probation. Teachers are given full responsibility at the start of the job, and new teachers have to cope with the demands of the job like any other experienced teacher.

The Ministry of Education does not issue Teaching Service Regulations to teachers, but advises new teachers that the terms and conditions of their employment are subject to these regulations. The appointment letter states:

> I take this opportunity to invite your attention to the Education (Teaching Service) Regulations, Chapter 39:01 of the Laws of the Republic of Trinidad and Tobago, in which are set out the terms and conditions of your employment as a member of the Teaching Service. (Director of Personnel Administration, personal communication, April 29, 1988)

None of the interviewees described any orientation to the legal and contractual obligations of the job from the Ministry of Education. As

Miss T&T explained:

> I was just sent here with a letter. I wasn't even given Teaching Regulations or anything like that. I was just plopped in here and that was it. (Miss T&T 1990)

However, the Trinidad and Tobago Unified Teachers' Association (T&TUTA), provides legal advice on terms and conditions of employment for those teachers who seek it.

No interviewees described involvement in an orientation program that focused on the history of the educational system in Trinidad and Tobago. Salman was the only interviewee who said that he received a handbook specially designed for new teachers at his school. The handbook outlined the school policies and procedures and teacher regulations.

Many of the interviewees explained that they had little choice in where they are placed to teach, unless they were recruited by the principal of a specific school. Jesse, Adrian, and Bumper found that they were moved around to several schools before their appointments were confirmed. Jesse, who taught at three schools in her first year, found that this movement gave her a varied experience of teaching in different school systems because she was able to interact with different teachers. On the other hand, Adrian found that this movement hindered his ability to settle into the job. However, principals recruited Tiger, Cynthia, Smith, and Salman to fill vacancies in specific schools.

The interviewees who began their teaching careers at secondary schools were put into classrooms and expected to carry full teaching workloads. However, many of these interviewees mentioned that they did not receive much support or feedback on their teaching. The lack of formal support or feedback from principals or heads of the department did not mean that as new teachers the interviewees were not being covertly observed. Cynthia remembered that when she was a new teacher, a few other teachers "cast an eye," and chatted with her. In turn, as an administrator, she said that she and her principal:

> Follow the process in the sense that we kind of keep an "eye" on the teacher but the "eye" is not a sit in the classroom kind because we know it makes them uncomfortable. We encourage the Heads of Departments to do that, to make appointments and do some clinical supervision of the new teacher. Some of them have been doing it and some of them have not been doing it. But we make it a point of duty to pass by to listen in but you are outside of the classroom. The

principal and I we would confer on our observations. Or we might be next door in another class. Your class will be set to work because we still teach, and you listen to the teacher. It is a very informal method. We keep an eye... we make it a point of duty to keep an eye on the new ones, but it's the Head of Department who has primary responsibility. (Cynthia 1978)

There was, then, some form of surveillance of the work of new teachers by their colleagues and principals.

The Education Act of 1966 states that one responsibility of the Minister of Education is to:

Make provision for the professional training of teachers for the entire system of public education, and lay down the standards which are applicable to the recruitment of teachers, their training and conditions of service. (Laws of Trinidad and Tobago, Education Act, 1966, 10)

Yet, no interviewee felt that the Ministry of Education was in any way concerned about his or her progress as a new teacher. All of the interviewees perceived the support they received from the Ministry of Education to be minimal. Two interviewees concluded:

I don't think there is enough involvement by the Ministry. Of course, I suppose they probably don't see that as their role. I don't think enough is being done. I think the view is still held by the Ministry you qualify, jump in a classroom. (Cynthia 1978)

In other words, possession of academic qualifications signifies that one can teach. Similarly, Jesse said the Ministry of Education involvement with her as a beginning teacher was:

Zero. In terms of staff development? None. But in terms of problems getting money, and all of that, lots. But nothing in terms of staff development. No nothing at all. Nothing from the ministry. (Jesse 1985)

In Jesse's experience, the Ministry of Education was keen to fulfil its role as employer.

The Education Act of 1966 also recognized that one of the twelve "powers, duties and functions" of a supervisor of schools is:

the conduct and supervision of courses of induction and training for untrained teachers in service as well as courses for other teachers. (Laws of Trinidad and Tobago, Education Act, 1966, 18)

Maya, Salman, and Dot.Com mentioned that, as new teachers, they had some contact with Ministry of Education Curriculum Officers. Sid Chase recalled:

> In fact, I never saw a Curriculum Officer for years. In fact, in my entire career I only saw a Curriculum Officer once and that was well after ten years of teaching. (Sid Chase 1979)

Antonia was one of the few interviewees who recounted having had formal meetings with their principals when they first began to teach. She explained:

> The principal...briefed me about classroom management, what was expected of me as a teacher, the role, how you have to listen to the children. As a Form Teacher there are certain things that you have to do. You have to be there for the children. Plus he gave me some handouts to read. (Antoinia 1994)

On the other hand, Harold explained that he received very little orientation to what he had to do when he first began teaching. He explained:

> There were not any supports really. There was not any in terms of what to expect and what type of focus to adopt. There was not anything. It was more syllabus, scheme oriented. That was the sum total of it really. If I could remember the first day, I was just given the scheme. The other teacher said, "Well you have a Form One class first thing in the morning. You are doing 'mountains' and the classroom is in that direction. "Where is the textbook? "This is the textbook here. Flip through. This is the first chapter. It is on mountains." And you go. (Harold 1999)

These two stories indicate the level of variation between schools in terms of the role of the principal in terms of the preparation of new teachers to take on the task of teaching.

Some of the interviewees said that they also received some support from their heads of departments. However, again, the quality of support varied from school to school. For example, Smith stated:

> I have teachers...I have a good Head of Department on whom I—[*name of subjects*]—two good heads of departments. When I have trouble getting a concept over they can advise me how to go about it. Or they can advise me how to get out of a sticky situation in a classroom. So I tend to rely a lot on my peers or I did initially. (Smith 1997)

While some schools had well-developed systems of subject departments, others, especially schools with smaller teaching staffs, did not. In addition, in some smaller schools, some teachers may teach several subject areas, and this may complicate the departmental structure. For example, one interviewee explained:

> I was teaching Maths, Accounts, POB and Commerce. So I was in the Science department and I was in the Business department. Your Head would not really monitor you to say... although they would be checking with you. (Name withheld)

The most frequently mentioned area of support by the interviewees was from their colleagues, especially those who taught the same school-subject. Sid Chase explained:

> There was nothing structured but I found a lot of comfort in some of my colleagues whom I went to, who I would sort of observe as well respected teachers and who I thought were good teachers. I would go and I would ask them some questions and they would point out certain things to me. But, to a great extent there was actually no support. I mean, when I say that the support even from my colleagues that was quite sporadic as well, you know. But I did feel comfortable enough to ask them if I got into a jam. (Sid Chase 1979)

But new teachers cannot always depend on colleagues. In some instances, where there were many new teachers on the staff, some interviewees felt that they could not really get help from their colleagues. As Rhonda stated:

> You had other teachers who were in no position in terms of training, no position in terms of finances, no position in terms of equipment to offer that support themselves. You basically have people who are in the same position. The only thing is that other people have been there longer than you and they have probably learned to overlook, learned to be less frustrated, or they are more frustrated. (Rhonda 1995)

Comment and Conclusion

The discussion above illustrates that the recruitment practice between 1966 and 2000 was not as simple as described by Jesse. Two dominant discourses informed the activities of the recruitment practice. The first was that an ability to learn, as evidenced by an academic qualification, was equated to ability to teach. In other words, any "certified as knowledgeable" person would be able to teach. The second discourse was that teachers are capable of learning what they need to do as teachers on the job. They can learn on their own, and so, there is no need for a system of support. There was also an understated expectation that the new teacher can do it all on his or her own with little help. For example, the Ministry of Education expects that the new teacher would seek out the Teaching Service Regulations and interpret his or her contractual obligations. But in reality, beginning teaching was for these 29 teachers (and still is for new entrants) a very confusing time for the new teacher. Many of them still enter the profession without any idea of their rights and responsibilities.

In Trinidad, between 1966 and 2000, the Ministry of Education and the Teaching Service Commission called forth persons to be specialist school-subject teachers in secondary schools. These persons possessed a minimum academic qualification of Advanced Level. They were classified and ranked as teachers based on their academic qualifications, rather than practical competence of being able to teach or work with young people. The graduate secondary teacher was ranked at the top of the various levels of secondary teachers. Possession of an additional teacher education qualification, such as the primary-school teacher's diploma or the Diploma in Education, did not enable them to be ranked any higher.

Like Hale and Starrat did in their study, I found that a lack of ceremony or weak rites of passage (Hale and Starratt 1989) marked the interviewees' entry into the teaching profession. The interviewees' orientation to the job and school context was on an ad-hoc basis and varied, depending on the principal's or head of department's professional commitment. As new teachers, the interviewees' ability to teach was not observed beyond a few questions in an interview. There was also an absence of formal supervision of the interviewees when they were placed in schools. The recruitment practice provided few official opportunities for the interviewees to think about what they were required to do as teachers. The practice does little to help the graduate secondary teacher see beyond himself or herself as a specialist school-subject teacher.

Notes

1. J. Mendes (1984), p. 202.
2. The term *graduate* to describe teachers denotes that the teacher is the holder of at least an undergraduate degree. It is a legally binding term for a specific classification of a specific category of secondary school teachers.

3. See De Four-Babb (2004), for an expanded version of the research project.
4. The 29 teachers, interviewees, are identified by a shortened name or pseudonym and the year they first began teaching in Trinidad and Tobago.

References

Althusser, L. (1971). *Lenin and Philosophy,* translated by B. Brewster. London: New Left Books.
Bristol, L., L. Brown, and J. De Four-Babb. (2010). "Teacher Education in Trinidad and Tobago: An Issue of Quality Imperatives." In *International Handbook on Teacher Education Worldwide: Issue and Challenges,* vol. 1 and 2, edited by K. Karras and C. Wolhuter. 747–764. Athens: Altrapos Editions.
Britzman, D. (1991). *Practice Makes Practice.* Albany, NY: University of New York Press.
Campbell, C. (1997). *Endless Education: Main Currents in the Education System of Modern Trinidad and Tobago, 1939–1986.* Kingston: University of the West Indies Press.
Darling-Hammond, L., and E. Sclan. (1996). "Who Teaches and Why? Dilemmas of Building a Profession for Twenty-First Century Schools." In *Handbook of Research on Teacher Education,* 2nd ed., edited by J. Sikula, T. Buttery, and E. Guyton, 67–101. New York: Simon and Schuster.
De Four-Babb, J. (2004). "Talk Yuh Talk: Making Sense of How Graduate Secondary Teachers in Trinidad Learned to Teach without Pre-Service Teacher Education." Unpublished doctoral thesis, University of Waikato, Hamilton, New Zealand.
Ellsworth, E. (1997). *Teaching Positions: Difference, Pedagogy, and the Power of Address.* New York: Teachers College Press.
Foucault, M. (1972). *The Archaeology of Knowledge and the Discourse on Language.* Translated by A. Sheridan. New York: Pantheon Books. Original work published in French in 1969.
Foucault, M. (1977). *Discipline and Punish: The Birth of the Prison.* Translated by A. Sheridan. New York: Vintage Books. Original work published in French in 1975.
Gore, J. (1998). "Disciplining Bodies: On the Continuity of Power Relations in Pedagogy." In *Foucault's Challenge: Discourse, Knowledge and Power in Education,* edited by T. Popkewitz and M. Brennan, 231–251. New York: Teachers College Press.
Government of Trinidad and Tobago. (2011). Service Commissions. Accessed August 15, 2011. doi:http://www.news.gov.tt/index.php?news=329.
Hale, L., and R. Starratt. (1989). "Rites of Passage: A Case Study of Teacher Preparation." *Journal of Educational Administration* 27 (3): 24–29.
Kemmis, S., and P. Grootenboer. (2008). "Situating Praxis in Practice: Practice Architectures and the Cultural, Social and Material Conditions for Practice." In *Enabling Praxis: Challenges for Education,* edited by S. Kemmis and T. J. Smith, 37–62. Rotterdam: Sense.
Laws of Trinidad and Tobago. Education Act Chapter 39:01, Act 1 of 1966. Port-of-Spain, Trinidad: Government Printery.

Llamas, J. (2006). "Technologies of Disciplinary Power in Action: The Norm of the 'Good Student.'" *Higher Education* 52 (4): 665–686. doi:10.1007/s10734-004-1449-1

Lortie, D. (1975). *Schoolteacher: A Sociological Study*. Chicago: University of Chicago Press.

Mackinnon, F. (1960). *The Politics of Education*. Toronto: University of Toronto Press.

Marchack, S. (n.d.). *Alternative Recruitment Strategies: Case Study of Contact Employment in the Public Service of Trinidad and Tobago*. Accessed August 15, 2011. doi:http://unpan1.un.org/intradoc/groups/public/documents/UN/UNPAN021826.pdf

Marshall, J. (1989). "Foucault and Education." *Australian Journal of Education* 33 (2): 99–113.

Mendes, J. (1986). *Cote ce, Cote la: Trinidad and Tobago Dictionary*. Port-of-Spain, Trinidad: Superb Publishers.

Ministry of Education, Vacancies. (July 29, 2000). *The Trinidad Guardian*, 8.

Page, G and J. Thomas. (1977). *International Dictionary of Education*. London: Kogan Page.

Reilly, R. and G. Chao. (1982). "Validity and Fairness of Some Alternative Employee Selection Procedures." *Personnel Psychology* 35 (1): 1–62.

Rizvi, F., B. Lingard, and J. Lavia. (2006). "Postcolonialism and Education: Negotiating a Contested Terrain." *Pedagogy, Culture and Society* 14 (3): 249–262.

Schatzki, T. (2012) "A Primer on Practices: Theory and Research." In *Practice-Based Education: Perspectives and Strategies*, edited by J. Higgs et al., Rotterdam: Sense Publishers. Accessed June 10, 2011. doi: http://www.csu.edu.au/research/ripple/publications/publications/Schatzki-110721-Primer-on-Practices.pdf.

Stewart, S. (1981). "Nationalist Educational Reforms And Religious Schools in Trinidad." *Comparative Education Review* 25 (2): 183–201.

Taylor, P., and M. Driscoll. (1995). *Structured Employment Interviewing*. Aldershot, UK: Gower.

Trinidad and Tobago Government. (1960). *Cabinet Proposals on Education: Approved by the Legislative Council on 25th July, 1960*. Port-of-Spain, Trinidad: Government Printing Office.

11

Comparative Collaboration: A Transgressive Academic Practice of Being and Becoming

Laurette Bristol, Joyanne De Four-Babb, Talia Esnard, Jennifer Lavia, and Lisa Perez

Introduction: Inside Universities— Regimes and Responses

This narrative highlights our discourse of being and becoming early and mid-career researchers and academics within the practice traditions of the modern university. As we respond to the demands of the university, we interrogate our epistemological assumptions, our practice as researchers, and our actions as academics from the Caribbean, yet living and working in spaces outside the Caribbean region. Our central and continuing question: What are the sayings, doings, and relatings that prefigure our being and becoming as early career academics? In responding, we interrogate and construct the means through which we develop a supportive professional learning community within the flows of being and becoming academics and researchers in university settings. Additionally, we address notions of becoming Caribbean intellectuals and challenge the location of our intellectual habitus through the application of transgressive academic practices.

We are five black women in the university; in common, we share a Caribbean educational and professional experience. We met each other at different stages of our careers and have continued to support each other, acting as supervisors, critical friends, and mentors as our professional and emotional needs required. As individuals, we faced the demands to publish and build a rigorous research profile within the conundrum of heavy teaching loads. Responding to these demands, in September of 2010, we formalized our relationship through a research collaborative network we named Caribbean Educators Research Initiative (CURVE). Our CURVE relationship is one that emerges from and within connections and relationships forged over time and space and linked through our common experiences of a Caribbean heritage and teacher education. Our individual and collective selves are continuously formed and re-formed by and within our colonial past, our postcolonial present, our post-independence educational experiences, our global positions, and our academic lives. As we live the academic life, we choose not to prescribe to the prevailing discourses that suggest, "female academics are often at a particular disadvantage as they negotiate academic culture" (Tynan and Garbett 2007, 413; see also Barrett and Barrett 2011). Rather, while we recognize this reality, we want to instead suggest, from the outset, that female academics can actively transcend the political, social, economic, and cultural conditions of their careers through practices of collaboration. To do so, our research inquiry begins with and incorporates the historical conditions that have informed us as black women in the flows of globalized knowledge. We recognize the uniqueness of this experience and use it as the source of our creativity (Thomas, Mack, Williams, and Perkins 1999). As black women from the Caribbean, our histories construct, but do not limit, our areas of research interest, the ways in which we relate to each other and other female academics, and the modes of inquiry that we adopt.

CURVE is a praxis-oriented relationship that allows us to collectively name and claim the reflective and transgressive projects of our practice as academics, as educators of teachers, and as researchers. Mann and Clarke suggest that naming is a function of "learning reflexively through explicating transparently [our] own and others action," as such, we become conscious of the tensions that construct our professional lives and use them to 'create, not to contract' research and professional action (Mann and Clarke 2007, 15). As early to mid-career researchers, the practice of collaboratively naming experience is particularly useful because it allows us to identify whom we hope to become as Caribbean academics and intellectuals, determine our professional trajectories, develop a publication agenda, and transgress the traditionally isolating, competitive, and outcome-driven practices of the academy through a mentorship that spans across disciplines and universities (Tynan and Garbett 2007; Foote 2010). Acknowledging the globalized, market demands for increased knowledge capacity, Smith, Salo, and Grootenboer (2010, 55) have suggested that academic work has been constructed by, "fiscal constraints, escalating competition, demands for greater accountability from external sources, growing enrolments, increasingly diverse faculty appointments and the continuous expansion of new technologies." The economic currency of knowledge and the transmission of that knowledge have largely been shaped by forces of globalization and internationalization. International competition between universities for the best minds, innovative research, and cutting-edge practices has come to challenge academic freedom (Hayes 2009), problematize notions of internationalization and academic mobility (Saltmarsh and Swirski 2010) and called into question "knowledgeability" as a contested terrain (Smith 2010, 580). Yet within this constant state of flux, what has remained eternally consistent are the responsibilities of academics, that is, teaching, research, and service (Reybold and Alamia 2008).

In this context, the identity and practice of the academic can be compromised or enabled, depending upon how the individual academic chooses to respond. The rule of thumb for research-intensive universities is publication. Boyd and Harris (2010) suggest that for new members of staff, the university can be constructed as a "collective, dynamic, object-oriented system in which rules, tools and division of labour influence activity"; however, they add that the "contributions by participants are able to shape the system" (Boyd and Harris 2010, 10). All is not lost. Under the weight of regimes of performance, some, like Boyd and Harris (2010), argue that the academic can respond in alternative ways to reshape the system. These are responses which reenergize and sustain the innovative, moral, and intellectual vigor of the academic. Within the drama of global universities, Smith et al. (2010, 57) suggest that "collective praxis" is an alternative response that encourages "groups of academics within and/ or outside of their own institutions [to create] sites for the practice of communicative action by extending individual praxis into the realm of collective activity". Collective praxis facilitates the collective displacement of practices within the university that work to dumb down the voice and spirit of the academic. The academics engaged in collective praxis are then able to respond to neoliberal forces in the international university, which constrain knowledge generation. Instead, it emancipates a practice of collective-knowledge action. Collective-knowledge action is the use of knowledge to respond to, critique, transform, transgress, and transcend the world in which we live. This is the collective public sphere that we, as Caribbean academics, occupy through our collaborative practices.

In light of the above, we progress the argument that our condition of becoming is shaped through a consideration of our present state of being. Thus, we actively make sense of who we are as social and cultural agents working in international universities (Best 2003; Hostetler, Macintyre Latta, and Sarroub 2007).

Being and Becoming: Transgression, Culture, and the Academy

So what does it mean for us to be in a state of being and becoming as early and mid-career researchers and academics? Our stories will show that being as a state of existence is open to a multiplicity of interpretations. Our stories will identify the commonalities of our understandings, but they will also highlight the uniqueness of our interpretations of being early and mid-career researchers, operating within the modern university. More so, these narratives will show that our being (in the present) is only temporary; be-ing morphs into be-coming at the precise moment we begin to name, discern, and question our "essence (Dasein)" (Heidegger 1962), as historical beings and returns to be-ing when we examine who we are be-coming. Heidegger (1962), in describing being and becoming as an evolutionary formation, suggests:

> In so far as Being constitutes what is asked about, and "Being" means the Being of entities, then entities themselves turn out to be what is interrogated... Looking at something, understanding and conceiving it, choosing, and access to it—all these ways of behaving are constitutive of our inquiry, and therefore are modes of being for those particular entities which we, the inquirers, are ourselves. (Heidegger 1962, 26–27)

This naming and questioning of who we are, how we are being formed, and who we would like to become is a condition of learning. For Heidegger (1951), "Learning means actively allowing ourselves to respond to what is essential in that which always addresses us, that which has already claimed us" (in Thomson 2001, 259). How do we respond to that which always addresses us? What is it that demands our attention within the modern university?

As researchers employed with the university, we are labelled "academics." Depending on whether the university is research-intensive or teaching-intensive, this label identifies the sets of practices that orchestrate and prefigure the political nature of our work and the type of knowledge we are expected to consume and generate as academics, as researchers and as intellectuals (Kemmis, Edwards-Groves, Hardy, Wilkinson, and Lloyd 2011; Kemmis, Edwards-Groves, Wilkinson, and Hardy 2010; Kemmis and Grootenboer 2008). In naming the practices, which contribute to our evolving within the university, we argue that it is necessary to make sense of the historical *pre-sense* (presence) of our being, the cultural knowledge that frames our potential for action and the resource of language that constructs the ways in which we are able to make a cohesive inventory of our existence as Caribbean women who are early and mid-career researchers, academics, and intellectuals.

For us, being and becoming is not only an aspect of orchestration and prefiguring, but a characteristic of social, political, and economic alliances and affiliations (Glissant 1999). We cannot understand who we are, nor can we imagine who we will and can become, 'apart from [our] lived experience and that lived experience must acknowledge cross-cultural exchange and the creolized identities which have resulted' (Burns 2009, 101). As a part of this process, we acknowledge that we have been claimed by and cling to the Caribbean. In admitting this, we reflect upon the ways in which our Caribbean education systems, the particular histories within which they have emerged, and the contemporary challenges and opportunities that such represents, have shaped our Caribbean existence and our multilayered identities. These identities influence and determine the extent of our cultural and moral action as Caribbean academics and Caribbean intellectuals; expressions that appear synonymous but that are overlapping yet distinct and contextualized by the geographical spaces in which we live, the positions we hold within the academy, and the political demands and practices of the work in those positions.

Lamming (1995) constructs the space of the intellectual as a field of conflict. He argues that Caribbean intellectualism is seen through four types of personalities or activities that overlap. Intellectual behavior is consistent with a preoccupation with ideas, the communication of those ideas, the development and consumption of artifacts connected to the ideas, and the use of ideas in problem solving and survival. Lamming (1995) goes on to argue that the labor of the Caribbean intellectual has been restricted by a colonial legacy that constructs our mode of inquiry as well as the areas of interest, so much so, that he accuses the Caribbean intellectual as being:

> Fixed in the habit of digging up exclusively the small island enclave whose language zone corresponds to the particular metropole whose institutions have largely fixed [her]/his agenda of discourse and made [her]/him one of their own. (Lamming 2995, 22)

He goes on to suggest that the knowledge generated is:

> Largely archival. It is locked up in an enclave of scholars and research workers, consultants and technocrats. It is a knowledge which still awaits mass-distribution, and which, therefore, has not yet become the shaping influence on the consciousness of those whose recent ancestors had made it possible. It is not inscribed in consciousness...the most urgent task and greatest intellectual challenge [is] how to control the burden of this history and incorporate it into our collective sense of...future. (Lamming 1995, 25)

Best (2003), on the other hand, accuses the Caribbean intellectual of work that is often irrelevant to the conditions of home. He constructs the intellectual habitus of the Caribbean academic as a symptom of the colonial condition. He argues that the Caribbean intelligentsia acquires its legitimacy through a demonstration of:

> Technical competence in the methods and procedures of what is their own habitat, western scientism and western propaganda. [It is] largely abstract [and] tends to lack practical political content. (Best 2003, 21)

Best (2003) continues his indictment of the Caribbean intellectual by locating intellectual habits in the arena of the plantation. He suggests:

> The plantation mind—is the refuge which our intellectual classes take in a sterile scientism on the one hand, or in a cheap populism on the other. (Best 2003, 25)

Best (2003) like Williams (1946), believes that for Caribbean thought and action to be transformed, as a society, we must understand how we make sense of ourselves within the flows of the wider world in which we live. Thus, Caribbean intellectualism can be a form of transgressive cultural action. In the practice of Caribbean intellectualism, we are mandated to collectively and publicly interrogate Caribbean experience (Best 2003). Thus, Best (2003) provides us with an insight into our obligatory moral-cultural action as Caribbean academics and intellectuals. However, what is required is for us to move beyond the critique to reconstruct the theoretical tools with which we must *make sense of* and *act upon* our conflicted professional realities and sociocultural responsibilities.

Kemmis and Grootenboer (2008) provide us, as CURVE, with such a theoretical tool through their conceptualization of "practice architectures." Practice architectures are the cultural-discursive arrangements (sayings); material-economic arrangements (doings), and social-political arrangements (relatings) that hang together in a cohesive way to constrain or enable the sets of professional practices and research projects that we engage in. Given that our sayings, doings, and relatings are so much a part of our lived experiences, we need to find ways through which we move them from the realm of the everyday unconscious to the field critical action. To do this, we are required to deconstruct the sociopolitical, economic, and historical-cultural conditions that shape our practices as early and mid-career researchers, academics, and intellectuals. Thus, we are able to name the conditions that influence our be-ing and direct our be-coming. As a community of professionals who engage intellectual practices in this way, we establish the source of our individual and collective agency and create the spaces for critical, practice-oriented responses that are culturally insightful, to the demands of university work.

In capitalizing upon the explicatory capacity of "practice architectures," we recognize: first, the need to reflect upon our own understandings of the conversions and tensions embedded within the relationship between our academic work and our cultural responsibilities. Second, we need, as Caribbean intellectuals and academics, to promote a transgressive and progressive understanding of educational research in the Caribbean as a practice that emerges out of the conditions of our lived experiences and is interrogated by and within the community practices that have sustained us. We accept that our critical and cultural obligation is not only to engage in research on the Caribbean, but more importantly, to promote research for the Caribbean as a project of decolonization (Smith 1999). As workers within the university, the nature of this obligation calls the ways and reasons for which we practice research in the academy into question.

As CURVE, we respond to both the society and the academy through intuition and instinct. This allows us a *re*-turn to our "public spheres" (see Kemmis 2005) for comfort and community action through conversations. We are aware of the ways in which particular conversations (sayings) shape our reflection (doings), and we appreciate the ways in which conversations become the tool through which we name who we are and who we are yet to become (relatings) as researchers within the academy.

Collective Naming— A Transgressive Methodology

In our discussions, we agreed that as five female, black educators we need to be mindful of our history in the interpretation of our research, as the present is built on the past, in particular our colonial and post-independence past. We need to be up front about who we are and how we came to be that way and be constantly engaged in that reflection on and of self. We sought to dig deeper, unravel, unearth, and deconstruct the underlying issues and not accept the usual explanations. We sought to make sense of self, each other, our relationships, and the complexity of the context through our discourse and dialogue. These principles of historical and cultural awareness in and through research, personal reflective disclosure, and talk in community are fundamental to the practice architectures of our research and academic practices. Thus, the theory of practice architectures in collaboration with critical notions of Caribbean intellectualism has worked to shape our methodological practice of comparative collaboration. For us, *comparative collaboration* is a methodological approach that draws on the historical and cultural features of the group. In this methodological approach, we draw upon the concepts of critical friends, narrative inquiry, collaborative discussion and dialogue, personal reflection, and mining minds as ingredients for our methodology. This approach guides the ways in which we talk with and to each other, the ways in which we encounter other members of our professional community, and the ways in which we engage in research *for* and *in* the Caribbean.

We draw upon narrative inquiry in the form of storytelling and value our storied experiences (Clandinin and Connelly 2000).

> For us, narrative is the best way of representing and understanding experience. Experience is what we study, and we study it narratively

because narrative thinking is a key form of experience and a way of writing and thinking about it. (Clandinin and Connelly 2000, 18)

Narrative inquiry places value on people's stories and taps into *their* knowledge from *their* perspective. Clandinin and Connelly, and those who are influenced by their "narrative inquiry" approach to research, use teachers' stories in three ways: as a "phenomena under study" (Clandinin and Connelly 2000, 4), as a method of study, and as a way of thinking and writing their research (Clandinin and Connelly 2000). In this paper, our narratives are used as expressions of the practical understanding that we have of being academics, imagining ourselves becoming intellectuals. Our narratives are situated "within particular personal, social, professional, institutional and cultural stories" and help us to better understand each other, "learning about ourselves and each other" (Chiu-Ching and Yim-mei Chan 2009, 21). "As experience is rooted in the past, developed in the present, and enacted in the future, it is embedded in temporality and context, and is ever changing, fluid and dynamic" (Chiu-Ching and Yim-mei Chan 2009, 21).

Narrative inquiry enables us to honor our varied life histories, and because we are all at various ages and stages of our professional development:

> By examining our storied experiences, we can see our personal philosophy in action, leading us to understand how our views, values and beliefs were formulated and now direct our actions in [our research]. (Chiu-Ching and Yim-mei Chan 2009, 19)

In narrating our professional, personal, and cultural lives, we compare experiences as we collaboratively make sense of our experiences and engage in research. Comparative collaboration points to the dialectical arrangements that are a part of collective engagements. As we interrogate difference through comparison, we collaborate in the reconstruction of multiple yet individual professional identities and practices. We compare our stories across time, space, place, and context, and we compare our stories in terms of the places from where we sit; that is, our present personal and professional spaces that we each occupy. As we engage in comparative collaboration, we reveal to ourselves and others what may have been hidden; we reflect upon what we knew; we reimagine new possibilities and pathways for ourselves; and we reconstruct our practices as Caribbean individuals and professionals within the university.

Comparative collaboration is a narrative practice which involves conversation, reflection, and interrogation that links past, present, and future and builds on cultural knowledge. It is culturally located, and as we move forward, in our professional and research activities, we continue to refine and define our methodological and academic sayings, doings, and relating.

Naming Our Condition— The Beginnings of Transgression

The vignettes that follow provide a snapshot into the hours of talk: talk on Skype across three international time zones, squeezed into the hours before taking kids to swimming or music lessons; talk which went past closing hours in restaurants, whose owners and workers cleaned around us while we littered their dinner tables with paper among the Mongolian dishes; and talk during beach-house weekends walking along the shore, keeping an eye on children playing in the surf. In presenting these, we demonstrate a practice of naming unique to women who are mothers and wives. In naming our challenge, we engage a practice of (re)searching for spaces of intellectual practices and supportive academic communities outside domestic responsibilities and outside the isolation of university silos (Grant 2006). In sharing professional talk (Hardy 2010b), we engage in mentored transgressive and praxis-oriented responses to university managerialism (academic programming and policing the academic mind) practices that present a challenge for early and mid-career researchers, especially female academics (Ewing et al. 2008; Hardy 2010a; Waitere, Wright, Tremaine, Brown, and Pause 2011). We share aspects of our individual selves and our collective identity as CURVE. In this sharing, we acknowledge an extension of the collective community that is between ourselves as CURVE and our readership. In naming our positions of *being* early and mid-career researchers, we claim *becoming* as a beginning transgressive practice.

Laurette's current research builds on her doctoral study, which explored how teaching as a practice of education can be used to subvert the colonial legacy of plantation pedagogy. Focusing on teacher education in Trinidad and Tobago, she has proposed the notion of "plantation pedagogy." For her, plantation pedagogy offers a philosophical and methodological critique of teacher education in postcolonial settings that brings beginning, new, and in-service teachers

Comparative Collaboration   245

into critical dialogue and collaborative practice (see Bristol 2010). Laurette articulates her understandings thus:

> *I entered academia in an era where the internationalization and massification of university education in the late half of the twentieth century ensured increased class sizes and increased course workloads. As such, the intellectual activity of the university is now dominated by managerial concerns. Measures of accountability have been put in place to ensure quality education and an increase in the numbers of graduating trained professionals. As an early-career academic, I am constantly bombarded with the stories of assessment committees, timelines, deadlines, students' evaluations of the course, students' evaluations of my performance, annual performance reviews, the chronicle of university league tables, the legends of those who publish in A+ or A-listed journals, and the psychological yarns of those who win (access), on the behalf of the university, a source of major research funding to ensure their continuance within the university. These accounts have served to deflect and distract me away from an authentic consideration of the ways in which I should be as an agent of knowledge. Instead, I find that I express great anxiety over the question of results. I am concerned about the results of my students at the end of a semester, not because I worry about the quality of my teaching and my ability to engage the students in critical thinking, but because I agonize about whether or not the final scores would fit into the prescribed normative learning curve determined for the particular university, because of the peculiar needs of the students. I wrestle with my research activities, because many times the self-management of my teaching distracts me from an authentic interrogation of my practice. More so, the reports of yearly research outputs makes me want to cling to the production of comfortable research rather than engage in the discomforting, time-consuming research activity that I would prefer.*
>
> *I am concerned that I am beginning to lose the plot for teaching and research at this level, and with it, an authentic self-story. In a foreign country (Australia) so far away from home, I am constantly seeking the buzz of a research revival, an association for research direction, and an intellectual connection between home and the space within which I work. I find that I need to identify and relocate the story of a practice community that would sustain, enhance, and interrogate my teaching and research practice, as well as, my understandings of international Caribbean academic identity performances.*

Joyanne uses narrative-inquiry methodology to analyze the experiences of beginning and practicing teachers in Trinidad and Tobago with particular reference to the practicum aspect of their training. Additionally, she adopts narrative inquiry in her research on school leadership, persons with Alzheimer's, and the involvement of women in the clergy in the Caribbean (De Four-Babb and Tenia 2011; De Four-Babb and Beck 2011). Joyanne begins her expression by positing a central question:

> When does one begin to become an academic? When did this journey begin for me? When I was six and decided that I wanted to be a teacher at the university? When I entered the teaching profession in 1981 and recognized that indeed teaching would be a career of lifelong importance to me? When I completed the master's degree and realized that there were many paths that a teacher can choose to develop? After completing doctoral work, or now that I am in the academy? My journey as a student and teacher converged at my point of entry into academia (university teaching). For me, those childish decisions to be a teacher at a university realized themselves as being a teacher of geography at secondary school for many years before I began teaching college students who were becoming teachers. I have found that, for me, each end of one journey was a new beginning in becoming an academic. So it is not the points of change, but the continuum of changing philosophy, marked shifts in directions, the curves in my thinking that have brought me to this place as a becoming academic.

Talia's research is in the sociology of leadership, both in education and entrepreneurship, with specific reference to understanding the Caribbean context. She has been involved in research that aimed to advance a social cognitive approach to the examination of contextual and psychosocial factors that affect nascent and established entrepreneurs. Although her research interest spans the exploration of entrepreneurial attitudes, orientations, intentions, perceptions, and experiences, one particular interest is the experience of gender, leadership, and entrepreneurship (see Esnard-Flavius 2010). Talia relates her understanding of being an academic to her teaching:

> I am an academic; therefore, I teach. I am part of an educational faculty with a strong sense of student centeredness and a focus on pedagogy. In this working university environment (as a stark departure from my previous one), I have been forced to make the compulsory and uncontested shift from the use of the endorsed lecturer-centered instruction within my previous academic institution to the use of the promoted student-centred instruction within my present one. As part of that ideological and intellectual shift, I continue to struggle with

the pitfalls of becoming consumed with advancing the art and craft of planning, creating, and using resource materials; engaging students to come out of their comfort zones; revising and revisiting strategies for teaching and learning; and providing rapid detailed student-performance feedback within a work schedule and teaching load that exceeds the average among academic faculty.

I am an academic; therefore, while I acculturate the academy within these walls, I remain subsumed within the bowels of teaching.

I am an academic; therefore, I write. I write about elements of my doctoral thesis as my starting point. However, my research interest in entrepreneurial education as an applied field continues to be affected by the burdens of over-teaching, the lack of a defined entrepreneurial research agenda within regional institutions, the challenge of accessing external research and social networks though conference facility, the related lack of institutional funding and incentives for such a research agenda, and the upheld dominant expectation of mainstream educational research among academic administrators and senior academic staff.

I am an academic; therefore, as I write, I continuously negotiate a space for accepted educational research within the faculty and my preferred eccentric, driven educational focus.

Jennifer's focus has been on developing a sustained approach to teacher education via her involvement with the University of Sheffield's Caribbean Programme. Working with students from the Caribbean (most of whom are education professionals across all sectors of education) she is developing a collaborative, decolonising approach to interrogate the problems and issues of education in the Caribbean. Her current work involves a collaborative study of the lives and careers of Caribbean teachers in the United Kingdom. Her work is based on the application to understanding education in the Caribbean (see Lavia 2006). Jennifer interrogates being and becoming within a wider social context of practice:

My formal commitment to developing an academic life began when I started my PhD. This is a commitment that I had resisted for a long time, primarily because I had been wary of what I thought academic life would do to me. I had viewed academics as elite professionals who had lost touch with the real world. I did not want to lose what I saw as my core purpose – that is, using my skills as a teacher to work with those who are marginalized and silenced. During my undergraduate years and living overseas, I became involved in the mass political movements of the time. This interest was actually carried over from

> my high-school years in the 1970s, and in any case, it was difficult not be "involved," in or at least be influenced, by the mass movements of the 1970s. Having the practical experience of working with communities for social justice and against domination, poverty, and discrimination in all its forms, I did not want to be involved in a disengaged practice that separated theory and practice and fail to make a difference in the lives of people. By the time I began my doctoral studies, I had been an activist in the teachers' union, was involved in curriculum change at school and national levels, had been involved in the women's movement nationally and internationally, and had worked for many years in developing traditional and progressive forms of the local cultural arts. I had also been involved in a movement of teachers who were committed to self-determination in relation to their professional lives and careers. It is this latter episode that brought me into direct confrontation with the tensions I had previously resisted between "the academic" and "the intellectual." I came to realize that my life's work had been very much that of a public intellectual. If we are to claim the right of working for education, then what we are called matters less than what we do and why we do what we do– that is our moral purpose.

As a doctoral candidate, Lisa is interested in developing innovation in teacher education, particularly among teachers of business studies and agricultural science. She also has research interests in assessment and the experiences of beginning teachers. Lisa introduces the relevance of gender:

> My particular field of study is male dominated. I found myself in a unique situation where in my department at the university I am the only female. My colleagues are males, all over fifty years; I am female, in my thirties. The dynamics of our relationships are very interesting: the coordinator for my department is a former classmate of one of my uncles; another colleague is a family friend who knew me as a child and another taught me at Teachers Training College. One of my challenges in the beginning was how to relate to my colleagues. How would they perceive me? Is it as the student, the child of a friend, or classmate they had known, or was it as the professional I was striving to become in this world of academia. I found it difficult in the beginning to fit into their space. I could never be one of the boys; nature ruled that out. Therefore, I found myself having to create my own space and once again having to prove myself, to earn their respect as a colleague, and in so doing, becoming part of the team. How was my voice to be heard? I had ideas with regard to how some of the courses could be implemented and improved, as well as areas of potential research for

> our department. In the beginning, I offered my suggestions, which were listened to, all the appropriate responses were made; however, at the end of it all, none of my ideas were taken aboard. At this stage, I became somewhat frustrated, because in my mind, I felt that there was this invisible barrier or wall between myself and my colleagues. Many questions came to mind: Was there a problem in the way I communicated to my colleagues? Did I talk down to them? Did they have a problem with accepting my ideas? Is it because I am young and female? Is it the old boys' club coming into play? How was I to break through this barrier? I knew that I had to find a solution to this problem. I felt at the time that if I voiced my opinions to them, there would be too much tension among ourselves. I decided to observe how they communicated for a semester and discovered that all ideas were discussed with one key person in the group, who would then inform the coordinator, and suggestions were implemented. I finally understood the method by which things were communicated and implemented in our department. Did I agree with it? No, Did I try it? Yes, and it worked. On this journey, I am constantly reflecting, and changing as I find my niche in academia.

Collectively, we recognize that our talk defines our interpretations of our being and becoming. More specifically, we are aware of the ways in which our own efforts at self-reflection and collaborative comparisons have shaped our understandings of our being and becoming. In that regard, we realize that our academic and intellectual be-ings are a part of larger social-conditioning processes and experiences that are tied to the sociocultural realities of our historical and current institutional interactions. Thus, in the early stages of this transgressive process, we reflect on these comparative experiences and interpretations, we identify the central and organic notion of being as a process of becoming "a public intellectual"; this academic emphasis and professional understanding has, in itself, roused many varied tensions for us. On the one hand, our personal trajectories highlight the concerns of formalized labeling of "space and place" through processes of institutional convergence, internationalization, accountability, output, and conventional research. On the other hand, it underscores the tensions that are forged through our own interactions and personal interrogation of "academic place and space," and the related engagement of selves into processes of conscious, transformative self-reflection, and learning where we begin to question the (non)authentic nature of some of our professional practices. As a result, we name and make familiar with the very "practice architectures" (as identified through the doings, sayings, and relatings of institutional others) that have prefigured our understandings of academia and ourselves as discovered through related processes of self-reflection and learning. In these interrelated processes, we not only question our own sayings, doings, and relatings, but we also deconstruct and reconstruct our own notions of being and becoming as prefigured by institutional and cultural sayings, doings, and relatings. Thus, we see our being as part of our becoming, and our being and becoming as temporal, spatial, methodological, and continuously evolving. We also see ourselves as giving voice to the process of being and becoming through the naming of ourselves as early career Caribbean academics and intellectuals.

Conclusion

We have made an argument that suggests that, for us as members of CURVE, the Caribbean Educators Research Initiative, being and becoming is much more than an evolutionary process. Rather for us, who we are *be-ing* as early and mid-career researchers and academics and who we are *be-coming* as intellectuals is implicated within our cultural and historical obligations as Caribbean individuals within the university. These obligations shape the epistemology, axiology, and methodology of our research and academic projects and the content and nature of our intellectual activities. For us, the key learning moments of this transgressive experience revolve around two key questions: How are we becoming Caribbean intellectuals? And where do we locate our intellectual habitus?

In addressing the first question, we emphasize our conceptual position that we engage in an authentic becoming of Caribbean intellectuals through our methodology of comparative collaboration. Here we refer to our research methodology as well as to the practices and projects of connecting, networking, and collaborating with other academics. In saying this, we do not prescribe one methodology for Caribbean intellectuals, as we do not speak for the Caribbean, but rather, we speak *from* and *to* our particular experiences of being Caribbean individuals operating within international universities. Through our methodological and academic strategy of comparative collaboration, we provide an alternative response to the university. Our reaction functions outside the isolating projects of *knowledge generation* and promotes community projects of *knowledge action*. As Caribbean women, the intention of these projects revolves around identifying, interrogating, deconstructing, transforming, and transgressing the conditions that enable our sayings, doings, and relatings as actors within the academy.

In locating our intellectual habitus, we recognize that it lives in the structures within which we operate, and it is also a condition of our being and becoming. However, rather than locating this intellectual habitus only within the internationalization of the university or within the conditions of our history as colonial, postcolonial, and post-independence individuals, we prefer to shift the source of our intellectual habitus and relocate it within community. Our methodology (research and academic disposition), the nature of our explorations, and our recognized positionality of Caribbean women is given birth *through* and *within* community relationships. In saying this, we also recognize the internal contradiction of this statement. That is, we recognize that the community cannot be abstracted from the social and political structures that frame it, nor can it be abstracted from the historical conditions within which it sits. Rather, we posit, that our intellectual habitus, located within community, is one that recognizes the limitations of its own conditions but yet constructs new pathways of *being* and *becoming* through new ways of saying, doing, and relating with each other in community. A way of academic unfolding that is critically conscious yet intellectually transgressive.

References

Barrett, L. and Barrett, P. (2011). "Women and Academic Workloads: Careeer Slow Lane or Cul-de-Sac?" *Higher Education* 61: 141–155.

Best, L. (2003). "Independent Thought and Caribbean Freedom." In *Independent Thought and Caribbean Freedom: Essays in Honour of Llyod Best*, edited by S. Ryan. St. Augustine, Trinidad and Tobago: Sir Arthur Lewis Institute of Social and Economic Studies, University of the West Indies.

Boyd, P., and K. Harris. (2010). "Becoming a University Lecturer in Teacher Education: Expert School Teachers Reconstructing Their Pedagogy and Identity." *Professional Development in Education* 36(1–2), 9–24. doi:10.1080/19415250903454767

Bristol, L. (2010). "Practising in Betwixt Oppression and Subversion: Plantation Pedagogy as a Legacy of Plantation Economy in Trinidad and Tobago." *Power and Education* 2 (2): 167–182.

Burns, L. (2009). "Becoming-Postcolonial, Becoming-Caribbean: Édouard Glissant and the Poetics of Creolization." *Textual Practice* 23, no. 1: 99–117.

Clandinin, J. D., and M. F. Connelly. (2000). *Narrative Inquiry: Experience and Story in Qualitative Research*. San Francisco: Jossey-Bass.

De Four-Babb, J., and S. Tenia. (2011). "From the Pantry to the Pulpit: Anglican Clergywomen in Trinidad and Tobago." In *Breaking the Stained Glass*

Ceiling: Women as Religious Leaders, a special issue of *JENDA: A Journal of Culture and African Women's Studies* 20 (in press).

De Four-Babb, J. and M. Beck. (2011). *Narrative Inquiry as a Culturally Relevant Method of Understanding Caribbean Teachers' Experiences.* Paper presented at the Biennial Conference in Education, University of the West Indies, Mona, June 15–17, Ocho Rios, Jamaica.

Esnard-Flavius, T. (2010). "Gender, Entrepreneurial Self-Efficacy, and Entrepreneurial Attitude Orientations: The Case of the Caribbean." *International Business and Economics Research Journal* 9 (13): 17–31.

Ewing, R., M. Freeman, S. Barrie, A. Bell D. O'Connor, F. Waugh, and C. Sykes. (2008). "Building Community in Academic Settings: The Importance of Flexibility in a Structured Mentoring Program." *Mentoring and Tutoring: Partnership in Learning* 16 (3): 294–310.

Foote, K. (2010). "Creating a Community of Support for Graduate Students and Early Career Academics." *Journal of Geography in Higher Education* 34 (1): 7–19.

Glissant, E. (1999). *Caribbean Discourse.* Charlottesville, VA: University Press of Virginia.

Grant, B. M. (2006). "Writing in the Company of Other Women: Exceeding the Boundaries." *Studies in Higher Education* 31 (4): 483–495.

Hardy, I. (2010a). "Academic Architectures: Academic Perceptions of Teaching Conditions in an Australian University." *Studies in Higher Education* 35 (4): 391–404.

Hardy, I. (2010b). "Teacher Talk: Flexible Delivery and Acdemics' Praxis in an Australian University." *International Journal for Acdemic Developement* 15 (2): 131–142.

Hayes, D. (2009). "Academic Freedom and the Diminished Subject." *British Journal of Educational Studies* 57 (2): 127–145.

Hostetler, K., M. Macintyre Latta, and L. Sarroub. (2007). "Retrieving Meaning in Teacher Education." *Journal of Teacher Education* 58 (3): 231.

Kemmis, S. (2005). "Knowing Practice: Searching for Saliences." *Pedagogy, Culture and Society* 13 (3): 391–426.

Kemmis, S., C. Edwards-Groves, I. Hardy, J. Wilkinson, and A. Lloyd. (2011). *On Being "Stirred In" to Practices: Observations of "learning" How to Go on.* Wagga Wagga: Charles Sturt University.

Kemmis, S., C. Edwards-Groves, J. Wilkinson, and I. Hardy (2010). *Ecologies of Practices: Learning Practice* Paper presented at the Annual Conference of the Australian Association for Research in Education. Paper Code: WIL091156, 28 November – 2 December 2010, Melbourne, Australia.

Kemmis, S., and P. Grootenboer. (2008). "Situating Praxis in Practice: Practice Architectures and the Cultural, Social, and Material Conditions for Practice." vol. 1. In *Enabling Praxis: Challenges for Education (Pedagogy, Education, and Praxis), edited by* S. Kemmis and T. J. Smith. Rotterdam: Sense Publishers.

Lavia, J. (2006). "The Practice of Postcoloniality: A Pedagogy of Hope." *Pedagogy, Culture & Society* 14 (October 2006): 279–293.

Mann, P., and Clarke, D. M. (2007). "Writing It Down—Writing It Out-Writing It Up: Researching Our Practice Through Action Learning." *Action Learning: Research and Practice* 4 (2): 153–171.

Lamming, G. (1995). "Western Education and the Caribbean Intellectual." In *Coming, Coming, Coming Home Conversations II Monographs by George Lamming*, edited by R. Nettleford. Philipsburgh, St Martin: House of Nehesi Publishing. Reybold, L. E., and J. J. Alamia. (2008). "Academic Transitions in Education: A Developmental Perspective of Women Faculty Experiences." *Journal of Career Development* 35 (2): 107–128. doi:10.1177/0894845308325644

Saltmarsh, S., and T. Swirski. (2010). "'Pawns and Prawns': International Academics Observations on Their Transition to Working in an Australian University." *Journal of Higher Education Policy and Management* 32 (3): 291–301.

Smith, J. (2010). "Forging Identities: The Experiences of Probationary Lecturers in the UK." *Studies in Higher Education* 35 (5): 577–591.

Smith, T., P. Salo, and P. Grootenboer. (2010). "Staying Alive in Academia: Collective Praxis at Work." *Pedagogy, Culture and Society* 18 (1): 55–66.

Smith, L.T. (1999). *Decolonising Methodologies: Research and Indigenous Peoples*. New York: Zed Books.

Thomas, K. M., D. A. Mack, K. L. Williams, and L. A. Perkins. (1999). Career Development Strategies and Experiences of "Outsiders Within" in Academe. *Journal of Career Development* 26 (1): 51–67.

Thomson, I. (2001). "Heidegger on Ontological Education, or: How We Become What We Are." *Inquiry* 44 (3): 243–268.

Tynan, B. R. and D. L. Garbett. (2007). "Negotiating the University Research Culture: Collaborative Voices of New Academics." *Higher Education Research and Development* 26 (4): 411–424.

Waitere, H. J., J. Wright, M. Tremaine, S. Brown, and C. J. Pause. (2011). "Choosing Whether to Resist or Reinforce the New Managerialism: The Impact of Performance-Based Research Funding on Academic Identity." *Higher Education Research and Development* 30 (2): 205–217.

Conclusion: Postcolonial Strivings

Jennifer Lavia and Sechaba Mahlomaholo

> "Despite or perhaps because of the fragmentation and relativism of our time, it appears that we must reach for a conception of the good that will affect the directions of our lives."
>
> —Maxine Greene, Releasing the Imagination[1]

We have offered the reader eleven critical essays, through which contributors have formulated, argued, proposed, and critiqued subject positions in response to the questions: Can education contribute to cultural confidence of peoples and communities who have endured centuries of oppression and marginalization? If so, what is education, and what is education for, given such historical circumstances? In reviewing the historical circumstances that have been referenced, it is important to note that the contemporary circumstances of globalization and imperialism of colonized peoples are rooted in the historical relations with colonial encounter. In this light, a project of postcolonial imagination emerges to expose and provoke dialogue and action to articulate new imaginaries and agendas for change.

In bringing together the collective narratives in this book, we have shown that interpretations of colonial encounter are varied and experienced in particular ways by different communities. One the one hand, we can say that the aim of this book was simply to offer these varied interpretations as further accounts of the intersections of historical circumstance and contemporary conditions of globalization and neoliberalism. But we have argued differently, by positioning the work in this volume to acknowledge the centrality of the past to informing the present; we also dared to envision futures. In this way, our collective imagination can be seen as a site of resistance that transforms and recreates alternative ways of knowing, being, doing, and relating. By interrogating the shifts in cultural forces, we have positioned postcolonial thought as moving beyond temporal frames of reference to reclaim a radical agenda for self-determination and liberation. In this sense, our postcolonial strivings reside in a commitment for decolonization, mindful that we live in dangerous times, which demand urgent responses to pervasive and familiar inequalities that seek to entrench differences as a reason for exclusion. We are also cognizant of the opportunities that have emerged by the decentering of hegemonic structures, weakened by the crisis of capitalism and imperialism, and the unceasing struggles of subaltern communities demanding the right to live in this world on their own terms.

In the introduction, we claimed that one of the main intentions of this volume is to push the boundaries of postcolonial thought. As we come to the end of the volume, we want to elaborate on the insights gained seeking to expand the discourse by locating the next steps as those that will guide us to actioning theories of decolonization. We do add the caveat that there is no knowledge that is waiting outside the embodiment of liminal spaces of struggle for us to simply pick up, apply, and measure. Rather, theories of decolonization reside in spaces of diasporas, hybridity, multiculturalism, and cosmopolitanism, informed by "global interconnectivity" that is neither "systematic nor structured around some central locus of power, but is much more about popular consciousness, a form of social imagination" (Rizvi 2006, 23). Learning, unlearning and relearning, therefore, take place within a culture of difference, imagined as a collective sense of ourselves, and providing coherence between ideas and action "to provide a basis for the content of social relationships and the creation of categories within which to understand the world around us" (Rizvi 2000, 223) (see also Appadurai 2003). Maxine Greene also calls for "a mode of utopian thinking" that refuses "mere compliance":

> That looks down roads not yet taken to the shapes of a more fulfilling social order, to more vibrant ways of being in the world. This kind of reshaping imagination may be released through many sorts of dialogue: dialogue among the young who come from different cultures and different modes of life, dialogue among people who have come together to solve problems that seem worth solving to all of them, dialogue among people undertaking shared tasks, protesting injustices, avoiding or overcoming dependencies or illnesses. When such dialogue

is activated in classrooms, even the young are stirred to reach out on their own initiatives. Apathy and indifference are likely to give way to images of what might be arise. (1995, 5)

The dialogue created in this volume has allowed us to foster understandings about the postcolonial that communicate the lived experiences of everyday lives. Our strivings are shared within our consciousness about "diversity and background" and our commitments to transgress against socially unjust practices. In our view, such a movement straddles a decolonizing intent by upholding ontological commitments to re-visioning identity, community, and practice. For us, then, we see this volume as a provocation to elaborate on the postcolonial as a decolonizing project and to perceive these "next steps" as philosophical and methodological endeavors.

First, when we speak in terms of decolonization, we refer to a commitment to re-visioning identity, and we share with Kincheloe that such an engagement is to experience "the excitement of attaining new levels of consciousness and 'ways of being'" (2006, 182), juxtaposing "difference [to] create a bonus of insight...[which] becomes extremely important in any cognitive, epistemological, social, pedagogical or self-production activity" (2006, 184). The organic nature of such encounters has the potential to resuscitate and reappropriate indigenous epistemic systems, cultivating cultural confidence in the course of the struggle to articulate new understandings, structures, and identities.

Second, we refer to a commitment *for* community. We share with Kincheloe the notion of "a more textured concept of the relational individual" (2006, 192). This view is amplified by Rizvi (2006) and Appardurai (2003), both of whom agree that the transnational and global flows of people, capital, goods, and technology has the effect, over time of transforming cultures. Indeed, Rizvi claims, "A few people from a particular community has the potential to transform the entire community—its economic relations, it social order, its links to the outside world and most fundamentally the subjectivities of both the few who travel and the most who do not" (18). Community understood in this way is not to be deemed as homogeneous, but rather as a complex collective of difference, expressed through collective and individual actions. Both implicitly and explicitly, decolonization becomes a process of unlearning and relearning that is embedded in cultural relationship, interactions, and collective engagement. This has direct significance for understanding the relationship between the teacher and the learner as a decolonizing project where openness to dialogue becomes "an ethical, political and pedagogy basis" for conscious cultural inquiry and knowledge production.

Third, is an axiological commitment that is undergirded by moral agency. In elaborating on the third and final ontological commitment to elaborating a decolonizing agenda, we argue for an ethic of practice that resists structures, policies, and practices that seek to reduce education to a technical and mechanistic activity that responds primarily to the transfer of knowledge. In preference, we place moral practice—the desire to do good, to contest values, and to seek justice as fundamental to the purpose of education.

Education alone cannot redress the indignities, violence, and oppression of the past. The undermining of the past, as Fanon has advised, has deeply impaired the psyche, shackling mind and body (and at times spirit), rendering the colonized less than human. The deep implications for unlearning, given the resultant loss of cultural confidence, reinforced through historical and contemporary social, economic, cultural, and political structures and arrangements, does, however, locate education as a central cultural force for dislocating these epistemic regimes of power and control. The requirement for reconceptualizing new ways of being human and learning to be, do, know, and relate, places an emancipatory agenda upon education, with teachers being active agents for transformation. More specifically, cultural confidence is achieved though a practice of decolonization that works to make public the private lived experiences of silenced, marginalized, and excluded communities. In addition, we assert that postcolonial imagination provides a critical basis for creating futures, for reconstructing the person and community, and for re-appropriating indigenous knowledge through a politics of difference. We have argued that a practice of critical cultural inquiry acts as the methodology and pedagogy that provides the fluidity for such conscious deconstruction and reconstruction. Given that we have also argued that the postcolonial imagining is unfinished and urgent business, rather than admit that we have come to the end of the text, what we will do is to urge the reader to consider this juncture as a pause for reflection and reflexivity.

Note

1. Greene, 1995, 1.

References

Appardurai, A. 2003. *Modernity at Large: Cultural Dimensions of Globalizations*. Minneapolis: University of Minnesota Press.

Greene, M. 1995. *Releasing the Imagination: Essays on Education, the Arts and Social Change*." San Francisco: Jossey-Bass.

Kincheloe, J. 2006. "Critical Ontology and Indigenous Ways of Being: Forging a Postcolonial Curriculum." In *Curriculum as cultural practice: postcolonial imaginations*, edited by Y. Kanu. Toronto: University of Toronto Press, 181–202.

Rizvi, F. 2006. "Epistemic Virtues and Cosmopolitan Learning." Radford Lecture, University of Illimois at Urbana-Champaign, November 27, 2006. doi:http://www.aare.edu.au/aer/online/0801c.pdf

Rizvi, F. 2000. "International Education and the Production of Global Imagination." In *Globalization and Education: Critical Perspectives*, edited by N. C. Burbules and C. A. Torres. New York: Routledge, 205–225.

Contributors

Laurette Bristol, PhD, is a teacher-educator from the Republic of Trinidad and Tobago. She is currently a postdoctoral research fellow with the Research Institute for Professional Practice, Learning and Education (RIPPLE), Charles Sturt University, Australia. Her research interests include application of postcolonial theory to empirical educational projects in the Caribbean; explorations of the ways in which the organizational structures of plantation societies condition the pedagogical practices of teachers; leading and learning practices of teachers; and academic practices of early career researchers.

Antonia Darder is Distinguished Professor of Education and Latina/Latino Studies at the University of Illinois at Urbana-Champaign. Her research focuses on issues of racialized inequalities, with an emphasis on questions of identity, language, culture, the body, and social class. Her writings on critical pedagogy, cultural politics, and schooling are internationally recognized. She is the author of *Culture and Power in the Classroom* (1991), *Reinventing Paulo Freire: A Pedagogy of Love* (2002), and *After Race: Racism After Multiculturalism* (2004).

Joyanne De Four-Babb, a former secondary school geography teacher, is currently an assistant professor at the Centre for Education Programmes at the University of Trinidad and Tobago. She teaches three geography courses at both the Valsayn and Corinth campuses. She is also the coordinator of the Practicum Programme for all full-time students. Joyanne's uses narrative inquiry methodology to analyze the experiences of beginning and practicing teachers.

Talia Esnard is an assistant professor at the Center for Education Programs, University of Trinidad and Tobago (UTT), Trinidad and Tobago. Dr. Esnard is an educator who focuses on secondary and higher education. She holds a doctorate in sociology from University of the West Indies and has a unique eye for educational and entrepreneurial issues affecting Caribbean development. Her early research explored issues of educational inequalities and aspirations and her current research explores the sociology of leadership in education and entrepreneurship. She is interested in entrepreneurial culture, attitudes, intentions, and education.

Dennis Francis is a professor and dean at the University of the Free State, Bloemfontein, South Africa. Dennis holds a doctorate in sociology and teaches in the fields of social justice education and sexuality education. He has written extensively in the areas of race, education for social justice, and youth sexuality. Dennis is a National Research Foundation-rated researcher and currently serves as the Chairperson of the Kenton Education Association.

Jennifer Lavia is director of the Caribbean Programme and lecturer in Education in the School of Education at the University of Sheffield in Sheffield, England. Jennifer is interested in examining how postcolonial theories might contribute to how we understand education. Her studies emphasize perspectives of what she considers the "colonised," and she is interested in examining how evidence can be generated through cultural artifacts, practices, and rituals. Her practice focuses on critical pedagogies. She has published widely on postcolonial theories and Caribbean studies in education. She is member of the Editorial Board of *Disability & Society* and has co-edited a special issue of *Pedagogy, Culture, and Society,* on Postcolonialism and Education, 13 (3), October 2006.

Bob Lingard is a professor in the School of Education at the University of Queensland, Australia. He has also been a professor at the Universities of Sheffield and Edinburgh. His most recent books are *Globalizing Education Policy* (2010), co-authored with Fazal Rizvi; and *Educating Boys* (Palgrave, 2009), co-authored with Wayne Martino and Martin Mills. He is the co-editor with Terry Wrigley and Pat Thomson of a forthcoming collection, *Changing Schools.* Bob is an editor of the journal, *Discourse: Studies in the Cultural Politics of Education* and co-editor with Greg Dimitriadis of *Key Ideas and Education.*

Sechaba Mahlomaholo is professor in the Faculty of Education at the University of the Free State, South Africa. He leads the *Sustainable Learning Environments* research team comprising over 20 academics, 15 PhD, and 15 MEd candidates. He has served as guest editor of three accredited journals in 2011 and has published extensively on how quality schooling grounded on principles of equity, social justice, freedom, peace, and hope can be created across the world, especially in formerly marginalized contexts.

Elizabeth Mackinlay is a registered nurse, a priest in the Anglican Church, and the director of the Centre for Ageing and Pastoral Studies at St Mark's National Theological Centre, Canberra, Australia. She is also a professor in the School of Theology, Charles Sturt University, Australia. Her recently completed research includes an Australian Research Council project: *"Finding Meaning in the Experience of Dementia: The Place of Spiritual Reminiscence Work,"* and an ANZ Charitable Foundation, and a J. O. & J. R. Wicking Trust grant 2007–2010, *"Minimising the Impact of Depression and Dementia for Elders in Residential Care."*

Milton Molebatsi Nkoane is the senior lecturer and head of school in the Faculty of Education at the University of the Free State, South Africa. He teaches in the field of Educational Studies. He has a strong research interest in praxis as an operationalization of critical emancipatory discourses located within the postcolonial, poststructural, and postmodern. He is the editor of co-editor of academic books and journals and has written extensively in the areas of special-education needs and social justice.

Lisa Perez is currently a lecturer at the University of Trinidad and Tobago in Republic of Trinidad and Tobago. She began her teaching career in the primary school, later branching into higher education, concentrating on agricultural and business studies. At present, she is pursuing a Doctorate in Education with the University of Sheffield.

Gordon Rohlehr, professor emeritus of Literatures in English, University of the West Indies, St. Augustine campus, Republic of Trinidad and Tobago. Prof. Rohlehr specializes in West Indian literature and oral poetry expressed through his sociohistorical interest in Trinidad as well as in calypso and Caribbean popular culture. In his published work he has pioneered academic study of calypso, documenting its genres and tracing its history over several centuries. He has and has been the recipient of the University of the West Indies' Vice-Chancellor's Award for Excellence in the combined fields of Teaching, Research, Administration, and Public Service (1995).

Lorraine Singh is Discipline Coordinator for Drama Education in the Faculty of Education at the University of KwaZulu-Natal, South Africa. Her previous work includes 20 years as subject adviser and curriculum specialist in speech and drama for schools. She has served on two ministerial committees to write new schools' curriculum for arts education. She was a Fulbright scholar, holds a master's and a doctorate in Educational Theatre. Her doctoral study focused on the application of narrative inquiry and applied theatre to arts education policy.

Miren Uriarte is a professor at the McCormack Graduate School of Policy Studies at the University of Massachusetts. Her research in applied sociology focuses on race and ethnic relations. Her areas of expertise include institutional development in minority communities; differential impact of social policy on minority communities, particularly Latinos in the United States; and program development and evaluation research in education, health care, and human services in the United States and abroad. She is the co-founder and former director of the Mauricio Gastón Institute for Latino Community Development and Public Policy.

Greg Vass is currently a full-time doctoral candidate at the University of Queensland, Australia, researching the making of race in classrooms and schools from a critical race theory perspective. He has served as a secondary-school teacher and has been exploring the relationship between the education system and indigenous students.

Simon Warren has served as an educator, researcher, and advocate for education and race equality. Simon is currently Lecturer in Critical Policy Studies in the School of Education, the University of Sheffield, England. Simon is co-convenor of the European Society for Research in the Education of Adults, Migration, Racism, and Xenophobia Research Network.

Index

Aborigines, *see* indigenous education
academic research and researchers,
    see research
African indigenous knowledge
    systems (AKIS), 8, 63
    see also indigenous education
Afrocentric education, 60, 63–4
    see also indigenous education
Anti-Racism Network in Higher
    Education (South Africa), 33
apartheid, 33–46, 52
    education system in South Africa
        after, 37–41, 164–80
    education system in South Africa
        during, 49–65
    see also biracialism; racism
arts and culture
    in South Africa, 168–80
arts education
    in South Africa, 163, 166–80
autobiography, 2, 8, 147, 152–7, 243
    see also life-history research;
        storytelling

Bantu Education Act 1953
    (South Africa), 37, 52–5
bilingual development, 76
    see also bilingual education
bilingual education, 69, 71, 74, 76,
    80, 86–97, 109–21
    in Ireland, 103–21
    in the USA, 69–74, 78–97

biracialism, 147–61
    in South Africa, 147–54
    see also racism

calypsos
    as commentary on education
        (Trinidad and Tobago),
        192–207
Caribbean academics and
    intellectuals, 235–51
Caribbean Commission,
    see Caribbean Research
    Council of the Caribbean
    Commission; Williams, Eric
Caribbean Educators Research
    Initiative (CURVE), 236–51
Caribbean region, 15–29, 183–207,
    235–51
Caribbean Research Council of the
    Caribbean Commission, 103,
    185–7
Caribbean thought, 15–29, 235–51
Celtic Tiger years (Ireland), 106–9,
    115–16
class and race
    relationship between, 72–6
class inequalities, *see* class and race
closing the gap strategy
    in Australia, 125–43
collective praxis, 237–8
colonialism, 15–20, 35–7, 50–65,
    183–207

community, 1–7, 20–1, 27–9, 41–6, 69–97
  in Australia, 125–43
  in the Caribbean, 183–207, 235, 241–51
  harmonious, 202
  in Ireland, 103–21
  in South Africa, 51, 61–5, 163
community cultural wealth, 34, 41–6
community empowerment, *see* community
community of telling, 29
community participation, *see* community
comparative collaboration, 12, 235–51
comparative education, *see* education, comparative
cosmopolitanism, 256
  see also multiculturalism
creative arts, *see* culture and creative arts
creolization, 22, 180, 188–9, 200–1
critical communities, 27
critical pedagogy, 60–4
critical race theory (CRT), 42
  see also racism
critical theory, 33–46
cultural capital
  in South Africa, 41–4
cultural confidence, 2, 7, 8, 9, 11, 12, 23, 255–8
  in Australia, 141, 147
  in Ireland, 103–27
  in South Africa, 62, 163–9, 180
cultural contexts, 16, 43, 130, 136, 171
cultural critique, 3
cultural/historical practice, 3–4, 7, 11–12, 25, 29, 52–3, 59, 132, 143, 149, 163–4, 168, 171–4, 179
cultural identity, 6, 56, 83
  in Ireland, 103–21

  in South Africa, 163–80
  see also identity; racial identity; teacher identity
cultural imperialism, 76, 108
culturally ethical research, 24–5, 108–11
cultural pedagogy, 23
cultural performance
  teaching as, 27
cultural politics of education, 1, 3, 7, 17
cultural politics of language
  in Ireland, 103–21
cultural resistance, 22, 26–7, 164, 168, 175, 255–6
culture, 20–9, 107–8, 163–80
  national culture (South Africa), 165–80
  see also culture and education; culture and learning
culture and creative arts, 10, 163–80
culture and education
  relationship between, 16, 20–9, 163–80
  see also culture
culture and learning
  relationship between, 2, 3–5
culture of confidence, *see* cultural confidence
culture of silence, 26–7, 39, 43
CURVE, *see* Caribbean Educators Research Initiative

decolonizing practice, 9, 12, 60
democracy, 38, 40–5, 49, 96, 97, 111
  in Ireland, 117–21
  in South Africa, 57–63, 164–71, 176–9
dissonant acculturation, 84
dual language, *see* bilingual education

education
  in Australia, 125–43

Index   267

in the Caribbean, 183–207
historical analysis of, 2, 7, 10–11,
    17, 43–4, 52–5, 184–207
in Ireland, 103–21
in South Africa, 37–46, 49–65,
    163–80, 258
in Trinidad and Tobago, 183–207,
    211–32
see also arts education; culture
    and education; indigenous
    education; teachers
education, comparative, 16
education, post-independence,
    23, 251
in the Caribbean, 11, 201–7,
    211–32
educational practice, 3, 18–20, 23,
    26–9, 70–2, 238–51
in South Africa, 49, 50, 52–3, 55,
    57–9, 61–5, 163
in Trinidad and Tobago, 212–32,
    235–51
educational research, 16–29, 125,
    241–7
*Education in the British West
    Indies*, 183–207
English as a "world language," 116
English language learners, 8–9,
    69–97
see also restrictive language
    policies
ethics, 108–11
see also culturally ethical
    research
exclusion, *see* social exclusion

Funds of Knowledge Project, 5–6,
    10, 137, 142
see also education; knowledge

globalization, 15–20, 29, 50, 82,
    127, 140, 143, 237, 255

higher education, 38–41, 44, 56
hybridity, 22, 167, 256

identity, 2, 4, 10, 16–17, 50, 138–9
in Australia, 129–43
in Ireland, 103–21
in South Africa, 147–61, 163–80,
    237, 244
in the USA, 79–97
see also cultural identity;
    racial identity; teacher
    identity
identity pedagogy, 138–9
see also identity
imagination, *see* postcolonial
    imagination; social
    imagination
indigenous communities,
    see community
indigenous education, 60–5,
    125–43
in Australia, 125–43
in South Africa, 61, 63–5
see also Afrocentric education
indigenous knowledge, 8, 42–3,
    49, 55, 63–4, 126, 132, 137,
    143, 258
indigenous research, 27, 125–7,
    130–1
intergenerational conflict, 84

knowledge, 2, 3, 5–7, 19, 24–7,
    39–41, 50–2, 59–65, 125,
    236–40, 243–5, 256, 258
knowledge action, 250
knowledge generation, 250

language, 21, 55, 59, 69–97,
    103–21, 163, 167, 239
language acquisition programs,
    see restrictive language
    policies
language proficiency, 93, 94
language revival
in Ireland, 104–21
language rights, 3, 6, 72, 80, 82,
    113–21
see also minority rights

268 Index

Latinos, *see* restrictive language policies
liberation pedagogy, 49–52, 59–60, 63–5
　in USA, 63–5
life-history research, 10, 61, 147, 152–7, 243
　see also autobiography; storytelling
linguistic conservation, 116–17
linguistic minority, 113, 116
linguistic racialization, 69–97

marginalization, 1–2, 12, 78, 107, 155–61, 247–8, 255
　in Australia, 125–7, 141–2
　in Ireland, 112–13
　in South Africa, 35–6, 42–6, 49–65, 147–52, 163–6
　see also racism; social exclusion
mental mapping, 22
minding minds, 53, 242
minority language communities, 77, 78, 80, 83, 84–5, 97
minority languages, 78, 104
minority-migrant culture, 115–16
minority rights, 9, 104, 110–21
　see also language rights
multiculturalism, 115–21, 201, 256

NAPLAN, *see* National Assessment Program for Literacy and Numeracy
narrative inquiry, 15–16, 28, 59, 152, 158–9, 169, 230, 242–6
National Assessment Program for Literacy and Numeracy (NAPLAN) (Australia), 128, 141
National Association for the Advancement of Colored People (NAACP), 133
National Qualification Framework (NQF) (South Africa), 57, 58
nationalism, 112–16, 164–6, 189

nativist interests, *see* restrictive language policies
neocolonialism, 16, 50–1

oppression, 1–2, 9, 12, 23, 49, 77–8, 107, 199, 255, 258
　in Australia, 125, 141
　in South Africa, 10, 35–6, 63–4, 147, 148, 167

pedagogy, 8, 23, 57, 60, 62, 129, 139, 141, 167, 179, 187, 257–8
　see also critical pedagogy; identity pedagogy; liberation pedagogy; plantation pedagogy; transformative pedagogy
People's Education Movement (Trinidad and Tobago), 185–9
　see also Williams, Eric
plantation pedagogy, 244–5
positionality, 29, 108–11, 251
postcolonial aesthetic, 2
postcolonial discourse, 18, 59, 60
postcolonial imagination, 1–3, 6–7, 114, 255–6, 258
postcolonialism, 1, 6–7, 15–29, 59–60, 64, 142, 211
postcoloniality, 1, 2, 64
postcolonial methodology, 7, 19, 25, 27
postcolonial praxis, 57–60
　see also praxis
postcolonial research, 15–29
postcolonial subjects, 11, 50, 207
postcolonial theory, 16–29, 51, 142
postcolonial thought, 6–7, 15–29, 256
practice architectures, 64, 241–2, 249
practice theory, 3–6, 15–29, 49–65, 108, 243–4, 251–8
　see also under individual forms of practice theory
praxis, 3, 5, 6, 51, 57–60, 236, 237–8, 244

queer politics, 160

racial identity, *see* identity; racism
racism, 33–46, 49–65, 72–97,
    147–61, 164–80
    see also apartheid; marginalization
religion
    relation to race, 154–5
research, 5, 7, 12, 15–29, 44–6,
    49–65, 71, 75, 83, 125–30,
    139, 147–9, 152, 211–35
research action, 27–8
resistance, 1, 7, 22, 27, 43, 255–6
resistance arts, 175, 177
restrictive language policies, 69–97
    English language learning
        programs, 74–97
    Latinos (USA), 73, 79–97
    nativist interests (USA), 81–3
    in Ireland, 103–21
    in the USA, 69–74, 78–97

situated practice, 3–4, 6, 50
social exclusion, 5, 8, 39–40, 63,
    64, 69, 72, 75, 81, 127, 179,
    214, 256
    see also marginalization
social imagination, 16, 49–50, 256
Soudien Report (South Africa), 39
South African Population
    Registration Act 1950, 153
storytelling, 28, 242
    see also autobiography; life-history
    research

teacher education, *see under* teachers
teacher identity, 20, 211–12
    see also cultural identity; identity
teacher-researchers, 12, 19–29,
    44–6, 52, 59, 125, 130–1,
    153, 235–51
    see also teachers
teachers, 5, 16–21, 50–65, 86–7, 91,
    129, 133–9, 211–32

as agents of change, 8, 12, 61, 65
in Australia, 133–8
education of, 244–50
role of, 6, 20, 57, 243
in South Africa, 50–65
in Trinidad and Tobago, 193–207,
    211–32, 244–51
    see also education;
    teacher-researchers
Teachers' Economic and Cultural
    Association (TECA)
    (Trinidad and Tobago),
    see People's Education
    Movement (Trinidad and
    Tobago)
Third Education Research
    Colloquium (South Africa)
    2010, 33
transformative pedagogy, 63, 179
Trinidad and Tobago, 183–207,
    211–33, 244–6
Trinidad and Tobago Education Act
    1966, 191, 196, 212, 216, 229
Truth and Reconciliation
    Commission 1995
    (South Africa), 56

United Nations Millennium
    Development Goals
    (MDGs), 34, 61

voices, 2, 26, 53–5, 58, 60, 61,
    126–7, 131, 142, 169, 171, 175,
    184, 195, 201, 211–12, 237,
    248–50
    of students, 62, 72, 77
    of teachers, 26, 62, 211–12, 231,
        237, 248–50

Williams, Eric
    ideas on educational reform,
        183–207
"world language"
    English as, 116

GPSR Compliance
The European Union's (EU) General Product Safety Regulation (GPSR) is a set of rules that requires consumer products to be safe and our obligations to ensure this.

If you have any concerns about our products, you can contact us on

ProductSafety@springernature.com

In case Publisher is established outside the EU, the EU authorized representative is:

Springer Nature Customer Service Center GmbH
Europaplatz 3
69115 Heidelberg, Germany

www.ingramcontent.com/pod-product-compliance
Lightning Source LLC
LaVergne TN
LVHW011807060526
838200LV00053B/3685